Managerial job change: men and women in transition

Work role transitions are among the most significant yet least understood forms of social change, and how they affect individuals' careers, self-concepts and organizational adjustment is of great practical and theoretical importance. This book provides the first comprehensive, large-scale study of the causes, form and outcomes of job change.

Focussing on one of the most influential segments of society – middle to senior managers – the book offers a new theoretical approach to the analysis and understanding of job change. The authors ask how much job change is taking place, assess who is most affected, and evaluate the psychological consequences for the individual manager. They discuss organizations' handling of job transitions, and provide a unique focus on women in management, evaluating how their experience of careers and job change differs from men's.

This book presents important new findings to specialists in life-span development, careers, managerial performance and organizational behaviour. It also offers the non-specialist insights into wider questions, such as the relationship between social change and organizational life, and the individual's experience of changes in industrial society's structures, practices and values.

NIGEL NICHOLSON is Senior Research Fellow MRC/ESRC Social and Applied Psychology Unit and MICHAEL WEST is Lecturer at the Department of Psychology and Research Officer at the MRC/ESRC SAPU, University of Sheffield.

Managerial job change: men and women in transition

NIGEL NICHOLSON
and
MICHAEL A. WEST

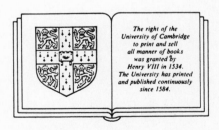

The right of the
University of Cambridge
to print and sell
all manner of books
was granted by
Henry VIII in 1534.
The University has printed
and published continuously
since 1584.

CAMBRIDGE UNIVERSITY PRESS

Cambridge
New York   New Rochelle   Melbourne   Sydney

Published by the Press Syndicate of the University of Cambridge
The Pitt Building, Trumpington Street, Cambridge CB2 1RP
32 East 57th Street, New York, NY 10022, USA
10 Stamford Road, Oakleigh, Melbourne 3166, Australia

First published 1988

Printed in Great Britain at Woolnough Bookbinding, Irthlingborough,
Northampton

British Library cataloguing in publication data

Nicholson, Nigel
Managerial job change: men and women
in transition.
1. Executives – Great Britain
2. Executives – Training – Great Britain
I. Title II. West, Michael A.
658.4'09   HD38.25.G7

Library of Congress cataloguing in publication data

Nicholson, Nigel.
Managerial job change.
Includes index.
1. Executives. 2. Career changes. 3. Organizational
change. I. West, Michael. II. Title.
HD38.2.N53   1988   331.12'72   87-11752

ISBN 0 521 33459 4

BO

Contents

Contents

Tables

Tables

viii

Tables

Figures

Acknowledgements

This book was a team effort, and could not have been produced without the assistance and expertise of many people apart from ourselves.

Thanks are especially due to Beverly Alban-Metcalfe for her unstinting and expert efforts in helping to design the first survey, the CDS-I, for enlarging our sampling frame so that it provided the large number of women respondents, and for her assistance with initial organization and analysis of material. Without these contributions the project could not have borne fruit. Professor T.F. Cawsey's most valuable input to the second phase of the study, the CDS-II, was similarly indispensable. Jan Jackson and Anne Rees were enormously resourceful in making light of the heavy work of data processing and analysis, and Kathryn Beadsley was unfailingly patient and skilful in transforming our seemingly chaotic scribblings and endless revisions into a pristine manuscript. Thanks also to Francis Brooke and Anne Rix of Cambridge University Press for their support and advice at all stages of the publication process.

We would also like to express our appreciation to John Wilson and Hano Johannsen of the BIM for providing access to most of the managers in the study, and to the several professional women's organizations and journals through which we secured our additional sample of women in management.

Last but not least, we would like to express our heartfelt thanks to all the managers who took part in the study. We hope that their donation of hard-pressed time to answer our questions may be repaid in some small way by any contribution this book makes to spreading enlightenment about what they do and how the quality of their working lives, and that of their successors, can be enhanced.

1

Men and women in transition

We live in times of change – rapid and radical change – and much of it centres on our working lives. Even if we lived in times of tranquil stability we would still be confronted with the task of adjusting to transitions, compelled by the perpetual motion of the life cycle. People would still have to undergo training and socialization to acquire occupational competence at the start of the life/career cycle, have to maintain and reform skills in the middle years to be able to fill the slots vacated by departing seniors, and eventually move on into retirement, renewing the cycle by passing on their positions to junior successors. Transitions are, to this degree, inevitable, but, as we shall be seeing in the pages that follow, such orderly and measured change is not the normal experience of most managers.

What do we know about how people adjust to the demands of change? Within the various literatures on people at work, change is too often treated as a troublesome aberration – an external force that disturbs the stable patterns of daily life. The snapshots of survey designs and case studies are often used to deduce and uncover these patterns, for example, in the search for law-like relationships between such factors as job characteristics, personality, work satisfaction, and performance. Social scientists seem to be more comfortable studying the world with an assumption of stability than they do in confronting the problem of how such patterns may be disturbed or reformed by change. Indeed, given the pervasiveness of change perhaps it would be better to assume that change is the constant and stability the exception. One might even argue, like some post-Freudian and existentialist writers, that one of the main functions of culture is to cushion and protect us from our fundamental insecurities about change (Fromm, 1942). The most anxiety-inducing questions about the meaning of our existence, the uncertainty of the future, and the nature of identity, are solved for us, partially at least, by the mechanisms of cultural transmission – the socialization of values, beliefs and behaviours and the institutionalization of social relationships.

Change and constancy are bound together through various dynamics, and their interaction can often appear paradoxical. In many spheres of life

1

we engineer changes in order to reinforce the status quo, for example, changing jobs to maintain our professional status and skills. Conversely we can see how stability is a cause of radical change, for example, where rigidity in the face of environmental challenges leads individuals and organizations to experience breakdown or revolution. These dynamics can be looked at from various perspectives within the social sciences: from the macro level of social strata, economic systems and cultural forces, through to the micro level of individual growth, adaptation and decline.[1]

Our concern in this book is primarily with the micro level, but setting individual adaptation firmly within the context of organizational life and environmental change. The notion of *transition* is central to our analysis as a concept that can help us achieve a new understanding of a wide range of issues in social science. We shall be arguing that the literatures of lifespan development, careers, the study of work behaviour and attitudes, occupational socialization, and organizational change, are all deficient in their attention to the particular causal dynamics of adjustment to change. In many writings in these areas change is either ignored completely, or described in overly broad thematic terms. The notion of transition allows us to look more closely and precisely at the fulcrum of the change process.

This then is one of the two main aims of this book – to shed fresh light on how people experience transitions, and what happens as a result of that experience. The second aim is more particular – to offer the first systematic analysis and commentary upon a ubiquitous and important social phenomenon – job change – as it affects one of the most influential segments of society: middle to senior managers. As we shall see, job changes are frequent events in managers' lives, and are also events of great personal importance to them and to their organizations. Yet we know almost nothing about the extent, form, and consequences of job mobility. In the remainder of this chapter we shall set the scene for our study of managerial job change. First, we shall look briefly at what we know about managerial work and how it may be affected by social change. Second, we shall use the model of the Transition Cycle to explore what various academic literatures have to say about the job change process. Third, we shall describe our research objectives and preview the contents of following chapters. Fourth and last we shall explain our research methodology for achieving these objectives and consider its strengths and limitations.

Change and the manager

In many ways the society we live in today is almost unrecognizable as a product of the society of our recent forebears. In other respects there is a remarkable continuity from former to present times (Halsey, 1978). Our experiences in organizations play a considerable part in providing us with a sense of continuity, and at the same time prepare us for the bewildering range of major changes we are witnessing in almost every area of our lives in industrialized society. The primary social institution of the family has a different appearance and some changed functions: family size has fallen, divorce and remarriage have risen, and forms of childcare have altered (*Social Trends*, 1985). The content and extent of education has changed: syllabi are more varied, training is more pragmatically oriented to a widening range of occupations and professions, and people are spending longer in educational institutions. There have been revolutionary advances in transportation and communications, and major shifts in the form of both product and labour markets. There have been parallel changes in how we use our leisure time and spend our money. Household technology and entertainments, the growth of the superstore, and the increasing use of private transport have all contributed to ways of living that are simultaneously more privatized and mobile (Fothergill and Vincent, 1985). All this has been accompanied by huge shifts in patterns of industrialization and social structure. Rapid advances in industrial and information technology, declining demand for the traditional products of manufacturing coupled with increasing demands for a widening range of services, have led to a major redistribution of employment from the primary and secondary sectors (extractive and manufacturing) to the tertiary (service and support) sector of the economy (Payne and Payne, 1983). At the same time organizational forms have changed. Increasingly, the equity of companies is owned by large institutions rather than private individuals (Britain, 1986). The size of enterprises has grown, to exceed in some cases the wealth of national economies, whilst there has been a continuing proliferation of small businesses, creating and filling more and more new market niches. The state and the law, despite whatever attempts are made to curb them, have had to evolve ever more complex and extensive systems to regulate these activities.

Although inequalities in wealth and power are little different in scale from those of half a century ago, standards of living have risen, and the identities of class and status groups have altered. The industrial proletariat and agricultural working class have declined in number, as has the size of the landowning plutocracy, whilst there has been great growth in the salariat at all levels. Menial white-collar jobs, service and technical functions, supervisory and managerial roles, and professional and executive jobs have all proliferated dramatically (Institute of Manpower Studies, 1986).

One of the most radical changes of recent years, and which directly concerns us in this book, is the changed role of women. Many of the changes we have described have meant that women have different opportunities for

3

time use and a changing sense of their own identity and motives. By virtue of reduced family demands, new technical aids to domestic labour, and more flexible work schedules and demands, women now have time to seek other forms of occupation (Martin and Roberts, 1984). The dramatic increase in the number of employed women, together with other changes in social behaviour and values, has initiated a far reaching revolution in the social identity of women. This is an area of considerable current ferment. Traditional gender roles and stereotypes are still pervasive in the family, the workplace and communications media, but large numbers of women are actively producing changes in each of these areas, consciously and unconsciously challenging traditional ways and assumptions, often with a new sense of their own purposes and needs (Alban-Metcalfe, 1985).

So we can see that the forces of change converge on human experience by altering the social structure, shaping social needs and values, and reordering the means by which needs are fulfilled by social structures. Here our interest is in management, since it is managers who are charged with co-ordinating and focussing responses to change while at the same time functioning as some of the most influential agents for change within organizations. Management itself has been fundamentally affected in three major ways by the social and economic developments we have described.

First, the number of people who are managers has been growing rapidly in this century (Parker *et al.*, 1981). But what is a manager? A simple definition might be: one who is required to facilitate and coordinate the efforts of others to achieve organizational objectives. Adopting such a definition, we can see how the shift from basic industrial processes to complex and varied information-based activities means that increasing numbers of people are managers: charged with the task of supervising, coordinating, integrating and interacting to fulfil organizations' goals. Managers are no longer a small minority in the community of occupations. They are the executors of many of our most valued and significant social processes.

Second, a corollary of the first point, the scope and variety of what managers are required to do has been continually expanding. The French writer, Henry Fayol, laid the foundations at the start of the century for management as a discipline by portraying managerial work as following the rationality of planning, organizing and controlling, but modern empirical studies by scholars such as Mintzberg (1973) and Stewart (1967) offer a different image. Any measured rationality in managerial work has to be forged out of a hectic and apparent chaos of unscheduled demands, fragmented interactions, and *ad hoc* decisions. Moreover, the boundary between the general or supervisory managerial functions and those of the technical or professional specialist is becoming increasingly blurred (Cullen, 1983). To be able to perform effectively general managers need to

4

have greater specialist knowledge than ever before about their organizations, markets and technology. Technical specialists, for their part, have increasingly to manage subordinates or coordinate their work within teams to cope with the expanding scope and complexity of their tasks and goals. No longer can technical managers so easily function within the splendid isolation afforded by their expertise. They are having to improve their ability to communicate, or to sell their knowledge to non-specialists and to manage relationships with client populations. The complexity of the modern organization and its multiple interdependencies with external groups, interests, and institutions has also meant that boundary-spanning roles have been growing in number and significance (Drucker, 1973). All of this amounts to a widening of challenge and opportunity for managers and professionals. The managerial career may have once looked like a clear and reasonably straight track towards a visible horizon, but now the paths have multiplied. Their courses are increasingly devious, with numerous lateral intersections, and the horizons they lead to are obscured by cloud. Managers today have more reason than their forebears to doubt whether they will get to a valued destination more quickly by staying on the main path than by taking some new diversion to the side.

The third manifestation of change is just this – uncertainty and danger constitute the darker opposite side to challenge and opportunity. Managers can no longer feel secure in the knowledge that their psychological safety and well-being will be provided for by life-long attachment to a single employer.[2] Organizations and careers are increasingly precarious, and the bleak landscape of unemployment is no more inhabited solely by the underclass: managerial redundancy has been increasing dramatically (Kaufman, 1982; Fineman, 1983). The rate of environmental change places imperative demands on organizations to adapt if they are to survive and prosper, reflected in the increasing numbers of mergers, business failures and new starts. For individual managers there is a constant pressure to update skills and knowledge, and to retain their status in organizational systems and the labour market. The galloping pace of the information technology revolution is a harbinger of profound uncertainty. How sure can one be that one's lifetime-accumulated skills will be needed tomorrow as they are today? To protect one's future it may be wisest to try to keep ahead of the game by making career choices that will enhance one's repertoire of marketable attributes.

Job change lies at the centre of this confluence of forces. Each of our three manifestations of change – the growth of management as a profession, broadening job opportunities, and the heightened uncertainty of career trajectories – all point in the direction of individual life changes. Changing jobs is both a voluntary and an involuntary response to these developments.

5

Involuntary job change is likely to follow from technological and structural change in organizations and their environments; voluntary job change from managers' desires to direct and control their destinies in the midst of turbulence.

So what can we achieve by studying managerial job change? First, we can attempt to gauge the extent of change, determine its origins, and identify which types of manager are most affected by it. In other words, managerial mobility is a lens through which we can obtain a fresh view of how social change is affecting organizational life.

Second, we can learn about the nature of job change as a personal experience. We can see how radical, onerous, unexpected and rewarding are managerial job moves.

Third, we can evaluate the consequences of change. This is perhaps the most important of our objectives for theory and for practice and should be briefly explained. It is a main aim of this research to investigate the dynamics of stability and change by analysing adjustment processes. In particular we contrast reactive and proactive adjustment strategies. These two modes were expressed aphoristically in *Man and Superman* by George Bernard Shaw, who wrote: 'The reasonable man adapts himself to the world; the unreasonable one persists in trying to adapt the world to himself. Therefore all progress depends on the unreasonable man.' The question we shall be asking is whether managers are 'reasonable' and undergo psychological adjustment in response to change – to become, in a sense, new men and women – or whether they are 'unreasonable' and try to shape their organizational worlds and roles to meet their psychological requirements (Nicholson, 1984). Reactive adjustment implies that job changing contributes to the evolution of social man, engendering shifts in consciousness, needs, and ways of living. Proactive adjustment implies that job change is not just an outcome of organizational change but is also a cause of it, for one can reason as follows: if human psychological attributes are resistant to change, and people seek to maintain stability in their identities, then adjustment processes will be externalized in the form of 'unreasonable' proactive adjustment. Rather than change oneself one changes the world.[3] The effect of proactive adjustment to job change then will be to accelerate evolutionary and revolutionary developments within organizations. However, it is in the nature of organizational design to absorb and neutralize most disturbances that individuals are capable of creating, so we need not assume that proactive adjustment will always have lasting or fundamental effects on organizational process. Nonetheless, the seeds of some major future developments in organizations may well be sown by proactive modes of individual adaptation.

A fourth reason for studying job mobility is that we can examine how

6

organizations recognize or fail to recognize its implications for individual or organizational effectiveness. Are managers who are contemplating or confronting the demands of mobility helped or hindered by their organizations? The wider question here is whether mobility is an opportunity organizations can exploit to their own advantage. Can enterprises enhance the value of their human resources by using job changes as opportunities for the personal development of their people (Brett, 1984; Pinder and Walter, 1984); and what might be the costs for employers and employees of inadequacies in how mobility is managed?

Fifth, and finally, the increasing representation of women in management raises important questions. Are they a force for change in organizations by bringing to managerial work new perspectives, needs, and ways of behaving, or do they replicate the attitudes and responses of their male counterparts? In particular, it is germane to all the questions we have raised here whether the women who are entering management have different career paths and mobility patterns to men, whether they enter gender segregated managerial specialisms or industries, and whether their experience of job change and modes of adjustment has a distinctive character.

We have framed all these issues in terms of the practice of management and the design of organizations. It is also apparent that each issue has deeper theoretical implications, linking in important ways with a number of major concerns in various social science fields of study. We shall now briefly examine these implications, summarizing what is known about the causes, processes and outcomes of transitions.

The Transition Cycle and the study of organizational behaviour

Our lives are full of transitions, and they take many forms. We are periodically confronted by major life changes, such as marriage, parenthood and bereavement, that signal movement from one social status to another (Glaser and Strauss, 1971). We also experience myriad minor transitions which affect our customary ways of life, such as new relationships, living arrangements, household aids and recreational media, all of which engender responsive shifts in our daily routines and interests. But it is in the sphere of work that significant role transitions can be expected to occur most often. Even here they have a varied appearance. Sometimes their approach is well signalled and their form clearly structured by surrounding institutional processes – as in the case of recruitment or retirement. In other cases they are unexpected or dramatic, as in many instances of job relocation, function change and job loss.

Is there any reason to hope that some unified theory of transitions could encompass this diversity, even if we limit our consideration to the work

7

sphere? Before attempting to answer this we need to assess our current state of knowledge and what analytical tools might be available for our use. We propose a simple cyclical model of adjustment to transitions as a basic framework to which can be added the richness of detail and diversity observable in people's experiences of transitions.[4] We are asserting here that work role transitions are a relatively unexplored primary unit of analysis which may offer diverse areas of social science the promise of a deeper and more precise understanding of the processes and outcomes of change.

Figure 1.1 illustrates the basic structure of the Transition Cycle. It has four stages: preparation, encounter, adjustment, stabilization, although the fact that it is a *cycle* allows us to see the first stage of any transition – preparation – as the fifth stage of the preceding cycle. In other words the notion of the cycle contains the assumption of *recursion* or perpetual motion. The experience of having undergone a transition and reached a new stabilized state is itself a preparation for the experience of the next transition. A second assumption contained in this model is *interdependence* – what happens at one stage of the cycle has a powerful bearing on what happens at the next stage. How well one prepares for change, for example, determines how cushioned or exposed one is in confronting the shocks of the encounter stage – the first hours, days or weeks of familiarization with new circumstances. The third feature of the cycle is *discontinuity*, i.e. the cycle has discontinuous stages, each having qualitatively distinct tasks, experiences, problems and solutions.

The characteristics of each stage can be summarized as follows:

Preparation

In the preparation stage psychological readiness is the key concern. How much forewarning does one have of a transition? How clear or detailed are one's expectations? With what feelings and motives does one anticipate change? How well equipped in skills and knowledge does one feel in the face of the known and the unknown of future change? A number of academic and practitioner literatures have focussed on the preparation stage, but there is little conceptual unity among them. Within Industrial/Organizational Psychology, motivation theory has attempted to predict people's approach to future change. In particular expectancy-valence theory (Vroom, 1964; Mitchell, 1974) seems especially applicable to this stage. The theory is complex and highly specified, predicting that one's motivational force towards some future outcome is jointly determined by how much one values possible outcomes, and how confident one is that one's efforts will result in

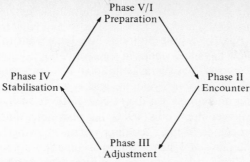

Figure 1.1 The Transition Cycle.

desired outcomes. Sociologists have taken a longer-term view of preparation through the notion of 'anticipatory socialization' (Merton, 1957). From this perspective readiness for change is a function of how appropriately one's values and customary modes of behaviour have been shaped by previous experiences in education, employment and the sub-culture of one's social stratum (Van Maanen, 1976).

The contrast of the psychological and sociological accounts of preparation emerges as a conflict of competing perspectives within the careers literature (Watts *et al.*, 1981). Psychologists have devoted their energies to describing the process of occupational choice, and how personality characteristics predispose people toward different career preferences. Sociologists have emphasized how class-based inequalities of opportunity structures allocate individuals to different work roles and statuses (Esland and Salaman, 1980). However, it can be said that the conflict between these approaches only exists by virtue of each side's caricaturing the extremity of the other's theoretical position. A middle position is tenable. People do attempt to make job choices and wrest some control over their destinies, but against a background of structural forces over which they have little or no control: what has been termed 'bounded discretion' (March and Simon, 1958).

Finally, a more practical approach to the question of preparation is to be found in the literature on selection and recruitment. Much has been written on how new recruits, especially people approaching their first jobs, form their impressions of prospective employers and conceive of the recruitment process; how the interview process is conducted by both parties, and how selection decisions are made (Wanous, 1980; Herriot, 1984; Lewis, 1985; Schneider and Schmitt, 1986). The effectiveness of the recruitment procedure has a direct bearing on readiness in two ways. First, it determines how accurate is each party's view of the other. Second, it determines whether people selected will 'fit' with their new milieux.

Encounter

Until recently, relatively little attention has been paid to the encounter phase, the first few days and weeks in a new job, but it is clear from recent writings on the subject that the assumptions of interdependence and discontinuity in the Transition Cycle are widely recognized. The degree of 'reality shock' in encounter is a direct consequence of the psychological readiness of the newcomer. Louis (1980) has provided a detailed account of the cognitive processes of the encounter phase, showing how the task of 'sense-making' in one's new surroundings assumes paramount importance. The magnitude of this task is a function of three factors: change – objective differences between one's new and previous role requirements, status, and work environment; contrast – how much person-specific carryover there is from past experience to one's new position; and surprise – one's positive and negative disconfirmed expectations. An important implication of this analysis is that even when one is well prepared, there will still be surprises in store for the job changer.

The immediate task of coping in the encounter stage is portrayed by Louis in cognitive terms, i.e. sense-making through thought and reasoning. Attributions are important inputs to this search for meaning. Newcomers draw upon their own wishes and needs, the 'scripts' they have accumulated, modified and carried over from situation to situation, the interpretations of significant others, and the shared 'interpretative schemes' available in the local sub-culture. The process is thus highly subjective, with consensus as well as distortions forged out of interactions with others. This clearly locates Louis' ideas within the symbolic interactionist tradition of social psychology (cf. Meltzer *et al.*, 1975).

The other main account of the encounter process to be found in the literature provides a complete contrast, by focussing on feelings. This is the stress-coping view of encounter. Some writers have approached this by extrapolating to job change from the study of other major life events and changes. Hopson and Adams (1976), for example, extend the Kubler-Ross phase model of coping with bereavement to describe adjustment to job change.[5] According to these writers psychological defence mechanisms, such as denial and withdrawal often will be evident in the early stages of encounter, before change can be assimilated and integrated.

A more research based approach has been taken by those scholars, notably Brett (1980, 1984), Pinder (1981), and Frese (1982, 1984), who emphasize the multiplicity of adjustment tasks facing job changers, especially where change involves geographical relocation. Stress arises as a function of the magnitude and content of these demands. Problems of family adjustment to relocation are a particularly critical focus, though the impact of stress can be mitigated by social supports in and out of the workplace. Friends and family are often more consistent and reliable sources of aid than authoritative figures to be found at the workplace. In organizations, people are typically starved of the kinds of structured feedback and resources that might be made available to help them over the encounter period, so informal help and advice from one's new colleagues are commonly solicited to make good these deficits (Louis *et al.*, 1983; Feldman and Brett, 1983). These are active rather than passive coping strategies, and this perhaps leads us on to the thought that, even though the experience of job change may be stressful, it is often mixed with feelings of excitement, the pleasure of discovery, and satisfaction that not all of one's worst fears have come true. Hans Selyé, a founding father of stress research, talks of 'eustress' to connote the positive stresses of life – those which we willingly embrace to enrich our experience and achieve our goals (1956). Much of the stress of job change may have this character.

So how generally useful is a stress-coping model of the transition process? From the research literature it would appear to have limited application. In many job changes, positive experiences outweigh or quickly supervene over the negative (Keller and Holland, 1981; Werbel, 1983; Latack, 1984; Kirjonen and Hanninen, 1986). The stress-coping model is appropriate to certain types of undesired and unwelcome job move, to some traumatic entry experiences to roles of particular kinds, and to changes at times of life when one's readiness for change is especially low. But, in many other work role transitions, problems in coping with strong feelings are short-lived and secondary to the positive experiences that emerge from the progressive cognitive and behavioural pathfinding on which the job changer is embarking.

This then leads us to the second discontinuity, or third stage of the Transition Cycle. The tasks of coping with the shock and surprise of encounter give way to a quite different set of priorities, which we shall call adjustment.

Adjustment

Once one's feet are under the desk, a rudimentary mental map of one's new world has been acquired, and an initial relationship with tasks and people has been formed, the real work of adjustment begins. This is the task of fitting in; of moving towards becoming a fully functioning member of an occupational community. There are three principal levels on which accommodation must be reached: with one's work role, with the people with whom one must interact, and with the culture of one's new environment. The three levels are, of course, highly interrelated, combining in what amounts to a process of resocialization (Strauss, 1959). In instances of radical job change one becomes, in a sense, a member of a new society, having to shed old and adopt new behaviours, relationships and views of the world.

This perspective accords transitions a central role in lifespan development, for it is apparent that adjustment processes may have long-term implications for the changing focus and direction of adult life. It is not so long since the field of developmental psychology was almost exclusively devoted to the study of children, adolescents, and old people. Theory and research seemed to embody the presumption that all the important psychological developments take place in the first or last two decades of the lifespan, and that the bulk of adulthood, sandwiched between these periods of major biological and social change, is stable and uneventful. But there has been a major reawakening of interest in the complexity, subtlety and importance of change in adult life, symbolized by an armada of basic developmental texts and advanced monographs flying under the new disciplinary flag of 'Life Span Developmental Psychology'.[6] These are mainly concerned with shifts in cognitive abilities and personality traits over adulthood, drawing upon longitudinal studies, many of which are impressive in their scale and sophistication (Baltes *et al.*, 1980; Eichdorn *et al.*, 1981). Yet whilst mention is sometimes made of changes in the work sphere as both 'normative' (culturally scheduled and predictable) and 'non-normative' (unscheduled and unpredictable) life events, the implications of job change have not been explored. We would argue that the study of work role transitions therefore offers the opportunity to shed light on some of the most common and significant turning points in the changing life course.

Within the study of organizations, the adjustment process has been analysed by a number of writers, under the heading of organizational socialization. It is within this literature that one finds closest attention paid to the transition process, though it must be said that most writers treat it as if it were a once-and-for-all occurrence, or only of practical or psychological significance at the points of career entry, exit or radical mid-career switches. It has less often been seen as a recurrent fact of working lives. Organizational writers also pay little attention to individual differences (Jones, 1983). It is rarely considered that the transition process may have different effects on people at the start, middle or end of their careers, on men versus women, dominant versus submissive types etc. However, we can find in the literature insights into what kinds of accommodations are made and through which agencies. For example, Schein (1971a, 1978) has provided a typology of transitions within organizational space: vertical moves between levels of the hierarchy, lateral moves across functional boundaries, and inclusionary moves away from or towards the centre of organizations. Schein predicts that informal socialization has most impact during vertical and inclusionary moves and formal strategies of education and training apply more to lateral moves. The nature and outcomes of different forms of socialization have been further developed by Van Maanen (1976) and Van Maanen and Schein (1979). There is insufficient space to give an account of the six dimensions to socialization that these authors identify, but what is of chief interest to us here is how these writers analyse the *outcomes* of socialization. They depict a contrast between 'custodial' responses, where the new occupant acts like a 'caretaker' in conforming to role expectations, and two sorts of innovation: (i) content innovation, changing the way the role is performed, and (ii) role innovation, changing the goals and basic objectives of the role. They predict that their six dimensions of socialization are differentially related to these outcomes, and Jones (1986) has provided partial support for the theory by demonstrating that 'institutionalized' and 'individualized' socialization methods produce, respectively, custodial and role innovative responses, moderated by individual differences in 'self-efficacy'. The important point here is that the adjustment process can be seen to have important organizational consequences, and these will differ from situation to situation.

Elsewhere in the literature the emphasis has been on adjustment via mentors and supervisors (Weiss, 1978), group dynamics (Moreland and Levine, 1983), job characteristics (Dawis and Lofquist, 1984) and sources of influence and evaluation (Feldman, 1976). A number of outcomes of the socialization-adjustment stage have been highlighted: satisfaction, group acceptance, motivation, commitment, and conformity. A more identity-focussed perspective has been taken by scholars undertaking ambitious longitudinal investigations (Mortimer and Lorence, 1979; Brousseau, 1983; Kohn and Schooler, 1983). These studies, plotting concomitant changes in the characteristics of the jobs and personalities of cohorts over periods as long as ten years, are in agreement about the evidence: psychological and job characteristics tend to converge over time. Personality development – shifts in people's values, intellectual flexibility and self-directedness – follow the directions set by job demands and vice versa. People grow to fit the scope and demands of the jobs they hold, and gravitate towards forms of work commensurate with their needs and self-concepts.[7]

This evidence provides a vital link in our chain of ideas. Adjustment to transitions not only influences organizational behaviour, it also shapes people's personalities and lives. Yet, how the relationships between individual differences and outcomes interact with the characteristics of transitions and other influences remains obscure and unresearched (Nicholson, 1984). To trace more clearly this web of complex and important relationships is a major objective of this book.

Stabilization and preparation

These can be briefly treated together, since it may not be uncommon to find that stabilization never occurs: where transitions of high complexity follow one another in rapid sequence, one has barely finished adjusting to the last change before encountering the next. But where adjustment has been able to run its course, then the stabilization stage sees the individual striving to maintain valued elements of the role, making fine-tuning adjustments to experience and action, and enjoying or suffering the fruits of success or failure. Clearly, the kinds of fitting or misfitting equilibria that are achieved as a result of stages I, II and III of the Transition Cycle create the climate for the life that will be lived in stage IV.

Perhaps the greater part of the literature of Industrial/Organizational Psychology (I/O Psychology) and Management is concerned with stabilization. Publications on leadership, work performance, assessment, management control and job satisfaction all tend to assume stabilized work arrangements and relationships. Some writers and researchers do explore dynamic changes within these areas, but for the most part the human subjects of their scholarship are treated as if they have no past and no future. There is little recognition of people's prior history of job changes and adjustments and, typically, little attention to their future goals and anticipated life changes.

For the manager, the crucial process in stabilization is relating across levels of the hierarchy to bosses and subordinates. The former are especially important for, in a very real sense, one's boss determines the contours of one's role, by setting the limits to controlled and discretionary performance. This can be thought of as akin to a length of rope between the boss and subordinate: too short and the latter feels over-controlled, too long and she may feel neglected and unsupported, or even, figuratively speaking, hang herself! Maintaining a mutually acceptable tension is, of course, a dual responsibility, and the subject of a continuing informal negotiation between the parties – what has been called the 'social contracting' relationship of leadership (Fulk and Cummings, 1984).

The interface between stabilization and preparation is perhaps most clearly represented in the literature on goal-setting and performance appraisal. Unfortunately, appraisal too often epitomizes the literal meaning of the term: the weighing and accounting of human attributes, which means placing primary emphasis upon the generation of reliable performance measures. These are important and legitimate functions, but they have the characteristic of being retrospective in orientation. Appraisal measures the past more easily than it controls the future. For stabilization to flow effectively into preparation, appraisal functions need to be allied with forward looking review activities. These can be highly focussed, as in goal-setting programmes, or more general and exploratory, as in career counselling interviews. The benefits of such approaches are well documented: they enhance and focus employee motivation, they help to integrate personnel and management systems, they aid planning and control, and they remove obstacles to change (Fletcher and Williams, 1985).

Our analysis of the Transition Cycle suggests that people's possible future job changes should be high on the agenda of performance review, even if no change appears to be imminent, so that employees are in a state of readiness for both expected and unexpected mobility. To be realistic, this should not be confined to thinking about within-company moves, but encompass some awareness of events, opportunities and pressures from outside the organization. Turning a blind eye to the possibility of a valued employee quitting does not make the event less likely; it is better to explore and face up to the reality of the uncertainties to which people and organizations are exposed and by reviewing them initiate dialogue that helps both parties to plan and control their destinies.

By looking at the causes of job change, the kinds of support and guidance people receive, and preparedness for change, we can better understand the stresses and opportunities it creates.

Theory, practice and the literature on transitions

The literature on transitions is in its infancy with a very thin empirical base on which theory might be built.[8] Our aim in this research was to enlarge this database significantly through one of the first large-scale studies of the causes, content and outcomes of job change. The notion of Transition Cycle may help provide a tentative start to the process of theory building. As we have seen the distinctive qualities of the stages of the Transition Cycle suggest that a number of different 'middle-range' theories may be needed to understand what happens at each stage (cf. Pinder and Moore, 1980). However the assumption of the Transition Cycle model that each stage is *distinctive* need not necessarily commit us to a fragmented perspective. The two other assumptions contained within the notion of a cycle have more integrative force. The assumption of *recursion* (the idea that cycles recur and have cumulative effects) and *interdependence* (what happens at one stage affects what will happen at the next) can lead us towards a more holistic appreciation of transitions and their theoretical implications. The three assumptions of distinctiveness, recursion and interdependence taken together have practical implications for people experiencing transitions and for organizations seeking to manage the transition process. We shall be attempting to draw out these implications from each chapter of the

15

book, and in the final chapter to point ways forward for theory and practice.

Each chapter asks and attempts to answer the questions we have raised in this introduction. In Chapter 2, we examine the character of managerial work and the people who undertake it. To understand managers' approach and reactions to job change we need to understand their motives and interests. How homogeneous are these and are they likely to facilitate or resist the change process? Next, in Chapter 3 we establish the baseline of change to which managers are responding. How often are managers changing jobs, what kinds of moves are they making, and under what circumstances are managers most exposed to radical job change? Chapter 4 extends the direction of the two previous chapters by examining the causes of job change. How much mobility is goal-directed and initiated by managers, and how much is it under the control of impersonal or ungovernable forces? How predictable is job change, and hence, how prepared are managers for it?

Chapter 5 brings into closer focus qualities of experience through the Transition Cycle. How anxious are managers before moving? What kinds of responses does job change draw from them, satisfaction, personal change or innovation? Chapter 6 enlarges the analysis of outcomes, examining the implications of job mobility for people's personal growth and development. We also consider the potential deleterious effects on mental health of downward status moves, a little studied but important negative job change. In Chapter 7 we give separate attention to moves into newly created jobs. These are a much more frequent but equally neglected and important kind of job change. We shall be looking at why they are so common, where they come from, and what kinds of adjustment they evoke.

Chapter 8 adopts a more organizational perspective, examining how transitions are handled, especially through the kinds of feedback and help in job learning that managers may or may not receive. Are there different career 'cultures' in organizations of differing types and sizes? Chapter 9 looks at the issue of women in management, drawing together ideas and findings from previous chapters and presenting some fresh insights from comparisons of the 800 women and 1500 men in the sample. In what ways do men and women managers have distinctive professional orientations and job experiences and do women have different career paths and patterns to men? Do they achieve status equality with men or are they assigned to segregated jobs and functions?

We conclude in Chapter 10 by drawing together and summarizing the practical and theoretical conclusions of the research. First the implications for managerial experience are discussed, then we review findings more theoretically through the Transition Cycle, and finally we consider how

16

they relate to various topics and areas of applied behavioural science. Overall, the view that emerges from this study of managerial job change is optimistic. There are costs to high mobility but for most the outcomes of job change are progressive – turning points or developmental steps in lives and careers. Yet it is also clear that the benefits of mobility could be greatly enhanced by helping both individuals and organizations to achieve better understanding of the transition process.

Research strategy

In science, methodology is the means by which we can achieve our objective of acquiring knowledge. Our strategy is that of the questionnaire survey, a much used and abused social science method. Its weaknesses are well known, though often overstated. Unrepresentativeness, bias, unreliability, and difficulties establishing the validity of responses are frequent criticisms, but these can be minimized when surveys are well-designed, use large samples, employ repeated administrations (longitudinal design), and incorporate qualitative as well as quantitative data; all features of the present survey. But without dwelling on technical issues let us anticipate any possible problems of interpretation our method may involve.

The first is representativeness, but representative of what? To claim that a sample is representative or unrepresentative entails some clear notion of a target population. Thus opinion polls extrapolate to the population of registered electors, consumer surveys to the total population of households, and so on. A survey of managers would seem to invoke the total population of managers, but, in the light of our earlier observations, what is a manager? There are many people in non-standard occupations or organizations, out of the mainstream of business and commerce, whose work is assuredly managerial and yet who might not recognize themselves under the title of 'manager'. Conversely, there are many technical specialists and professionals who are called managers but whose work is minimally concerned with the management of human resources. This means that any extrapolation to the world of managers 'in general' should be made cautiously, with an awareness of the limitations imposed by the ambiguous boundary around this target population.

It is methodologically sounder to take a more positive approach by deciding what types of managers are of interest and to target them accordingly. This was our strategy in the present study.[9] We set out to find people in industrial, commercial and service organizations with professional and managerial responsibilities for the work of others (e.g. subordinates) or coordinating with agents outside the organization (e.g. clients). We wanted to exclude people at the very start of their careers, and specialized professionals working on their own account or on exclusively technical problems within organizations (e.g. doctors and craftworkers), but not to exclude self-employed entrepreneurs, management consultants and the like. It seemed to us that the best way to dip into the mainstream population of people who consider themselves to be managers would be through the largest organization representing management in Britain – the British Institute of Management (BIM). With over 66,000 members in two grades of Members and Fellows, it claims to be 'the largest professional management institute in the world'. The qualifications for entry coincide with most of our criteria, and in particular exclude new entrants to management. Membership requires 'a balance of demonstrable management experience with educational achievement', and Fellowship 'a minimum of two years responsibility at board or general manager level, taking account of educational achievement', with applications being assessed individually. Sampling this population thus yielded for this study a sample of well-established middle to senior status managers.

Our initial mailing was to a randomly[10] selected 2,500 Members and 1,500 Fellows. Only a small number of women were in the responding sample; around 50 out of the 1,500 respondents, representing 1.25% of the mailed managers. There were around 800/900 women on the BIM mailing list at the time of the first survey,[11] 1.28% of the total membership, so our sample seems to have been representative in this respect. At this point we chose to introduce one specific kind of unrepresentativeness. We decided to increase the representation of women managers in the sample. Since women are entering management in increasing numbers (reflected in the growing proportion of BIM membership) and face unique challenges as a minority group, we felt it important to see if job mobility poses special problems or opportunities for them. So, a separate mailing of the CDS (Career Development Survey) was sent to all the women members of the BIM, as well as a mailing via other professional women's organizations and a mailshot in women managers' professional journals.[12] The final result was a sample of 2,304 managers and business professionals including around 800 women (an exceptionally large number of women managers compared with other studies in the literature). So in what sense is this a representative sample? Well, we know that our BIM male sample closely corresponds to previous BIM management surveys (Guerrier and Philpot, 1978; Melrose-Woodman, 1978) in its occupational and regional composition, but enjoys a slightly higher response rate.[13] There are no population statistics to assess how representative were previous surveys of the total BIM membership. Nor is there any way of assessing how BIM members might differ from non-BIM managers, except on the criteria for membership itself. Our female

18

sample cannot be sensibly evaluated for representativeness, for women in management are a growing population. We can confidently say, however, that we have included many of those at the leading edge of this growth.

So in terms of our strategy, we can say that our sample succeeds in drawing from a wide range of regions, managerial and professional occupations, and organization types, both private and public, large and small. Our sample size gives confidence that many of our results will be generalizable to other managers and professionals within this range of diversity.

The large sample size also enables us to use sophisticated statistical analyses for a variety of technical reliability checks. Furthermore, the repeat survey method – 1,100 of the CDS-I sample responded to the CDS-II just over one year later – allows us to crossvalidate the stability of findings.[14] This longitudinal characteristic is also important for other reasons. Our topic is change over time. Most surveys have to infer the dynamic qualities of their data from relationships observed at a single point in time. Here we have the capacity to observe changes more directly. It is for this reason that longitudinal research designs – always practically and technically demanding – are increasingly valued in social science.

Finally, there is the perennial anxiety about the truthfulness of respondents and consequently about the validity of findings. We are confident that we have high quality findings in most areas covered by the survey, and can correctly identify and discard those items and scales where validity is in doubt. Such assessments can be made by performing various cuts and correlations on the data, particularly where there are known indicator variables that one can be confident have been reliably measured (such as biographical and occupational data). In addition, the questionnaires contained several areas where respondents could respond freely. Their comments clearly verified information measured by scales in a number of areas, and, overall, strongly confirmed that the two surveys went to the heart of some of the most pressing concerns of our respondents. Managers care deeply about their career development and it seems they often found completing our questionnaires a thought-provoking and insightful experience. Two typical expressions of this from the free comment last page of the CDS-I were: 'I feel that merely completing the questionnaire has helped me focus more clearly on my attitudes to myself as a manager and my relationship with superiors, subordinates and to the organization'[15] and 'As the Managing Director of a relatively small company this has been an interesting exercise, insomuch as it has produced an opportunity for me to take a look at myself as objectively as possible, and also as how others see me.'

There is also an *a priori* case for arguing that our respondents were interested, self-revealing and honest. After all, if they had misgivings about responding they had recourse to a simpler and less time-consuming way of dealing with a voluntary mail survey – they simply need not respond. This argument does not dispose of those who would wilfully distort and mislead us. Such people could be undetectable if they answered skilfully, so we must take it on trust that they are few and far between. We are comforted by the fact that careful scrutiny of the raw data revealed not one suspicious or improbable set of responses.

Yet, it remains a valid objection to surveys that they rely on subjective data. How can we be sure that when people report on, for example, the characteristics of the jobs that they hold that their perceptions are accurate? We cannot, but this is not always a weakness – for the important reason that for many measured variables there *is* no single or reliable external yardstick. Indeed there is a strong psychological case for arguing that subjective measures are entirely appropriate in many (though not all) of the areas covered by our investigation. For a variety of perceptual phenomena it is sensible to follow the dictum that what is perceived as real is real in its consequences. If we are concerned with individual action and reaction, then how the world is seen by the actor at the centre of the stage has causal primacy. Clearly, there are times when it is important to distinguish between false attributions and the real circumstances that give rise to them. This we shall endeavour to do wherever possible, and maintain a critical stance in our analysis.

So we would argue that the advantages of our method far outweigh its disadvantages. So large a data set from such a richly varied managerial population, with its longitudinal design and comprehensive measures, presents a valuable opportunity. From descriptive analytical procedures we are able to present a panoramic view of managerial job change, and from predictive multivariate techniques we can make substantial progress towards unravelling the complex causes and effects of mobility. Together, these strategies may help to give practical guidance to managers experiencing job change and organizations who seek to benefit from the process. They can help us to build grounded theory about the significance of transitions for personal development and organizational effectiveness.

2

A managerial profile

Peter Drucker has been one of the most articulate and effective missionaries for management as a profession and a discipline. His major works on the subject (1955, 1973, 1985) have given generations of managers a sense of purpose and self-respect, and helped to shape the expectations of the growing legions of young would-be managers in business schools. In his 1973 book on the tasks, responsibilities and practices of management, he set out to expunge the image of the manager that held sway in the prewar 'Heroic Age of Management' when it was identified with responsibility for the work of others. Instead of the bowler-hatted boss exercising authority on behalf of hierarchy, Drucker portrays the tasks of management as furthering the mission of organizations, making work productive and fulfilling social responsibilities. He writes: 'Management is a practice rather than a science. In this, it is comparable to medicine, law, and engineering. It is not knowledge but performance' (1973, p. 17).

The components of this performance he envisages as 'planning, organizing, integrating and measuring' (ibid., p. 393). Within the management literature one can find this approach represented by a proliferation of best-selling practitioner cookbooks for managerial excellence, ranging from the *reductio ad absurdum* of 'one-minute' recipes for success (Blanchard and Johnson, 1982) to considered appreciations of the complexities of the managerial role such as is represented in the work of Rosemary Stewart, depicting the manager's world as bounded on the one side by demands and on the other side by constraints, with 'choices' the operating zone of freedom between them (1982). Such works are consistent with the vision of management as a 'practice' and at the same time they are a response to what Drucker and others have identified as an unassuaged thirst for support and guidance in managerial performance.

Indeed in recent decades one can see that there has been a swelling flood of ideas, information and insights about work motivation, job characteristics, group dynamics, control systems, organizational design, and the processes of change, which has flowed out from the behavioural sciences into business education and into the practice of human resource management.

21

This informational revolution has been fulfilling Drucker's vision of the professionalization of management. Managers are no longer seen as a mysterious and remote elite but acknowledged as ordinary men and women charged with maintaining and directing the enterprises of an increasingly institutional society. Yet this development is by no means complete. Traditional stereotypes of management persist in Britain and the USA as a class-based vision of 'them and us', historically rooted in primitive forms of the capitalist division of labour, and still sustained today within some atavistic factory systems and the polarized images purveyed by political ideologies of both the extreme left and right. Managers themselves are not immune to such images, which are perpetuated by media caricatures of organizational life. These images can have the power to create the illusion of a superior idealized reality, even to the point of persuading managers to regard their own real experience as somehow atypical. This is not to deny that there are class divisions in society – not everyone is a manager. But the contours of occupational stratification are changing as we move from industrial to post-industrial forms of organization. One symptom of this is that managers are more ready to assume the militancy of white-collar wage labour than was conceivable fifty years ago (Bamber, 1986). Managers are less prepared to be satisfied with the authority vested in the role or to accept unquestioningly demands for loyalty and compliance from their organizations.

To understand the implications of these changes it is important that we have a comprehensive and accurate portrait of managers' situations and self-images. In this chapter we begin to paint this portrait and lay the foundations for our study of managers' job changes by describing their biographical characteristics, life circumstances, the organizations within which they work, and, most important, the values and needs that drive them. It is only from this knowledge base that we can begin to assess why and how they change jobs and with what possible consequences.

Who are the managers?

From our first analyses of the 2,300 managers who participated in the Time 1 survey (CDS-I) it is apparent that they are a highly heterogeneous population, covering a broad range of ages, industries, organization sizes, job types and organizational statuses. There are some major differences between the men and women in biographical characteristics, as will be discussed in detail in Chapter 9. Here we can briefly anticipate these in summary. They are predominantly middle aged,[1] though the men are older on average than the women (48 vs. 37 median age). Almost all the men are married with children, but far fewer women fit this norm. Almost all the

A managerial profile

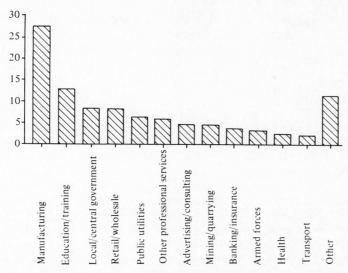

Figure 2.1 Managers' industrial groups. (*Source:* CDS-I, $N = 2,304$)

married women are in dual career partnerships, but far fewer of the men are in this situation. The managers vary considerably in their educational backgrounds – around a third have degrees of one kind or another – though the women are somewhat more highly educated than the men and the men more professionally qualified than the women.

Sex differences are less pronounced but still evident when we look at managerial occupations and organizational characteristics. Almost all the managers are in full-time employment (84%), with a much smaller number self-employed (8%) and the remainder in miscellaneous other categories of employment (fixed-term contract, part-time working, semi-retirement etc.). When we look at the types of jobs and organizations they are in, the enormous diversity of managerial roles becomes apparent. The largest number are to be found in manufacturing industry, but this still accounts for only about a quarter of the sample. The rest come from a variety of private and public sector institutions, service organizations, and business settings. A breakdown of these is shown in Figure 2.1.

Totalling up the managers who are in the private and public sectors places two thirds in the former and one third in the latter sector, roughly proportional to the distribution of employment more generally in the UK (Brown and Sisson, 1983). Company size varies enormously as well.

23

Table 2.1 *Percentages of managers in different organization sizes*

Number of employees in organization	Percentage of managers
0 — 30	15
31 — 100	10
101 — 500	16
501 — 1,000	8
1,001 — 3,000	11
3,001 — 10,000	12
10,001 — 50,000	13
50,000 +	15

(*Source:* CDS-I, $N = 2,304$)

Around a third of the sample come from companies with fewer than 500 employees, and a quarter at the opposite extreme: from companies exceeding 10,000 employees, as shown in Table 2.1. Again, this distribution is similar to the spread of the total work force across different size companies (Report on the Census of Production, 1982).

We looked at managerial roles in two ways. We asked people to indicate their job title, and, more subjectively, to say whether they considered themselves to be 'a functional specialist' or 'a general manager'. From the first of these classifications, role titles, we can see that their occupational diversity is even greater than their industrial diversity, with no single category out of some 29 job areas accounting for much more than 10% of the total. The most common job areas are: management services, personnel/training, finance/accounting, and general management, with sizeable minorities in the more traditional areas of production, sales, marketing, administration, engineering as well as growth areas such as R&D, management education, consultancy and computing.[2] In response to our second more general question about functional types, managers divide themselves roughly half and half into generalists and specialists, though here there does seem to be a notable sex difference (discussed in Chapter 9). Women managers are more likely to describe themselves as functional specialists than men.

The last biographical/occupational category to be mentioned is status. This is a difficult variable to measure with absolute accuracy. Role titles and salary levels are inconsistent indicators of levels of responsibility or organizational position, so instead of these we opted for a more direct self-report of status. We asked people how many levels there were between them and the top person in their company or organization in the UK, and how many levels below them to the level of first-line supervisor or equivalent. This measure is, of course, confounded by organization size, for it is, in general, 'easier' to be near the top of a small than a large organization, and of a 'flat' rather than a 'tall' organizational structure.[3] Putting these considerations to one side for the moment it does seem that we have netted a fairly senior sample: well over half (60%) are no more than two levels from the top of their organizations and one in seven are at chief executive level. A breakdown of status by organization size and by sex is provided in Chapter 9 (Table 9.9).

Taken together the statistics convey two general facts. First, they confirm the diversity of managers' personal and occupational characteristics. These men and women differ greatly in their circumstances and backgrounds, and the diverse managerial roles they occupy are found across a very broad range of organizational types. Second, within this diversity our sampling strategy has cut the range at the middle management level, so that here we are looking at the top half of the distribution of managerial statuses. The reflections that follow, therefore, are about the people who have the primary responsibility for the running of business in the UK. It is a matter of some interest, and indeed of some social importance, that we understand the values, attitudes and orientations of these people.

Values

Let us start by seeing what matters to managers in their lives. To do this we asked them to rank the following in order of *importance* to them in their lives: religious beliefs and activities, activities relating to political or community issues, family relationships, career or occupation, and leisure time social and recreational activities. Their results average ranks give a very clear ordering of family first and career second, with the rest far behind:

Family	62%
Career	28%
Religious	5%
Social/recreational	4%
Politics/community	1%

But if we look at these rankings taking into account people's domestic circumstances a more differentiated picture emerge, as is shown in Table 2.2.

It seems, not surprisingly, that family commitments have a preeminent bearing on the central life values of the married manager while career and leisure interests are of much greater importance to the single manager. Two observations may be made about these findings. First, they confirm the

25

Table 2.2 *Central life interests and family circumstances*

	Single $N = 331$ %	Married no children $N = 368$ %	Married with children $N = 1477$ %
Family	28	63	71
Career	50	31	23
Religious	9	5	4
Social/recreational	11	4	2
Politics/community	5	1	1

(*Source:* CDS-I, $N = 2,176$)

supreme importance of lives outside work for most managers, increasingly recognized in the literature (Dunnette, 1973; Evans and Bartolomé, 1980), and second, they signal clearly the need to take account of life circumstances when assessing people's work values, something organizational researchers have often failed to do (Dubin *et al.*, 1976).

In the CDS-II (the second phase of the survey 15 months after the first) we took this analysis a stage further by exploring how contented managers were with some of these areas. They were asked to indicate how satisfied they had been over the last year with their lives in each of the following areas: family, work, social/recreational, personal/emotional. Figure 2.2 shows the results. A very large percentage express high satisfaction with their family lives, but markedly fewer express similar satisfaction with work. The data on personal/emotional life suggest that all is not entirely well in the personal/emotional area where over one in five managers express some dissatisfaction. These results thus reveal some contrast between the quality of work and family life but also suggest the most potent difficulties arise in the private personal/emotional world of managers. What may be most important here for our understanding of management is how these satisfactions and problems interact, for it would seem that the most successful and contented managers are those who can hold the positive and negative experiences of work and non-work in a state of balance where they compensate for one another (Evans and Bartolomé, 1980; Korman *et al.*, 1981; Handy, 1984).

What is the source of these satisfactions and dissatisfactions? The literature on the question is extensive, and cannot be summarized here. But one can say that they emerge both from continuous processes, such as patterns of relationships, and from discontinuities, such as significant life events. We can shed a little light on the discontinuities from our questioning in the

A managerial profile

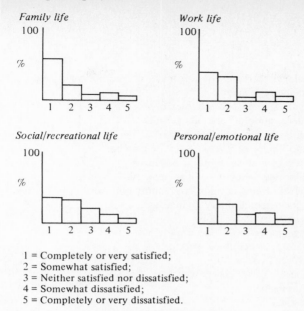

Family life

Work life

Social/recreational life

Personal/emotional life

1 = Completely or very satisfied;
2 = Somewhat satisfied;
3 = Neither satisfied nor dissatisfied;
4 = Somewhat dissatisfied;
5 = Completely or very dissatisfied.

Figure 2.2 Life satisfactions of managers in the last year.
(*Source:* CDS-II, $N = 1,067$)

Time 2 survey (the CDS-II) about what events took place in the 12–15 months[4] between the surveys.[5] The results are shown in Table 2.3.

Reviewing these events, normally treated as stressors in the life-events literature, it is striking that most arise in the work sphere. Moreover to this we can add that we know that nearly half of the managers also experienced the life event of a job change between the two surveys. If such discontinuities play a prominent role in managers' work lives, it seems from these data that they do not occur with nearly the same frequency in their non-work lives. Therefore one may reason that the non-work dissatisfactions we have observed are due more to continuous processes such as relationships, material conditions and so on rather than to discontinuous events. In the sphere of work continuous processes are also important, of course, but there would seem to be a more regular need to adapt to the discontinuities of environmental change. Yet if we take all these sources together, the need to adapt to change events is almost universal. For if we look at how many managers experienced *any* of these events, the total comes to fully 80% of the sample, and only 20% experienced none of the events in the short space of one year. We shall not dwell on non-work lives further, for our concern in this book is mainly with work and careers, and a first step to evaluating these is to look at how harmoniously or discordantly managers relate to their occupational environments.

Table 2.3 *Major life events reported between CDS-I and CDS-II*

	%
1 Business reorganization or major organizational change	33.4
2. Change of residence	15.1
3 Death of a close family member	14.8
4 Deterioration of relations at work	14.6
5 Son or daughter leaving home	13.5
6 Major injury or illness to family member	13.5
7 Death of a close friend or colleague	12.4
8 Major deterioration in financial state	9.0
9 Arrival of new or additional family member	8.8
10 Major personal injury or illness	8.4
11 Involuntary loss of job	5.2
12 Pregnancy of self/spouse/partner	4.7
13 Spouse/partner stops working	4.2
14 Divorce or separation	3.8
15 Spouse/partner begins working	3.7
16 Retirement	3.3
17 Marriage	1.9
18 Death of spouse	0.6

(*Source:* CDS-II, $N = 1,067$)

Person–role fit

There is increasing recognition in the literature on work psychology that mental health and performance depend upon the interaction of two sets of factors – individual differences and environmental characteristics (French *et al.*, 1982). We shall follow this reasoning by looking at how they match and mismatch. First, we shall look at managers' work related needs, from a series of questions asking for ratings of what is important to them in a job[6] (Table 2.4). From the results it is clear that managers place most importance on intrinsic values, plus the experience of working in a supportive environment.

This clear superiority of 'intrinsic' over 'extrinsic' work values is consistent with the results of a long history of similar studies (Hoppock, 1935; Houser, 1938; Jurgensen, 1948; Rosenberg, 1957; Herzberg, 1968). Above all else managers want challenge, recognition and self-development opportunities.

Using data reduction techniques[7] we were able to discover which of these work preferences tended to cluster together into coherent dimensions. One

28

A managerial profile

Table 2.4 *Work preferences: rank order of item average scores*

Most important
1 Challenging work to do
2 The quality of senior management
3 Work where individual accomplishment is appreciated
4 Opportunities to improve knowledge and skills
5 A job where I can be creative in doing things my own way
6 Opportunities for advancement
7 Working with people who are friendly and congenial
8 Opportunity to influence organizational policies
9 Job security
10 Belonging to an organization that is highly regarded
11 Opportunity for high earnings
12 A job where I get feedback on how I am doing
13 Location
14 Job which allows me to make a contribution to society
15 A job which fits in well with my life outside work
16 Work environments where tasks and responsibilities are clearly specified
17 Good fringe benefits
Least important

(*Source:* CDS-I, $N = 2,304$)

main dimension is what we have called '*need for growth*', comprising the items 'challenge', 'creativity', 'opportunities for advancement', 'acquisition of knowledge and skills', and 'opportunities to contribute to society'.[8] This seems to represent the work equivalent of what Maslow (1954) termed 'self actualisation', or the drive to achieve one's potential.

A second underlying dimension we have called '*need for predictability*', which embodies almost the opposite values to the expansive and expressive character of the first. This dimension comprises the items 'security', 'tasks and responsibilities clearly specified', 'feedback', 'quality of senior management', and 'belonging to an organization that is highly regarded'.[9] A third dimension composed of 'high earnings', and 'fringe benefits' measures '*need for rewards*'.[10] A comparison of the relative importance of these needs at work reveals that need for rewards is the least strong, and need for growth the most strong.

Now let us examine the extent to which work environments provide opportunities for managers to fulfil these needs. To do this we asked managers to rate their jobs on these same 17 items, this time saying how good or poor they found *their jobs* to be on each.[11] We can compare these

A managerial profile

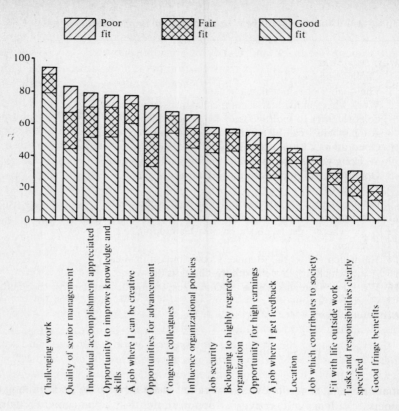

Figure 2.3 Fit of work preferences with actual work characteristics. (*Source:* CDS-I, *N* = 2,304).

two sets of ratings, for work needs and for job characteristics, to assess the overall degree of fit or misfit between managers and their jobs – where it is worst and where it is best. Figure 2.3 shows the results. On the whole, the managers rate their jobs as generally very high in challenge and in opportunities to be creative. Colleagues are seen as friendly and congenial and, for most, the location of work is also satisfactory. However, opportunities for advancement are seen as only fair by many, and opportunities for high earnings and fringe benefits are generally given low ratings.

30

The greatest discrepancies[12] between perceived and desired work characteristics are found in opportunities for advancement, the quality of senior
management, feedback and clarity of specification of tasks and responsibilities. In short these depict work environments in which challenge is high
but support is generally low. This is a potent combination: both risky and
stressful, and consequently potentially stifling to innovation. It is much
easier to try out new ideas and to take risks in environments which are
relatively predictable and when people around you support your attempts
regardless of whether or not those attempts are successful. This is true of
human behaviour right through the life cycle. The young child is far more
likely to explore new places and objects in a supportive atmosphere,
especially when exploration is encouraged (Ainsworth and Bell, 1974), a
finding that has been replicated for adults in clinical and counselling settings
(Rogers, 1961). In the work environment safety and support are no less
vital for individuals to be willing to take risks in trying out new ideas and
exploring the limits of their own potential. One may reflect that these misfit-
tings are causally linked in the minds of managers. In particular disappointment with the quality of senior management was widespread in our sample.
It may well be that our managers hold their seniors responsible for the
deficiencies they perceive in other areas, such as recognition, opportunities
for advancement and challenge.

Overall though, the fit between managers' work preferences and work
characteristics is good. Higher order growth needs are the most consistently
met, and it is therefore not surprising that on separate measures of
organizational commitment and work involvement[13] our data find managers
generally loyal and concerned to contribute to the good of their
organizations.

This analysis of managerial need fulfilment through their working
environments gives us only oblique insights into the personalities of
managers. To look more directly at this we can use other measures of how
they see themselves and their social relationships.

Managerial self-concept

First we asked the managers to reflect on their personalities and social identities through a series of self-perception items, shown in Figure 2.4.[14] We
then asked them to rate themselves again on the same scales, but this time
asking them how they saw themselves *at work*. Figure 2.4 shows the contrast between the two resultant profiles. In general (i.e. not at work)
managers describe themselves as creative, forceful, keeping feelings to
themselves, trusting, relaxed, sociable, fulfilled, happy, intellectual, confident, ambitious, optimistic, controlling, contented with themselves, and as

31

disliking uncertainty – what amounts to an overwhelmingly positive self-image. Although the ratings of 'self at work' were quite close to the ratings of 'self in general' there were some significant differences, and all of these are in a more negative direction. Managers tended to describe themselves as less creative, more forceful, much less trusting, more inclined to keep feelings to themselves, more reserved, more frustrated, less happy, more tense, and as less contented with themselves 'at work' than 'in general'.[15] There were no differences between managers' general and work identities on a smaller number of items: ambition, confidence, liking for uncertainty or intellect. These findings raise an important issue, generally not discussed in the organizational literature. Work affects how people see themselves, and the reflected self of working life seems undeniably less positive than it is away from work. What is it in the work environment that so impairs people's psychological adjustment?[16]

Some clues to this are to be found if we look back to managers' perceptions of work. The deficiencies reported in feedback and predictability are elements which could be expected to make them less trusting or open, and more tense. In short it seems reasonable to view these images of managerial working identity as the counterpart to work environments that are generally more threatening and unsafe than the world outside work.

Entrances to exits – differences by age and status

So far we have been looking at general trends amongst this heterogeneous management sample, but it is important also to keep in mind the diversity of their needs, experiences, and backgrounds. There are many possible ways of exploring this diversity, and we shall focus on three main dimensions of individual difference: age, sex, and status. We shall look first at age and status together, and then at sex differences.

Is managerial work a great levelling influence, homogenizing attitudes as people pass from work entry to retirement, or is their experience differentiated by age-graded eras which signify distinctive adaptive phases? And when we look at the effects of status, does the quality of working life change for those who attain the upper reaches of organizations? Does life get harder the higher you climb or are the peaks of power more fulfilling and rewarding places to be?

To investigate these questions we divided our sample into four age groups and three status groups.[17]

We examined how these groups differed in their self-perceptions (identity), work preferences (needs) and job characteristics (situations), using statistical methods that assess which group differences are meaningful and at the same time separate out the independent effects of age, sex and status.[18] The

Age:

'Young'	Aged between 20 and 35,	$N = 496$, 24%
'Young-middle'	Aged between 36 and 45,	$N = 567$, 27%
'Middle'	Aged between 46 and 55,	$N = 652$, 32%
'Senior'	Aged 56 and over,	$N = 354$, 17%

Status:

'Leaders'	People at the top of their organizations,	$N =$ 317, 14%
'Lieutenants'	People on the second or third level,	$N =$ 1054, 46%
'Juniors'	People on the fourth or lower levels,	$N =$ 905, 40%

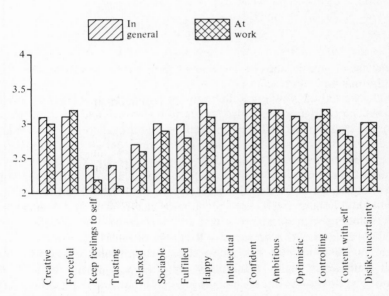

Figure 2.4 Managers' self-concepts – at work and in general.
(*Source:* CDS-I, $N = 2,304$).

results show increasing psychological security with age and status. Moreover, as Figure 2.5 shows, independently of status 'seniors' emerge as better adjusted than younger managers, and independently of sex. 'Leaders' are better adjusted and more dominant than lower status managers. One can see a clear increase in self-reported dominance[19] across the three status groups and an equally clear trend towards increasing adjustment across the age groups. Dominance appears to peak for all status groups in the 36 to 45

33

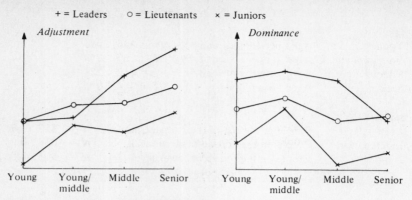

Figure 2.5 Self-concepts of managers by age and status groups.
(*Source:* CDS-I, $N = 2,304$).

year age group, perhaps at the time when managers are likely to be most ambitious and career centred.

The period of 'young-middle' age appears to be a watershed in other respects too. Figure 2.6 shows how need for growth and need for rewards from work also peak in this period, before declining thereafter for 'middles' and 'seniors'. It is among the older groups that, perhaps not surprisingly, need for predictability, i.e. safety, support, feedback and clarity, are greatest. Predictability is also most valued at middle and lower status levels, perhaps signifying the greater precariousness of these positions. Individual item analysis (not shown here) also reveals that 'leaders' concerns are becoming more pro-social, for they care significantly more about making a contribution to society. It is also of interest in Figure 2.6 that 'juniors' show much less evidence of strong growth needs. These differences (all statistically highly significant) serve as a powerful reminder that managers do not constitute an homogeneous group and that their needs are differentially shaped by qualities of experience that change over organizational levels and life stages.

We can gain a better appreciation of this heterogeneity of experience by looking at how these same groups evaluate their work characteristics, as shown in Figure 2.7. Individual item analysis also confirms that from 'juniors' up the status scale to 'leaders' there is a steady increase in positive evaluations on all the 17 items making up the work characteristic scales, with the sole exception of job security which only 'leaders' rate lower than other groups. Apart from this, the clear general pattern of results is that higher job satisfaction and greater well-being attend each successive

34

A managerial profile

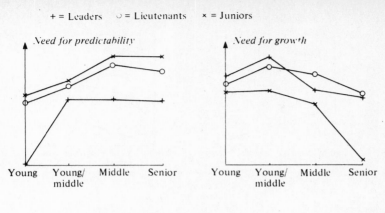

+ = Leaders   ○ = Lieutenants   × = Juniors

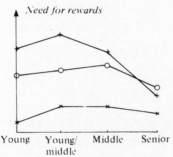

Figure 2.6 Managers' work needs by age and status groups.
(*Source:* CDS-I, N = 2,304).

category in the status hierarchy. Evidently the rewards of success are not just material.

The effects of age are less pronounced. However it can be seen that 'seniors' find fewer opportunities for rewards but greater predictability in their jobs.[20] This is an interesting trend when we consider that need for rewards also declines while need for predictability increases across the age groups (see Figure 2.6). This bears the interpretation that managers accommodate increasingly to work demands over their working lives; needs shape to fit what people have found organizations have to offer over a long period. So where opportunities for high earnings and advancement are not great, managers make adjustments in the value they place on these factors and so they continue to be fulfilled.[21] Desiring the unavailable is a recipe for frustration, alienation and dissatisfaction, and therefore it is in one's psychological self-interest to revise one's goals to levels which can be achieved within organizational settings.

A managerial profile

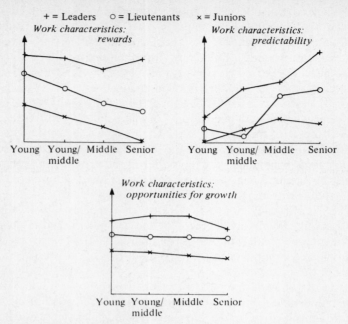

Figure 2.7 Perceived work characteristics by age and status groups. (*Source:* CDS-I, *N* = 2,304).

So, to summarize the age effects, it seems that managers nearing the end of their careers differ in a number of important ways from those at earlier stages. They appear more relaxed, fulfilled and less ambitious, and are less concerned with material rewards from work than they are with opportunities to influence and contribute to their environments.

The status effects we have found confirm the image of managerial elites as confident and powerful, with little evidence of strain being a common penalty of power. On the contrary, these managers see themselves as happy, fulfilled and creative, though of course one must allow for negative reactions possibly being suppressed by success, but periodically resurfacing as psychological dislocations from cumulative stresses (Cooper and Marshall, 1978; Hunt and Collins, 1983). We also found that the higher the status group the less likely respondents were to say they usually did what was expected of them rather than what they wanted.[22] It would appear that one of the chief rewards of high status is autonomy, a factor which has often been linked with psychological well-being and personal effectiveness (Mortimer and Simmons, 1978; Kohn and Schooler, 1983; Warr, 1987)

36

and its generally high levels in top managers' jobs probably serves to buttress their very positive self-images.

Within the last two decades job satisfaction has largely been supplanted as a measure of work attitudes by organizational commitment and job involvement. The reason is probably that job satisfaction has proved a poor predictor of work behaviour (Brayfield and Crockett, 1955; Nicholson *et al.*, 1976) and that commitment and involvement are motivational concepts more clearly linked with behaviour. Commitment and involvement can be seen as outputs of the psychological and behavioural investments people have made to their organizations and jobs, and as predictors of important organizational behaviours, such as performance and turnover (Mowday *et al.*, 1982). Commitment has been defined as having three components: identification with organizational values, willingness to expend effort on behalf of the organization, and loyalty (or intent to remain within the organization). Work involvement is the more focussed psychological investment a person has in their job. In the CDS-II we used standardized measures of commitment and involvement to look at the varying orientations of the managers.[23]

The results showed that most managers are very concerned to help their organizations and for their work to contribute to the good of the organization. Managers are also likely to express (though less emphatically) pride in and loyalty to their organizations. For example, a majority (68%) asserted that they would not seriously think of changing jobs even with the offer of more money (one of the loyalty items). Figure 2.8 shows the differing commitment and involvement of managers in different age groups and at different levels of the status hierarchy.

Older managers have higher levels of loyalty, commitment, and job involvement (independent of their status in organizations). This raises the question of whether managers develop increasingly favourable attitudes to organizations with age or simply that older managers have grown up in times when respect for institutions and authority was more unquestioning than today, i.e. they retain a legacy of positive attitudes to organizations acquired in earlier socialization and which they carry throughout their lives. If the latter is true then it would suggest that organizations will need increasingly to build effectiveness on more than simply the loyalty of their valued personnel, since one cannot expect new generations to have been similarly socialized. We cannot dispose between these two explanations from these data, but we are more inclined to accept the former (progressive increases with age and experience) from available knowledge about socialization and work attitudes. Commitment and involvement are relatively malleable psychological orientations, changing in response to altered life and career circumstances (Buchanan, 1974; Rabinowitz and

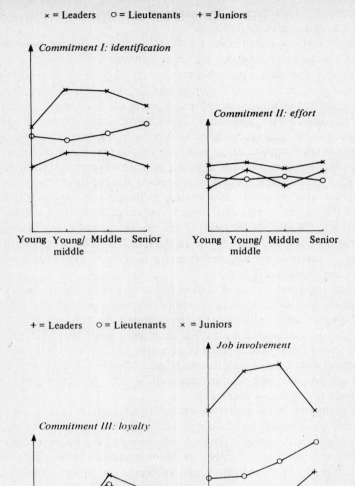

Figure 2.8 Organizational commitment and job involvement by status and age groups.
(*Source:* CDS-I, $N = 2,304$).

Hall, 1977). It seems reasonable therefore to assume that our managers have acquired more positive attitudes as their age and status have increased.

Figure 2.8 points in the same directions by showing that identification, effort and job involvement also increase across status levels. One may infer from this that career success has a positive feedback effect on attitudes, creating high levels of commitment towards the setting within which success is experienced. Or, more simply, we feel favourable toward the places where we do well, and we do well in the places we like. Identification, involvement and effort can be expected to be greater where one has some sense of ownership over work and organization. The vested interests of leaders in successful outcomes are not solely material.

Men and women in management

Lastly, let us look at sex differences. Chapter 9 explores in more detail the implications of the many observations made elsewhere in this book about the differences and similarities between men and women managers. Here we will focus particularly on the differences in the self-concepts and the expressed work needs of men and women. How does the woman manager see herself and in what ways is this different from the male manager? Are her needs in the work environment fundamentally different from her male colleagues and counterparts? Are women in management the victims of patriarchal norms, having to adopt a cold, aggressive, driving personality, in order to be accepted and succeed in a hostile environment, or, alternatively, are women constrained to conform to 'feminine' stereotypes of affiliative dependency?

Analysis of the self-concepts of men and women managers in the CDS-I revealed a number of significant differences between the sexes, shown in Figure 2.9.

Women managers were more likely to report showing feelings readily, and to see themselves as more sociable, fulfilled, intellectual and optimistic than the men. On the other hand they describe themselves as more tense and less confident.[24] These findings suggest that the female manager does not differ from the male manager in many of the ways some gender stereotypes would have predicted. The female manager appears to have a generally healthier self-image than the male manager. However exceptions to this are the women's higher levels of tension and unsureness, possibly symptomatic of the pressures encountered by female managers in a traditionally male dominated profession, for there is no doubt that women experience many obstacles in their careers which do not lie in the paths of men. The some-

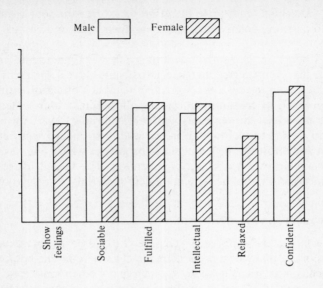

Figure 2.9 Differences in self-descriptions of men and women managers.
(*Source:* CDS-I, $N = 1,449$ males, 806 females).

what hesitant and cautious watchfulness we find among the women may reflect their less safe and supportive managerial positions.

Perhaps we should be more concerned to speculate why the men differ from the women in these respects, i.e. why should they be more reluctant to show feelings, see themselves as less sociable, as less fulfilled, as less optimistic, and as less intellectual. Certainly males in Western society have traditionally been socialized to conceal or control their feelings while women have been taught the value of affiliative behaviours to win approval (Tavris and Offir, 1977). For boys assertiveness has been the more socially acceptable way to succeed, and this pattern persists into adulthood.

The work needs of men and women managers also differ quite radically. Table 2.5 shows that women managers are less interested in fringe benefits, high earnings, and security. They are more interested in having friendly and congenial colleagues, challenge, work where individual accomplishment is appreciated, opportunities to acquire knowledge and skills, opportunities to be creative, contributing to society through their work, feedback, work which fits in well with life outside work, and employment in a favoured location. In more general terms it is clear that the women managers are less concerned than the men with material rewards from work and are more interested in fulfilling need for growth.[25] It might be suggested that this is

Table 2.5 *Differences in work needs of men and women managers*

	Men vs Women
1 Opportunities for advancement	ns
2 Working with people who are friendly and congenial	<<<
3 Challenging work to do	<<<
4 Work where individual accomplishment is appreciated	<<<
5 Belonging to an organization that is highly regarded	ns
6 Opportunity to improve knowledge and skills	<<<
7 A job where I can be creative in doing things my own way	<
8 Good fringe benefits	>
9 A job which fits in well with my life outside work	<<<
10 Job security	>>>
11 Opportunity for high earnings	>>>
12 Location	<<<
13 Job which allows me to make a contribution to society	<<<
14 Opportunity to influence organizational policies	ns
15 Work environments where tasks and responsibilities are clearly specified	ns
16 A job where I get feedback on how I am doing	<<<
17 The quality of senior management	ns

>   Men score higher than women ($p < 0.05$)
>>>   Men score higher than women ($p < 0.001$)
<   Women score higher than men ($p < 0.05$)
<<<   Women score higher than men ($p < 0.001$)
ns   No significant difference
(*Source:* CDS-I, $N = 2,304$)

because many of the women are partners in dual career families (441 of 806) and that, because their incomes are not the sole means of support for their families, material rewards are of less importance to them than for the men who are much more likely to be the family 'breadwinners'. We tested this by analysing dual versus single career men and women, and found no clear evidence to support this popular 'pin money' theory of married women's work motives.[26]

A more important sex difference is the major disparity in need for growth. One possible interpretation is that to succeed in management women require greater intrinsic motivation and commitment than men in order to overcome the gender-specific obstacles that lie in their managerial career paths (see Chapter 9). The other major difference between the sexes is the greater concern of women for the fit between work and non-work life and

41

with the location of their organizations. Women, even when holding full-time jobs, often retain primary responsibility for child-rearing and household management, so there is good reason for them to be more concerned than men about the fit between work and family life. Location of work is similarly important for schooling of children. However analysis shows that these factors are more important for single women too.

Men and women managers' descriptions of work environments do not differ as radically as do their work needs, though the women managers (whether single or married) are more likely than men to report that their jobs provide a good fit between work and life outside and that their work is in a good location. One may infer perhaps that women seek out jobs which allow them to integrate their work and non-work roles. They are also more likely to see their jobs as allowing them to make a contribution to society and providing good opportunities to acquire knowledge and skills. This reflects wider differences in the roles and career paths of men and women in management, which we shall be looking at further in subsequent chapters. For the moment we can conclude that these data reveal some quite pronounced contrasts in the ways that men and women managers view themselves and their working lives.

Summary and conclusions

We started this chapter with some thoughts on the changing role and image of management, taking Drucker's views as a reference point. Much of what we have observed here has confirmed the new image of management which he and other writers have been promoting. First and foremost we find that people from a bewilderingly wide array of organizations and occupations very clearly see themselves as managers. There is no hint in our findings to support the old two-dimensional stereotype of managers as authoritarian guardians of power, work obsessed and materialistic in their style and values. True, the managers in our study are generally highly committed to their organizations and involved in their jobs, but work is not all important to them in their lives. For a great majority of those with partners and families, career is secondary to family as a central life concern. Ideally work and family in the harmoniously ordered life should be mutually supportive: one works in order to uphold and enhance the quality of one's life outside work, and one orders one's home life to facilitate productive and satisfying contributions to occupational and institutional life. The need for fulfilment in both the spheres of work and non-work has always been important, but perhaps now there is increasing recognition that it needs to be an effective transaction in both directions (Dunnette, 1973; Handy, 1984).

When we look at what people value and want within their managerial roles, though, it is clear that however important life outside work might be, this diverse group of men and women are nonetheless looking for psychological fulfilment from their occupations. The high value placed upon challenge, recognition, learning opportunities and creativity amount to a desire for personal effectiveness and growth in the work sphere. Security, rewards, role clarity, and organizational prestige are of lesser importance. We may take some comfort from this image, and, to a lesser extent, that need for power ('opportunity to influence organizational policies') is not a prime concern, though the low rating given to being in a 'job which allows one to make a contribution to society' (especially for the men) is perhaps a little worrying. Drucker's emphasis upon this latter value as one of the three central tasks of management would thus appear to be idealistic, underestimating the degree to which managers today have a privatized and autonomous rather than a pro-social conception of their professional identities. We find further confirmation of this in Chapter 8 where it seems that managers accord task-related accomplishments greater importance than care for the well-being of others.

Drucker also highlights the need for management development, a theme much in evidence elsewhere in the literature (Pedler *et al.*, 1978; Colantuono, 1982; Kaye, 1982; London and Stumpf, 1982). We do find that managerial jobs are by and large need-fulfilling, but it seems that organizations are often judged to be inadequate in what they do to help managers. Recognition for achievement, feedback, opportunities for advancement, and learning opportunities, are often insufficient, and, subsuming these, the quality of top management is judged to be deficient. It would seem that for many managers the satisfactions they are able to extract from work are by virtue of their autonomous efforts and not through the supportive agency of well-designed human resource systems, a theme confirmed and enlarged upon in Chapter 8. This perhaps accounts for the self rather than social orientation suggested by our findings. It also may account for the fact that although the managers generally have highly positive self-images, they are less positive in the sphere of work. It is as if self-dependence in uncertain and unhelpful work environments fosters a public persona of watchful reserve.

Finally, it should be noted that these satisfactions and frustrations are not evenly distributed across the management population. Life gets better as you get nearer the top of organizations, and as you get older. The one suggests privilege – heightened access to the source of psychological fulfilments as one rises through the hierarchy; the other suggests adaptation – increasing equanimity through the life cycle, consistent with a number of accounts of life cycle adjustment, from Erikson (1950) onwards. We also observed sex differences which confound some stereotypes of men and women at work, though in other respects it seems as if women, as a minority in the managerial population, may develop distinctive orientations to survive and prosper in the face of inequitable circumstantial obstacles and the prevailing values of male-dominated sub-cultures. More of this later (see Chapter 9). Now it is time to look at one important kind of managerial behaviour, the central concern of this book, job changing.

3

All change: mobility patterns in management

The portrait of the managerial character painted in Chapter 2 has positive and reassuring overtones. Managers care more about their families than their jobs, and more about their higher order needs than their material satisfactions, though it might be said, without being unduly cynical, that most can afford to take this stance from a position of well-paid employment. At the same time there is considerable variation in managers' expressed needs and how likely these are to be fulfilled by the positions they are in. Although we found no evidence of widespread and deeply felt frustrations, there were a number of discordant notes in some of our findings. Psychological adjustment at work is less favourable than away from work. Managers often find organizations fail to fulfil their needs for achievement, recognition and feedback, and they are also often disappointed in their senior managers. Therefore, it would not be surprising if managers sought out job change as a way of removing frustrations and improving the quality of their work lives. One major aim of our study was to find out if managers do try to do this, and if they are successful in the attempt.

We also pointed out in Chapter 1 that job change is likely to be driven by more than just the needs and desires of managers. We observed that the twin facts of organizational hierarchy and human aging compel a continuing process of managerial succession, like downward rolling ripples through organizations, and that mobility is further accelerated by a variety of other social forces and changes. The introduction of new technology, the redesign of jobs, intra-organizational transfers, and the recruitment and shedding of personnel are all strategies entailing job change that organizations commonly use to maintain command over their destinies amid rising seas of uncertainty. So both of these sets of forces – managers' needs and environmental change – implicate job change as a primary outcome. Are these forces for mobility increasing their pressure historically? We have argued that the pace of environmental change has been quickening. Perhaps at the same time managers' tolerance for frustration is declining. Maybe people are now more inclined to quit one setting in search of another more satisfying than they were in times of more stoical loyalty to paternalistic enterprises.

Whichever of these changes is happening we would expect mobility trends to reflect them. In this chapter we seek to document these trends, and in the next chapter to reflect on their origins. The evidence from the USA has been of high and rising mobility, though research has not established its causes or whether the rate has continued to rise through the periods of recession and expansion in the later 1970s and 80s.

In this and the next chapter, we supply some answers to these questions from a British context, though we believe there are grounds for some cross-cultural generalization.[1] In this chapter we shall look at job change descriptively: (1) how much of it is occurring; (2) what form does it take; and (3) to whom is it happening? Briefly anticipated, our answers to these questions are: (1) it is a frequent event, whose rate has been increasing unabated by recession; (2) it is more often than not radical in form; and (3) different types of change happen to people in different circumstances, but that some types of change seem to have more beneficial career outcomes than others. In Chapter 4 we shall pursue the meaning of job change further by looking at managers' career perceptions and how they view the causes of job changes.

Mobility rates

First, then, we shall use our data to put to the test the proposition, from our analysis of the Transition Cycle and social change, that job change is a frequent and ubiquitous event, and to do this we shall take employer moves as a criterion (we shall look at other types of change subsequently). Employer moves are of particular interest as one of the most radical types of change, and probably the most reliably documented in the literature.[2] This indicator also enables us to look at whether they have become more or less frequent in recent times.

There are always difficulties in documenting historical change through social statistics, for often the measures taken and samples used are of doubtful comparability. But in the present study we have some grounds for confidence that historical trends in this one important index of job change, employer moves, can be reliably charted. The British Institute of Management (BIM) has had a large and general managerial membership for nearly four decades and its periodic surveys of members have been documenting managerial mobility since the 1950s. The most recent of these surveys prior to ours (Guerrier and Philpot, 1978) compared its findings with its three predecessor surveys and concluded that mobility rates had been consistently rising since 1958. So in order to update this record we took care in our study to adopt the same measure of mobility as used in these previous surveys by asking managers how many changes of employer they had

Table 3.1 *Historical change in mobility*

	Number of employer changes:				
Date of survey	0	1	2	3	4 or more
1958[a] (N = 646)	34%	24%	21%	11%	13%
1966[b] (N = 815)	33%	23%	19%	12%	13%
1971[c] (N = 964)	17%	16%	19%	14%	33%
1976[d] (N = 1304)	13%	16%	17%	17%	37%
1983[e] (N = 1364)	9%	13%	16%	18%	43%

[a] Clements (1958);
[b] Clarke (1966);
[c] Birch and McMillan (1971);
[d] Guerrier and Philpot (1978);
[e] Alban-Metcalfe and Nicholson (1984)

experienced in their careers to date; we also incorporated identical occupational and regional classifications to check the comparability of our sample with Guerrier and Philpot's. By restricting our historical comparison of employer moves to the male BIM Members who responded to our survey (i.e. excluding women and the higher status 'Fellows' of the British Institute of Management), a comparable sample was achieved in terms of two measured criteria: the distribution of the sample across 13 regional areas of the UK and across 16 occupational categories. On neither index did the distributions of our sample differ from its most recent predecessor,[3] i.e. our samples are demographically comparable. Table 3.1 shows how the numbers of job changes in managers' careers have been changing, as reflected in all the BIM surveys that have reported on them.

Table 3.1 shows that there has been a steepening decline over the last 25 years in the number of managers who have spent their entire working lives with a single employer: down from a third of all managers in the 1950s and 60s to less than one in ten now. In our 1983 survey we find that nearly two thirds are with their fourth employer – the comparable figure was less than 1 in 4 in the 50s and 60s and one in two in the 70s.[4] One might have expected the recession of the late 70s and early 80s to have held back mobility rates. Certainly this could be expected from the reasoning that recession restricts labour market opportunities and could cause managers to cling to their jobs. However, our findings contradict this logic. The same trend seems also to be visible in the USA, where the rate of occupational relocations doubled from the early 60s to the late 70s (Sell, 1983). Either the recession has not had an impact on managerial levels of employment or it has increased rather than diminished the pressures for mobility. All available evidence favours the latter explanation. A cold wind has been blowing through the managerial labour market but the effect of the recession on business has been to hasten reorganizations and cost-cutting to maintain profitability. These changes have both encouraged and enforced higher rates of employer change, as old businesses have declined and new ones emerged. Our analysis of reasons for job change in Chapter 4 confirms this.

But employer changes are only half the story. Many other important career transitions and changes of work roles are possible without moving between organizations. We tried to sample as wide a range as possible of these by asking our sample to adopt the following definition of job change: 'Any move between jobs or any major alteration to the content of your work duties and activities. This means we would like you to include among "job changes" times when there has been a major change in the content of your job whilst you were still in the same post (e.g. major work reorganizations, giving you new duties).'

We then asked people to fill in a work history matrix to describe their last five job changes, telling us: the year each change took place, the reason for the change, and whether each involved (a) a change of employer, (b) a change in status (up, down or no change), and (c) a change in function. These classifications provide a much more sophisticated analysis of job change than any previous survey, and give us data from our total sample on well over 10,000 job changes.[5]

Around 75% of all these job changes involved a change of function, around 70% were upward status moves (10% downward status and 20% no change of status), and about 57% were employer moves.[6] So it seems that employer change alone is inadequate as a measure of mobility since it captures only just over half of all job change.[7] It is also apparent that our managerial sample is predominantly upwardly mobile. From the dates of moves we can also tell how frequent they are. Three years is the average duration of job tenure, though there is wide variation around this average: as many as one in ten have had five or more jobs in the last five years – i.e. over one a year, while at the opposite extreme, a further one in ten are only on their second job in ten years. A three year average might not be considered a rapid mobility rate if the types of job change were simple and incremental, but we can infer that they are not. The percentages we have recorded for functional, employer or status moves (75%, 57% and 80%) logically require most moves to have involved change on more than one of these three dimensions simultaneously. To find out which combinations of these change dimensions are most common we shall now turn to look more

48

Table 3.2 *The 12 types of job change: frequencies for last move*

Rank	Symbol code (a)	Type name	Per cent
1	↑ F	in-spiralling	27.6
2	E ↑ F	out-spiralling	24.6
3	= F	in-lateral	10.0
4	↑	promotion	8.4
5	E ↑	out and up	8.3
6	E = F	out-lateral	6.9
7	E ↓ F	drop-out shift	5.0
8	E	out-transfer	4.3
9	=	job reorder	2.5
10	↓ F	drop shift	1.3
11	E ↓	out-demotion	0.7
12	↓	in-demotion	0.4

(a) Key:
E   Employer change (no E means no employer change)
F   Function change (no F means no function change)
↑   Upward status change
↓   Downward status change
=   No status change
e.g. ↑ F indicates an upward status and functional change but no change of employer
(*Source:* CDS-I, $N = 2,304$)

closely at types of job move and the kinds of demands they make on managers.

Types of job change

We shall start by looking at the relative frequency of twelve types of job change. Twelve types can be uniquely identified by combining our three basic descriptive dimensions of job change: employer (yes/no), function (yes/no) and status (up, no change, down); i.e. $2 \times 2 \times 3 = 12$ types. We have given each of these twelve types a name and a symbolic code, as shown in Table 3.2. Table 3.2 shows these 12 types in rank order of frequency, from most to least common, using managers' last job move as a criterion.

Two types of change account for more than half of all job moves. These are two forms of 'spiralling' (Watts, 1981) – moves that take managers up the organizational hierarchy and simultaneously give them a new function to perform. Spiralling moves are approximately equally divided between those that take place within an organization, *in-spiralling*, and those that take the manager out into a new organization, *out-spiralling*. Clearly both are amongst the most radical of all job changes, requiring simultaneous adjustment to the new demands of lateral and vertical movement, and for out-spiralling moves also requiring adjustment to the demands of a new organizational setting. It is striking that those moves conventionally considered to be 'normal' are much more infrequent, such as simple promotions (rank 4), lateral transfers (rank 3), moves to a new company to perform the same function (rank 5), and instances of job redesign (rank 9). These frequencies are based on analysis of managers' last job change. When we check their reliability by repeating this analysis for all previous job changes recorded, the patterns are stable; we get almost identical findings from all five recorded job moves. In short, managerial careers are typified by sequences of spiralling moves. Job moves upward in status entail a simultaneous functional change in almost every case, and about half of these also involve a change of employer.

But how radical are the demands of these different move types? For example, do changes in function really make highly novel demands on managers? One way we are able to answer such questions is from the reports people gave of how their present job compared with their previous job in (a) its novelty of demands, (b) the new skills it required the mover to develop, and (c) how much they were able to apply previously acquired skills in their new jobs.[8] Table 3.3 ranks the 12 move types on these three measures.

The first feature to note in Table 3.3 is the lack of any clear relationship between the ranks in columns A, B and C. One might have expected, for example, that high novelty would also mean high learning requirements and low transfer of skills, or that high skill transfer would be associated with low learning opportunities. We find no such relationships here, though some of these expected relationships can be observed in different types of analysis.[9] However, it is apparent that these rankings of novelty, learning and transfer are all fairly independent of one another. But this does not mean that these qualities are randomly distributed across job types. Far from it. Our analysis shows that each of our three main dimensions of job change is systematically linked with these three qualities of job demands.[10] Certain key features are readily identifiable in Table 3.3. In column A, for example, it is apparent that greatest novelty is experienced when managers simultaneously change employer and function (move types 2, 6 and 7: 'out-spiralling', 'out-lateral', and 'drop-out shift'). In column B, high learning requirements seem to be especially associated with upward status moves (moves 1, 2, 4 and 5: 'in-spiralling', 'out-spiralling', 'promotion', and 'out and up'). In column C, linkages between skill transfer and move types are less clear, though simultaneous employer moves and status changes do seem to involve an

Table 3.3 *Evaluating role demands for the 12 types of job change*

		A Novelty: difference in tasks, skills and methods (3 items)	B Learning: requirement to develop major new skills (1 item)	C Transfer: opportunity to use previously acquired skills (1 item)
Scale:				
Type	Code (a)	Rank	Rank	Rank (b)
1 In-spiralling	↑ F	7	2	8
2 Out-spiralling	E ↓ F	3	1	1 =
3 In-lateral	= F	6	6	9
4 Promotion	↑	10	3	4
5 Out and up	E ↑	9	4	3
6 Out-lateral	E = F	4	5	6 =
7 Drop-out shift	E ↓ F	1	7	11
8 Out-transfer	E =	12	11	5
9 Job reorder	=	11	8	6 =
10 Drop shift	↓ F	5	9	10
11 Out-demotion	E ↓	8	12	1 =
12 In-demotion	↓	2	10	12

(a) Key:
E   Employer change
F   Function change
↑   Upward status change
↓   Downward status change
=   No status change
(b) Here '=' denotes tied ranks
(*Source:* Last job move data, CDS-I, $N = 2,260$)

above average skill transfer (moves 2, 5 and 11: 'out-spiralling', 'out and up', and 'out-demotion').

It is clear that there are some complex relationships here. The best way of simplifying and integrating them is to pick out and to look at a few particular move types. The most interesting and important of these is out-spiralling, the second most common type of move, and one of the two most radical by our measured change dimensions (i.e. out-spiralling and drop-out shift both involve employer + status + function change). Out-spiralling exhibits a uniquely potent combination of high novelty, high learning requirements, and high opportunity to transfer skills, a mix that could be said to combine demand for change optimally with the cushioning of psychological resources. 'Out and up' (move 5) exhibits similar features, though here novelty is rated somewhat lower.

A complete contrast is move 7, drop-out shift, the other most radical move type (change occurs on all three dimensions of employer, status and function, but here the status change is downward in direction). This combination has a quite different and somewhat ominous kind of potency: high novelty combines with only moderate demands for skill development, and affords low scope for transfer of skills. If out-spiralling connotes confident exploration in adjusting to job change, drop-out shift suggests exposure to demands without compensations or supports: a psychologically threatening experience, as we shall see in Chapter 6.

Lying midway between these two extremes is the most common type of move, in-spiralling. Although it must count as a fairly radical move, involving as it does simultaneous upward status and functional change, it seems to offer neither the challenge of high novelty, nor the psychological cushioning of high skill transfer, though it does present major learning requirements. Turning to look at other move types, some interesting contrasts can be observed, for example between out-demotion and in-demotion, the two least common move types (11 and 12). In-demotion has all the appearance of being an acute stressor, like drop-out shift, with high novelty but low learning and transfer – in short, it contains strong overtones of professional obsolescence (Legge, 1973; Kaufman, 1974). Out-demotion, in contrast, looks safe but mundane, with high transfer of skills to situations of low novelty and low learning requirements.

These results raise an important question of interpretation. When a manager reports high transfer of skills, learning or novelty, how much is this judgement a reflection of the person or the job? All these findings could be due to personality differences if, say, confident types were more likely to make particular job moves and at the same time to report higher novelty, learning and transfer than non-confident types. We performed further analyses to check this, by incorporating several of our self-concept measures to see whether the links we have found between move types and job demands are (a) completely explained by personality, (b) unaffected by personality, and (c) a mix of the two. Our analysis confirms (c).[11] There are some clear links between such personality factors as dominance, confidence and adjustment with move types and with job demands, but the main relationships between move types and job demands we have been looking at are very strong and unaffected by these secondary personality effects, i.e. personality does have an influence but additional to and independent of the effects we have described.

How should we interpret this? A number of possibilities suggest themselves. Well adjusted and dominant individuals may be predisposed to seek out jobs of high novelty and with good learning opportunities. The most radical moves may be undertaken by people with the greatest confidence in the transferability of their skills. The experience of successful adjustment to job change may in turn reinforce and heighten some of these psychological qualities, such as adjustment and dominance. In other words, some kinds of job change may initiate or sustain a self-reinforcing cycle of personal development and achievement, akin to Hall's (1976) 'success syndrome', the tendency for early job success to create the conditions for later achievement.[12] This interpretation is also consistent with the longitudinal research of Kohn and Schooler (1983), Mortimer and Lorence (1979), Brousseau (1983) and others who have demonstrated that psychological self-direction is both a cause and a consequence of demanding work experiences. Before we jump to this conclusion we need to examine our own longitudinal data. This we shall do later in this chapter and in Chapters 5 and 6, but we can preview the results now. The evidence is mixed. Personality and success do seem to be linked in two directions, but it is more difficult to find specific links with types of job change. The short time scale of our longitudinal phase is insufficient to do more than suggest how job change may initiate personal change (see Chapter 6).

Before we look at factors associated with different types of change it is important that we establish more objectively what kinds of moves managers are making. From their reports it seems that functional moves have high novelty, and that employer changes do represent a radical switch, but how much credence can we put in these reports? We can check this through our two-stage survey design which provides data at both points in time on people's job areas and industries. This enables us to test for example whether function changes are minor moves between similar families of occupations, and whether employer moves are likewise taking place between similar kinds of organization. Of the sample who responded to both the CDS-I and the CDS-II (1,081 managers), 38% (411) changed jobs in the 15 months between the two surveys. The occupational categories of our detailed response alternatives can be grouped into eight broad functional areas.[13] Table 3.4 shows that functional changes are mostly major rather than minor shifts. Even defining job area broadly through this classification there is still a remarkably high rate of radical migration between groups.[14]

On this showing managerial careers are highly volatile, insofar as they are punctuated by major shifts between functional areas. The data also tell us something about specific occupational trends. Administration (G) is the most obvious growth area and the fields of technical services, line and human relations functions (B, D and E) are the areas of greatest loss.

Table 3.4 *Mobility between job areas for people who changed jobs between CDS-I and CDS-II*

Job area	Number in area at CDS-I	Number of moves within job areas = outflow	Number in area at CDS-II	Number of moves within job areas = inflow	Net change = number in area at CDS-I − number in area at CDS-II
A *Sales* (inc. purchasing marketing, sales, distribution)	66	48	73	48	25	+ 7
B *Line management* (production, engineering, maintenance)	30	13	18	13	5	− 12
C *Finance* (finance, legal)	34	22	34	22	12	0
D *Human relations* (personnel, PR)	54	30	48	30	18	− 6
E *Technical services* (design, R & D, computing, research)	31	12	24	12	12	− 7
F *Management services* (consultancy, professional services)	45	20	43	20	23	− 2
G *Administration* (office administration, general management)	55	34	93	34	59	+ 38
H *Education* (management education, lecturing)	18	10	21	10	11	+ 3

Management services (F) is the most generally mobile functional area, with high migration both in and out of it. Sales and finance (A and C) are the only areas approaching some stability, but even here around a third migrated in or out of them within the one year period between the surveys.

We conducted the same kind of analysis for employer moves. After reclassifying some 29 industry codes into five broad groups, we plotted the moves of those people who changed employer between Time 1 and Time 2. The results are shown in Table 3.5.

Table 3.5 reveals low stability in all industry groups except for the government group (E). Overall only 58% of employer-changing managers are switching between organizations of even approximately the same type, and if one excludes the stable government group, this figure falls to 46%. So, taken together, Tables 3.4 and 3.5 confirm the genuinely radical nature of much job changing.

The findings we have reviewed in this section confirm the importance of looking at the *form* taken by job changes. The global statistics on mobility often quoted by the media and researchers are unrevealing about the kinds of demands that job changes make on people. More particularly, we have established that job changes are frequent events in the lives of many managers, and more often than not they are radical events, involving change on more than one dimension. Upward spiralling moves seem to be especially common. These results raise the question of whether these different types of change are experienced equally by all types of managers. Let us now try to answer this question.

Who moves and how? Factors associated with mobility

If the amount of job change that is visible here is a product of the two forces of environmental turbulence and unfulfilled individual needs there is every reason to suppose these two forces will not be uniformly encountered across the managerial population. We have already seen that there is wide variation around the three year job change average, and that certain occupational and industrial groups are more mobile than others. Now we want to pinpoint more precisely who changes and who does not. Here we shall look at two sets of factors associated with mobility: biographical and occupational factors, drawing on our demographic indicators from the two surveys. Later on, in Chapters 4 to 6, we shall be devoting attention to psychological measures of individual differences. First, here we shall relate demographic factors to two types of mobility measure: managers' past histories of different kinds of mobility and their expectations of future job change. The first of these, past mobility, is constructed from managers' reports of their last five job moves. We are able to index for each manager:

Table 3.5 *Mobility between industry groups for people who changed employer between CDS-I and CDS-II*[15]

Industry group	Number in group at CDS-I	Number of moves within group	= outflow	Number in group at CDS-II	Number of moves within group	= inflow	Net change = number in group at CDS-I – number in group at CDS-II
A *Industrial* (inc. manufacturing, mining, quarrying, agriculture, contractors)	24	8	16	19	8	11	– 5
B *Traditional services* (transport, retail, wholesale, printing publishing, leisure)	11	3	8	9	3	6	– 2
C *New services* (prof. services, consulting, computing marketing, voluntary org)	23	9	14	21	9	12	– 2
D *Commerce* (banking, insurance, finance, investment)	6	3	3	9	3	6	+ 3
E *Governmental* (educ., civil service, utilities, public services, health	28	21	7	31	21	10	+ 3

how many of their last five moves involved a change of employer, function or status; how many employers they have had in their entire careers, and how fast they have been changing jobs over the past five moves (from the dates of each change). The second mobility criterion, expected future change is, perforce, more subjective, derived from managers' estimates of how likely they would be to experience different kinds of job change over the next twelve months.

Tables 3.6 and 3.9 show how these mobility measures relate to biographical and occupational factors. Note that these two tables are split for convenience of explanation; in reality they are the product of a variety of interconnected analyses.[16] Methods of analysis were used which reveal relationships independently of each other, e.g. so one can be sure that age effects are not due to status effects, or *vice versa*.

Biographical factors

Table 3.6 shows age and sex to be fairly constant predictors of mobility, while family situation[17] and education are not. Looking at age first, we can see that it tells us more about expected future mobility than about actual past mobility. Younger managers have greater expectations of all kinds of change, apart from dismissal/redundancy. The latter, not surprisingly perhaps, is more expected by older workers. Older managers also tend to have had more employers in their career lifetime ('Number of Employers'), again not surprising considering they have had longer careers in which to change employers. Younger managers have experienced more rapid change than older managers, consistent with the idea in the careers literature that youth is a time of exploration and rapid change (Super, 1957; Schein, 1978). The most interesting and unexpected finding is the Age × Sex interaction for employer changes. This interaction denotes that when men are young they have a high rate of employer changing which declines as they grow older, while women keep up a high rate of employer changing throughout their lives and careers – indeed, higher than men's at most ages. This can be verified by another method: calculating managers' ages at the time of their last job change (from age and date of change) and plotting for each age group the percentage of job changes which were employer moves. This analysis is shown in Table 3.7.

The results confirm that male managers' early careers are marked by a high rate of movement between organizations, which declines steadily into late middle age when there is a secondary peak. This peak is no momentary aberration. The same pattern emerges if we calculate equivalent data for each of the last five job changes: the same late career peak occurs. This is almost certainly due to enforced job change as men become more exposed

Table 3.6 *Biographical factors positively related to job change*

| Job change measures | Biographical factors | | | |
	Age	Sex	Family situation	Education
Past career mobility				
Employer changes (out of 5)	Younger males	Females	Single men, women with children	Highly educated
Upward status changes (out of 5)	Younger males	—	Married men and married women no children	Highly educated
Function changes (out of 5)	—	—	—	—
Number of employers in career	Older	Females	—	—
Speed of job change	Younger	Females	—	—
Future career mobility				
Expected in-company lateral change	Younger	—	—	—
Expected in-company promotion	Younger	Females	—	—
Expected employer change	Younger	Females	—	—
Expected dismissal/ redundancy	Older	—	—	—

— = No relationship
(*Source:* CDS-I, *N* = 2,304)

to the risks of redundancy in late middle age, and further analysis does in fact reveal that this late peak is associated with a late career rise in the frequency of downward status moves for men. The following interpretation seems plausible. Men typically engage in early career exploration, moving between organizations, before settling to a single employer. Thereafter, pressures to change employers increase in later life as managers become more vulnerable to forces for change. There is no similar pattern for women; they maintain a high rate of employer changing in all age categories, though with a slight dip in middle age.[18]

Table 3.7 *Frequency of employer moves by age of change*

Age of change	<31	31–5	36–40	41–45	46–50	51–55	55+
Males	61%	53%	52%	48%	41%	51%	44%
Females	54%	55%	57%	48%	58%	54%	52%

(*Source:* CDS-I, Last job change, $N = 2,117$)

The pattern is similar for upward status moves (not shown in the table): high rates of promotion for men in early career with a decline thereafter; women having uniformly moderate to high rates throughout their careers. Downward status moves are infrequent for both men and women – around 10% of all changes – but for men the rate jumps to around 25% in late middle age.[19]

Family situation and domestic responsibilities are increasingly recognized in the literature as important influences on work and careers (Yogev and Brett, 1985). This is perhaps especially important for women, who have to build careers against the competing demands of traditional gender role expectations. In Chapter 9 we shall be looking specifically at the nature of these special demands and challenges for women in management. Here we can look at one important indicator of these, 'family situation', to see if it is linked with types of job change. After removing the effects of age only two clear relationships remain: for employer changing and for upward status moves there are significant interactions between sex and family situation,[20] but in opposite directions, as Table 3.8 shows.

Men with low domestic responsibilities – single and married without children – have the highest rate of employer changing, but the lowest rate of upward status moves. In complete contrast, women with dependant children have the highest rate of employer changing and the lowest rate of upward status moves. What is particularly interesting about these results is that the effects for these two kinds of mobility are almost exactly opposite to each other. How is this striking pattern to be explained? The finding for the men is easier to account for than the finding for the women. Men with few domestic responsibilities are most free to make radical moves – in-company promotions become more common as men become embedded in settled family life (this is confirmed when later we come to compare in-spiralling with out-spiralling moves). Can this mean the converse is true for women – that domestic responsibilities *increase* their propensity for radical moves? There are two reasons why it might.

First, more women than men have marriage partners who are in full-time employment, which increases their susceptibility to relocation through their

59

Table 3.8 *Family situation and job change for men and women*

Family situation	Employer changes (out of five)		Upward status changes (out of five)	
	Men	Women	Men	Women
Single				
(*N* = 50/231)	2.9	2.5	2.9	2.8
Married, without children				
(*N* = 117/194)	2.4	2.6	3.1	3.0
Married, with children				
(*N* = 1,073/204)	2.3	2.9	3.2	2.7

High scores underlined
(*Source:* CDS-I, *N* = 2,304)

spouses' work demands. We tested this by looking at partner's occupational status, and found that managers of either sex in dual career marriages are significantly more likely than others (regardless of age) to change employers. This is true for all ages and both sexes, though the effect is not strong.[21] So we do find some limited support for this explanation.

The second explanation is more speculative and psychological. As we shall be showing in Chapter 9, women have to overcome a variety of gender-specific obstacles in our culture to pursue managerial careers, and these are undoubtedly greatest for women with families. It is plausible to speculate that only the most highly motivated women will seek to maintain managerial careers in the face of these competing obligations, and therefore the greater the domestic responsibilities they have had to contend with the more motivated they need be. In other words those women who stick with their managerial careers whilst child-rearing have above average motivational drive which makes them the most prepared to make radical moves to advance their careers. We shall return to this theme in Chapter 9. Suffice it to say at this point, that taken together, all the evidence from our analysis of biographical factors confirms that women's career patterns are generally quite unlike those of male managers.

The last biographical factor of note in Table 3.6 is education. The only outstanding finding here is that employer changing and upward movement are more common amongst highly educated managers.[22] To evaluate the implications of this we need to look at two related occupational predictors of employer change: specialism and status. We shall now look at these and other factors to help unscramble relationships.

Occupational factors

As Table 3.9 shows, some very strong and clear links are visible between occupational factors and job change.

It is evident that managers who describe themselves as 'functional specialists' make different types of move to those who see themselves as 'general managers'. Specialists change employers more than generalists. Generalists are able, it seems, to advance their careers through status and functional moves. Specialists, in contrast, are obliged to take their particular skills with them from organization to organization in the search for career advancement; this is borne out by the results in Table 3.9 for both past career moves and future expected job change. A more detailed and objective picture of these trends can be seen in the results for job areas, confirming our earlier observation that the newer managerial occupations are the most mobile. But here we also see an interesting reversal for expected future change: line managers, who have had the least mobile *past* histories, have the highest expectation of *future* change. This reflects their declining labour market opportunities: they owe their present positions as line managers to stable employment in the past with a single employer, but they anticipate turbulent futures and having to change jobs, consistent with our earlier observation of the one-way traffic from traditional line management to other newer areas. The findings in Table 3.9 for industry groups underline these general trends, showing most radical mobility in the new and growing sectors (mainly private) of the economy.

But it is the results for status and organization size that are the most striking and provocative. There is a consistent tendency for high status managers and managers from small organizations to have made the greatest number of employer changes and upward status moves. The finding for size is easily explained. The larger the organization the greater the opportunities for internal movement, therefore people in small organizations are more likely to come to their present position from outside.

A separate but related issue concerns movement between organizations of different sizes.[23] Using our longitudinal data we can look at this more directly to reveal the following:

Moved between organizations in same size category	30	23%
Moved to organizations in a larger size category	35	27%
Moved to organizations in a smaller size category	65	50%
Total	130	100%

Table 3.9 Occupational factors positively related to job change

	Type	Job area	Status	Size	Sector	Industry group
Past career mobility						
Employer changes (out of 5)	Specialists	Finance, management services, education (vs line)	High	Small	Private	New services (vs commerce)*
Upward status changes (out of 5)	Generalists	—	High	Small	—	Industrial, trad. services (vs new services, government)
Function changes	Generalists	Line, technical services, management services, administration (vs finance)	—	—	Public	Government (vs industrial)
No. of employers in career	Specialists	Finance, management services, education, (vs line)	High	—	—	New services (vs commerce)
Speed of job change	—	Sales, tech. servs. (vs line, education)	High	Large	—	Commerce, new services (vs industrial)

Future career mobility						
Expected lateral change (in-company)	Specialists	Line (vs. education)	High	Large	—	—
Expected promotion	—	Line, human relations (vs finance)	Low	Large	Private	Commerce (vs new services)
Expected employer change	Specialists	Sales, technical services (vs line)	Mid	Mid	—	—
Expected sack	—	—	Mid and high	Mid	Private	Industrial (vs commerce)

* Low scoring groups in parentheses, i.e. new services high employer changing, commerce low

— = No relationship

(*Source:* CDS-I, N = 2,304)

There is a highly significant 2:1 traffic from larger to smaller organizations. Why should this be so? It is not attributable to differential mobility rates in large and small organizations nor is it likely to reflect any general historical trend since there was no change in the average size of companies during the measurement period that could account for it. It is much more likely to reflect normative trends in the career paths of managers who make radical job moves. One may speculate as follows: many successful managers start their careers and acquire their managerial skills in large organizations, before finding their established career positions in smaller organizations where their talents can find greater expressive scope. Other findings indirectly support this interpretation. Small organizations do seem to provide psychological benefits not so readily found in medium size or large organizations. As Table 3.9 shows, it is also true that managers in small organizations are more likely to have made upward status moves to achieve their present positions. Yet the findings for speed of movement present an initially puzzling contrast – mobility is more rapid in large organizations. There is no contradiction here with the suggestion that managers in small organizations have more radical and upwardly mobile careers. It merely shows that, regardless of what types of change people undergo, large organizations tend to move people at a faster rate between jobs than do smaller enterprises. We can infer from this that in large companies a rapid succession of *minor* changes is a normal pattern. In small companies less frequent but radical moves are more common. The fact that managers in large organizations have higher expectations of future intra-organizational job change in the next 12 months than managers in smaller enterprises fits this explanation.

A more intriguing finding, though, is that it is managers in *middle* size organizations who most expect to change employer in the future. They are also more likely than others to expect to be made redundant. Analyses presented and discussed in Chapter 8 offer an explanation. Managers experience most career frustration and dissatisfaction in middle size organizations. There is something of a 'small is beautiful' effect here – intrinsic work satisfaction and career fulfilment are greatest in small organizations – while for managers in large companies there are compensatory benefits of variety, opportunity and the paternalism of responsive personnel systems. But middle size companies often have neither of these advantages: for frustrated managers within many of them the only way forward is the way out.

We turn last but not least to the findings for status. The relationships in Table 3.9 are very strong and highly consistent: top managers have had more radical, upward and rapid job changes than other managers. The obvious interpretation is that managers' careers are advanced by job changing. Before we pursue this further we need to dispose of the alternative possible explanation that high status managers tend to change jobs faster and more often than their junior counterparts. The findings for expected future change contradict this explanation. The fact that it is the junior and middle ranking managers who see themselves as more likely to change jobs in the immediate future suggests that high status managers made their radical and rapid moves in the past to get to where they are now, but are less likely to continue to make the same kinds of moves in the future. Indeed, it would seem that high status brings with it commensurately greater risks of downfall, for high status managers feel more vulnerable than others to the threat of redundancy and dismissal.

These important findings raise a number of questions about career paths and managerial success. Which aspect of mobility is most important to attaining high status: upward movement or inter-organizational movement? How might personality differences amongst managers account for these relationships? We shall devote the last part of this chapter to trying to unpick some of these tangled causal threads, but first let us briefly summarize what differences we have found between the three primary dimensions of job change: employer, status and functional movement.

First, it seems that the most common feature of change, functional mobility, is not confined to managers of any particular type or circumstances, apart from some scattered occupational/industrial associations. None of these is particularly noteworthy. In fact it is the absence of certain associations that is of interest. In particular, the results give no support to the idea that broadening managerial experience through lateral movement leads to high status positions. The results for upward status moves and employer changes tell a quite different story, for we have seen that these moves are strongly associated with individual biographical and occupational factors. Their linkage with age and sex carries the clear message that men and women have different career paths – job moves of different kinds are made at different career stages for the two sexes. Family circumstances also seem to impinge differently upon men's and women's mobility. But both upward and employer moves seem to lead to high status and positions in small organizations.[24] Let us now look into the relationship between status and mobility more closely.

Status and mobility

It has been claimed that frequent moves between organizations and employers are essential steps in the route to the top (Jennings, 1967), though elsewhere the relationship between career success and mobility has been questioned (Veiga, 1983). We are now in a position to test this more

rigorously than past research, by separating out the effects of upward status
and inter-organizational mobility. One way of doing this is by comparing
the two most common types of job change: in-spiralling and out-spiralling.
The reader will recall that these have in common both vertical and lateral
movement (simultaneous function and upward status change). The only difference between these two types is therefore whether or not the person
changes organizations. Out-spiralling involves a change of employer, in-
spiralling does not. Table 3.10 shows what happens when we compare
these two types of move.[25]

The results reveal that employer changing is indeed a highly critical
dimension to job change, for the factors associated with in- and out-
spiralling are almost mirror images of each other. In-spiralling moves may
look seductive as career routes within organizations, but they are typical of
managers who have plateaued at moderate to low status levels. They are
also characteristic of careers in large organizations, and in traditional
managerial occupations and industries. Again, it is important for the reader

Table 3.10 *Factors positively associated with in-spiralling vs out-
spiralling job changes*

	In-spiralling	Out-spiralling
Age	Up to late middle age	Younger males (all ages females)
Sex	Males	Females
Education	—	More qualified
Family situation	—	—
Status	Low status	High status
Type	Generalists	—
Job area	Sales, line, administration (low in management services, finance)	Finance, management services, education (low in sales, line, human relations)
Company size	Large	Small
Sector	—	—
Industry group	Industrial, traditional services, commerce (low in new services)	New services (low in industrial, traditional services)

— = no relationship
(*Source:* CDS-I, Last job change data, *N* = 2,304)

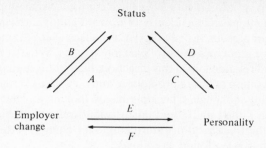

Figure 3.1 Possible causal links between status, mobility and personality.

to note that our analytical procedure ensures that these effects are independent of one another. Out-spiralling in contrast is a common move type amongst high status managers in small organizations, and in the new or expanding fields of management. There is an unmistakable implication in these data that if you want to get on in management you would be advised to change organization from time to time. Interestingly, this is something that men are prepared to do in their early careers, but not later, but which women do more of and more continuously throughout their careers.

A further implication of these results is that the upward status moves people make *between* organizations are larger vertical steps than the upward status moves they take *within* organizations. Further analysis of relationships amongst our various indicators have confirmed this.[26] One obvious mechanism for this that can be imagined is that the manager moving to a new organization will often be in a bargaining relationship with the new employer, and have greater leverage for status rewards than does the intra-organizational mover. In-company upward movers are less likely to be in a position to negotiate and more likely to have been successful supplicants or the grateful recipients of what is on offer. This interpretation also implies that out-spirallers will often be more proactive in their motivational orientation than in-spirallers. Let us now consider this.

The question is whether people's motivational orientations are a cause or an effect of their job move types, or whether status is a cause or effect of job change and achievement. We performed a series of analyses – both cross-sectional and longitudinal – to establish the possible causal links. These are depicted in Figure 3.1, and we set out to test paths *A* to *F*, as far as the data permitted.

Looking first at Paths *A* and *B* we have confirmed that employer change is linked with status independently of upward status movement.[27] Which path does this represent, *A* or *B*, i.e. which causes which? It must be *A* since present status cannot be a cause of past move types. What of Path *B*? Table 3.9 suggests no relationship in this direction: high status managers generally had low expectation of future promotion, and no above average expectation of future employer change. Checking this by looking at what actually happened between Time 1 and Time 2 also disconfirms path *B*: high status does not increase the likelihood of future employer change.[28] Relationships *A* and *B* have thus been found as follows:

Status

0   +

Employer change

Relationships *C* and *D* can be similarly evaluated. Amongst personality variables we find a link between status and two of them: adjustment, and need for growth.[29] The logic is more equivocal here, for personality could equally be a cause of high status and a product of it. Longitudinal analyses from the Time 1 to Time 2 reveal that people who moved upward in status did show an increase on two measures, need for growth and dominance, but not in any other personality measures (Path *D*).[30] But there was no indication that personality differences predict status increases over time (Path *C*).[31] So it would seem that Paths *C* and *D* look like this:

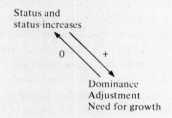

Status and
status increases

0   +

Dominance
Adjustment
Need for growth

Finally, Paths *E* and *F* can also be examined by longitudinal analysis. Here we found no predictive relationship between personality measures and employer change in either direction (with one minor exception).[32] So,

68

completing the picture we would seem to have arrived at the following pattern of relationships:

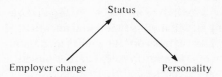

But we must be cautious in generalizing from these findings. Because of the short time scale over which we were able to assess change, we cannot be sure that some of the causal linkages we failed to find here might not have emerged over a longer period. This implies that the connections we have found represent the most immediate and visible outcomes of change. The model we have arrived at suggests that employer change, however it originates, is likely to enhance a manager's prospects, and that status attainment does in turn contribute to psychological development (see also Chapter 6).

One must also be careful in offering strong prescriptions from probabilistic data like these, i.e. no doubt there exist many managers for whom employer changing does *not* yield these benefits. But the principal connection between inter-organizational mobility and status emerges repeatedly from rigorous tests and seems to convey an unmistakable message: all other things being equal, employer moves do advance managers' careers. In the light of this it is notable that women are experiencing these moves more continuously through their careers than men. So why are they not achieving more than men? Earlier we speculated that one reason our women managers are not in positions of superior status to men is because they are younger and at earlier stages of their career. Does this mean therefore that the future belongs to them? Not necessarily – being on an upward fast track doesn't guarantee getting to the pinnacle. The career path of radical and rapid change may help women to achieve status equality with men in the middle ranks of management, but at the moment very few are getting to the top boardroom level of business in Britain (Davidson, 1985). We shall take up this theme further in Chapter 9.

Summary and conclusion

We have glimpsed the complexity of career patterns in this chapter, which few simple generalizations can adequately reflect. We have seen that there is a high and rising rate of management mobility – there are still some managers whose careers are stable and orderly but their numbers are dwindling. Most can expect to change jobs at least once every three years, and for the great majority job change also means a change of job function. More often than not job change involves either a change of status, a change of employer, or both, for over half of all management job change is 'spiralling' in character, involving simultaneous functional and upward status changes. And for around half of these, this spiralling takes managers out of their companies to new employers. In short, radical career moves are far and away the most common types experienced by managers.

The radical nature of most job change was illustrated by the fact that function changes are not usually just minor sideways steps, but take many people right out of one family of job titles into another. Likewise, employer changes are less often switches between similar types of organizations than they are radical migrations out of one sector of employment into another. From a more psychological perspective we have also seen how job changes usually impose on the manager truly novel demands and the need to develop new skills.

A sure sign of real advancement through mobility is where there is a significant increase in manager's discretion from old to new job, and, as we shall see in Chapter 6, all other things being equal, it is employer moves that most often bring this about. The tendency to move from large to small organizations undoubtedly aids this process, for job discretion is generally higher in small organizations.

Indeed, it is because of these and other concomitants that moves between employers are the most interesting and important kind of job change from a developmental point of view. Perhaps the most striking finding here is that employer changes are bridges typically crossed by successful travellers on the upward spiralling path to managerial success. Simply experiencing a series of promotions within an organization is less likely to lead to the top. On such conventional career paths the route may peter out well before the summit. The lesson for the ambitious manager would seem to be, boldness be thy friend. Taking the path of a radical transition, out of your company and out of your function, is part of the fast route to the top. Mere speed of movement is not enough.

It is also striking that proportionately more women than men, more young than old, and more specialists than generalists are following this route, a route that also passes through more of the new occupations and growing industrial sectors than the old and declining ones. It is in areas such as management services rather than industrial sector organizations and line management that fast and radical upward moves occur. It is apparent that these moves occur more in the private sector than in state sectors of the economy. This is also regrettable, perhaps, insofar as it confirms some gloomy stereotypes about careers in the public sector, an issue taken up in Chapter 8.

But now it is time to take a less detached view of job change than we have attempted in this chapter, by looking at how managers assess tneir own careers and job change influences.

4

The causes of mobility

Why do people change jobs? We have already reviewed in general terms how transitions are the product of various sources of turbulence and forces for change: people's unfulfilled needs, occupational opportunity structures, and organizational processes. But if we look to the literature of the applied behavioural sciences no coherent or integrated view of job change is to be found, which is perhaps surprising given how ubiquitous, radical and significant an event it seems to be. This is not because job change has been of no interest to social scientists, but because it has been viewed from the highly separated vantage points of different sub-disciplinary fields. Each has commented on distinctive aspects of mobility, but with quite different assumptions and methods. The result has been diverse and generally non-complementary insights.

Writers on careers constitute one group for whom mobility is a central concern, but their interest in transitions has almost exclusively focussed on early career choice processes, and beyond that they have looked for broad patterns in the development of careers (cf. Brown and Brooks, 1984; Watts *et al.*, 1981). Their analyses, deriving from the traditions of counselling and differential psychology (the study of measurable individual differences), have focussed on how relatively stable individual factors such as personality, interest, social class, and gender, influence the career course. Industrial psychologists, in contrast, are mainly interested in human performance and well-being in organizational contexts, concentrating on the interaction between job conditions and relatively short-range individual differences in such factors as attitudes, motives and skills. Job change has been studied as both an input to this interaction, as in job redesign studies, and as an output of them, as in turnover studies, but without any common theoretical base between these two orientations. It is the latter field that relates most closely to our current concern, where writers on turnover have generally viewed it as a rational and largely reactive response to perceived environmental deficiencies and opportunities for movement (Mobley *et al.*, 1979; Mowday *et al.*, 1982). Finally, organization theorists are a third group with an interest in job change. Some of the most insightful published work to date has come from this quarter, where from a predominantly micro-sociological perspective the processes of socialization and adjustment to change have been studied (Glaser and Strauss, 1971; Van Maanen, 1976), but without much attention to the causes of change. Macro-organizational scholars have had more to say on this, but only within the broad purview of an interest in the causes of managerial succession and how it relates to the performance of the organization as a whole (Grusky, 1963; Allen *et al.*, 1979).

So it seems that the kinds of mid-career job changing we have been recording have been generally neglected or subsumed under some other concern. If one looks closely at all these literatures, one finds that they tend to use many different data sources to draw inferences about job change and its causes, but surprisingly and regrettably they rarely make use of individuals' own reports of changes in their working lives.

In this chapter we seek to remedy this imbalance in two ways. First, we shall look at managers' descriptions of their own careers. These enrich our understanding of the different career patterns we have been looking at, and the kinds of decision processes that underlie them. Second, we sharpen the focus by examining the reasons managers give for different types of job change. Both these methods show that career decision-making is a complex process, resting upon mixed motives and uncertain environmental forces. The simple conceptual accounting that is deployed to draw distinctions between, for example, voluntary and involuntary turnover, or between occupational choice and environmental selection, appears difficult to sustain in the face of the reality of managers' reports. These reveal a much more shifting, contingent set of relationships between needs, circumstances and actions than would fit any simple push–pull theorizing. We conclude the chapter by using our longitudinal data to unique effect, mapping managers' expectations of change onto their subsequent experience of change. This reveals a generally poor ability on the part of managers to predict their own immediate future career moves, raising some disquieting questions about how misleading or inaccurate may be commonplace conceptions of 'careers'.

Career paths

In the previous chapter we have been able to use work history data to uncover some themes and variations in managerial job change, but work histories are not the same as careers. The former are objective records of change, the latter are the subjective social constructions people put upon sequences of occupational experience. How people evaluate their work histories as 'careers' is important if we are to understand their motives towards, and reactions to, stability and change.

Therefore we set out in the CDS-II to augment our records of managers' work histories with an investigation of how *they* would characterize their careers. Open ended questioning would have been unsatisfactory for this purpose, since we wanted to know what proportion of managers experience career problems and satisfactions of the distinctive kinds that have been discussed in the literature. For example, we wanted to know how many felt they had experienced 'orderly' or 'conventional' careers, following some well-defined path; how many might consider themselves to be 'plateaued', how many felt at the mercy of identifiable external pressures, and how many are consciously value-driven in their career choices. A series of questionnaire items were devised to tap these and other dimensions of careers in a standardized fashion, but which at the same time offered managers a wide range of different ways to describe their careers. We also used a single item measure for managers to rate their overall career satisfaction. Table 4.1 shows the scales developed for this purpose, and the column under (A) in Table 4.1 summarizes the general pattern of results (we shall be considering column (B) shortly).

We have grouped items according to four distinctive dimensions to careers.[1] First, in group A, what we have called 'orderly' career paths, denote careers that are on recognizable 'tracks', whether fast or slow, and do not involve radical choices or changes: i.e. one's profession, occupation or organization determines the overall career course. The most widely endorsed item of this group is A1 which confirms the generally upwardly mobile character of the sample – note the contrast with item D13 where only a minority say they have experienced degraded skills (see Chapter 6 for a discussion of downward mobility). So it seems that the 'orderliness' of careers exhibited in group A is the kind of order that comes from a sense of progress, from knowing and understanding the compass bearings of one's trajectory.

Group B items represent careers where directional bearings are more internally set and consequently more moveable. The fact that item B5 is the most widely endorsed of all the items confirms that functional mobility is the most common characteristic of managerial careers. However this item differs from the other two in this group in an important respect. In items B6 and 7 people are saying their job changes have been driven by their interest in finding a better relationship with their work. Item B5 suggests that self-directed choices are driven by some conception of an end-state or career goal. Items B6 and B7 convey the image of more immediately apprehended subjective standards and values creating fluidity and variability of career movement. The distinction between these two modes is, as we shall be arguing, akin to a contrast between goal-directed (rationalist) and value-driven (existentialist) modes of motivation and choice. More of this in due course.

Group C are labelled 'externally-directed' because choices have been overtly at the mercy of pressures and opportunities rather than goals and interests, but at the same time these forces have not imposed any evident order on careers. It is particularly notable that around half of all managers seem to have been 'planless' in their career paths (C8), though far fewer are prepared to say that they have been 'careerless' (C10).

Finally, group D items denote careers which have come to a halt, whether temporary or lasting. It is striking that even though the great majority of the managers have been experiencing upwardly mobile careers by both subjective and objective indicators, for half of them their upward mobility has led them up onto a career plateau (D11).

It is apparent from the percentages in Table 4.1 that substantial numbers of people must have given 'agree' responses to more than one of the top four ranked items (since around 50% gave agree responses on the highly rated items). We investigated these overlaps further through correlational analysis, confirming the complexity of people's career types. We can see for example that many managers' careers have been goal-directed but plateaued, steadily progressing but planless, and so on.[2] However, one excluded combination stands out amongst the top four items: managers who were likely to agree that their career moves had been towards a career goal (B5, rank 1) tended to *disagree* with the statement that their careers had been planless (C8, ranked 4). This supports our inference that the former item embodies a rationalistic motivational orientation to career development.

What is not clear from these items is how managers *feel* about their career development, for which we may turn to look at the single item measure of career satisfaction.[3] This conveys an image of overall contentment – though around one in ten managers do express outright dissatisfaction with their career progress. This measure also allows us to evaluate how satisfied or dissatisfied managers are with the different career types represented by the items of Table 4.1. The last column of the table – labelled 'B' – shows the results of correlating the 'career types' items with our measure of career satisfaction. A positive correlation means that people who agree with a particular career type item are career satisfied, and a negative correlation indicates that those who agree with an item are career dissatisfied. Where there is no significant relationship this means that there is no difference in the career satisfaction of people who agree and disagree with the statement.

This analysis gives an interesting new slant to our view of careers. Let us again focus first on the four most widely endorsed statements (numbers A1,

Table 4.1 *Career types*

	A			B
	Strongly agree %	Agree %	(Overall rank)	Correlation with career satisfaction
A Conventional career paths				
1 My career has consisted mainly of steady progression within my organization or profession	11	42	(3)	0.15***
2 My career has consisted of rapid upward moves within my organization or profession	8	31	(6)	0.31***
3 I have done much the same kind of job throughout my working life and my career has consisted of learning how to do it better	6	19	(9)	−0.06*
4 My current career line is just beginning and I am finding my way in my organization	3	12	(12)	ns
B Self-directed career paths				
5 My career has consisted of moves designed to broaden my experience in a variety of settings while making progress towards a career goal	19	40	(1)	0.18***
6 My career has consisted of one or more changes in fields as I searched for a better fit between myself and my work role	15	28	(5)	−0.06*
7 My career has consisted mainly of choices based on personal interests rather than on ambition	7	23	(8)	ns
C Externally-directed career paths				
8 There has been no pattern or plan to my career. I have simply picked up opportunities as they occurred	18	29	(4)	−0.13***
9 My work history has consisted of modifying my career plans to fit in with the needs of my spouse/family	6	13	(10)	−0.17***

10 The jobs that I have had do not really form a career	3	7	(13)	−0.34***
D *Impeded career paths*				
11 My career was upward and has now reached a plateau	18	32	(2)	ns
12 My career is blocked. I feel 'stuck' in my present position	15	20	(7)	−0.38***
13 My professional skills have declined in value during my career	3	13	(11)	−0.24***

*$p < 0.05$; ** $p < 0.01$; *** $p < 0.001$
(*Source*: CDS-II, $N = 1,087$)

B5, C8 and D11). There is a slight tendency for the steady progressors (A1) and the goal-directed (B5) managers to be more satisfied, and for the planless (C8) to be dissatisfied, but the most notable finding is the absence of any relationship for the plateaued (D11). In other words, people who say they have reached a career plateau are no more likely to be dissatisfied than those who are not plateaued, which, one may suppose, is a sure sign that some plateaus may be comfortable and welcome resting places while others are not (Veiga, 1981). Indeed one might surmize that the higher the climb, the more welcome the resting place, though our data provide no clear support for the idea that high status managers are any less concerned about status immobility than low status managers.[4]

However, it is apparent that an important distinction needs to be drawn between being 'plateaued' and being 'stuck', for the latter is strongly associated with dissatisfaction (see the negative correlation in Table 4.1 for item D12). Similarly feeling 'careerless' (item C10) is more dissatisfying than believing one has had a 'planless' career (C8). On the positive side it is also apparent that having experienced fast upward mobility (item A2) is what most managers consider satisfying.

Now let us turn to look briefly at how these career types relate to our measures of work histories. These relationships are summarized in Table 4.2, along with a repeat of the career satisfaction findings.[5]

The results are reassuring about our measures insofar as they reveal some predictable patterns, e.g. both the steady upward progressing and the fast upward movers (A1 and A2) have experienced multiple upward status changes, and low mobility on other dimensions. More noteworthy is the finding that these 'conventional' upward mobiles tend to be in-spirallers rather than out-spirallers, whereas in contrast, the self-directed types are more out-spiralling than in-spiralling. So we see that the in- vs out-spiralling dimension is important in distinguishing career motives, as well as the career destinations we have considered. Within groups of items there are also some interesting differences. Within the 'orderly' group A there is a clear distinction between those whose careers have involved a tangible status progression (A1 and A2) and those whose have not (A3 and A4). It is particularly noteworthy that managers who say they are 'just beginning' their career line have already had an above average number of employer changes: indicating that this item is picking out some mid career managers who have recently switched to new career lines. Within group B there is a disjunction between the goal-directed (B5) and the other self-directed types (B6 and B7). The former have had high rates of change on all work history dimensions except employer change, and high rates of both in- and out-spiralling; the latter are more exclusively out-spiralling: employer changing is the outward expression of their search for fulfilment.

In group C the 'planless' (C8) have no distinctive work histories, as one might expect, while the other two externally-directed types (C9 and C10) have generally not yet experienced much upward status mobility. Last but not least, there is one finding of outstanding interest in the 'impeded' group D of items. This is that managers who say they have plateaued are less likely than others to have changed employer or to have out-spiralled, providing further confirmation that employer changing and out-spiralling are the routes to high places in organizations, though it should also be noted that this is not a cause of career dissatisfaction among the plateaued. It is the in-spirallers, orderly and goal-directed types who are the most satisfied and this deserves brief comment. Employer changing, though it may yield long-term benefits of status attainment, is more driven by a continual search for need-fulfilment and by circumstantial pressures (see later in this chapter). As such it may be characteristic of people with higher thresholds for career contentment, while more conventional upward movers visualize their career goals within their organizations and are satisfied by being brought closer towards them through successive promotions.[6]

To explain these patterns further we need to look at causes, effects and other accompaniments of these career types. To do this we related the career type measures to the biographical and occupational factors we have found to be influential in previous analyses.[7] Table 4.3 shows the results.

Looking at biographical factors first, there are some clear, though not particularly surprising effects, such as the tendency for older managers to have reached career plateaus and blockages, and younger managers to be experiencing rapid upward movement. Sex effects are more intriguing. It is noticeable that men seem to have more orderly career paths, insofar as they are more likely to have moved steadily upward within a career track (item A1) or to have been making more divergent moves with a particular career goal in mind (item B5). Women, on the other hand have made more unconventional and value driven career choices (as reflected in items B6 and B7). At the same time they are forced to be more opportunistic (item C8) and directed by family considerations (item C9). We discuss the implications of this further in Chapter 9. It is interesting to note that there are no age or sex effects for career satisfaction.

These differences are complemented by the findings for managerial type. Specialists exhibit more of the intrinsic pattern we find for women (though our analysis ensures that this finding is not just because more women are specialists). This finding is surprising and important. It disposes of the myth that technical managers have predictable and orderly careers while generalists are more exploratory or adventurous. Our results show quite the opposite, and indeed complement our finding in the last chapter that

79

Table 4.2 Career types and work histories

Career types	Employer changes	Upward status changes	Function changes	In-spiralling moves	Out-spiralling moves	Career satisfaction
A Conventional						
1 Steady progress	Few	Many	Few	Many	Few	High
2 Rapid upward	Few	Many	—	Many	—	High
3 Much the same	—	—	Few	Few	—	Low
4 Just beginning	Many	—	—	Few	—	—
B Self-directed						
5 Toward career goal	—	Many	Many	Many	Many	High
6 Searching for a fit	Many	—	Many	Few	Many	Low
7 Interest not ambition	Many	Few	—	Few	—	—
C Externally directed						
8 Planless, picking-up opportunities	—	—	—	—	—	Low
9 Family fit choices	Many	Few	—	Few	—	Low
10 Careerless	—	Few	—	—	—	Low
D Impeded						
11 Upward but plateaued	Few	Few	—	—	Few	—
12 Blocked and stuck	Few	Few	—	—	—	Low
13 Skills declined in value	—	—	—	—	—	Low
Career satisfaction				High		

— = No relationship

(*Source:* CDS-I and CDS-II, correlational analysis, N = 1,070)

Table 4.3 *Career types and biographical/occupational factors*

		Age	Sex	Type	Status	Size	Job area	Industry
A	*Conventional*							
1	Steady progress	Old	M	—	Low	Large	Line, finance, mgt services	—
2	Rapid upward	Young	—	Generalists	High	Small and large	—	—
3	Much the same	Young & old	—	—	—	Small	—	—
4	Just beginning	Young	—	—	—	—	—	—
B	*Self-directed*							
5	Toward career goal	—	M	Generalists	—	Small and large	—	—
6	Searching for a fit	Middle	F	Specialists	—	Small	Education	—
7	Interest not ambition	—	F	Specialists	—	Small	—	—
C	*Externally-directed*							
8	Planless, picking-up opportunities	—	F	—	—	Small	Line, education	Traditional services
9	Family fit choices	Old	F	Specialists	—	Small	—	—
10	Careerless	—	—	—	Low	Small and medium	Line	—
D	*Impeded*							
11	Upward but plateaued	Old	—	—	—	Medium	Line	Government
12	Blocked and stuck	Old	—	—	Low	Medium	Line, education	—
13	Skills declined in value	Old	M	—	Low	—	Line	Industrial
	Career satisfaction	—	—	Generalists	High	Small and large	Finance, administration, education	New services, commerce

— = No relationship
(*Source:* CDS-II, N = 1,067)

specialists tend to make more radical career moves in pursuit of their career goals. However at the same time it is well known that specialists tend to encounter career ceilings at lower levels than generalists, unless they can 'convert' themselves to general managers (Bailyn, 1980). Our data confirm that they are less likely to get to the higher strata of organizations than are generalists – which no doubt partly accounts for the generally lower career satisfaction we see here among the technical specialists.[8]

The findings for status are unremarkable: highly placed managers are more satisfied, less stuck, and have enjoyed more rapid upward progression. But the findings for company size are more interesting. Again they point to there being special problems in middle size companies, where we can see that career dissatisfactions and blockages are evidently greatest (see items A2, B5, C10, D11, D12 and the measure of career satisfaction). Finally, Table 4.3 shows that the job areas of line management and education, and the industrial groups of traditional services, government and industrial sector are the areas of greatest career impedence and dissatisfaction. The situation in new services and commerce is noticeably brighter.

So let us take stock of what these self-report career descriptions have told us about managerial job change. They confirm many of the trends we observed in Chapter 3, but in a different way, shedding some fresh light on types of managerial careers, their origins and outcomes. We have confirmed, for example, the generally upward mobile paths of most managers, though speed of movement varies and many who have enjoyed past success now consider themselves to be 'plateaued'. We have also found that large numbers of managers are making radical job switches to find work that fits their values and interests, though it is also true that there is a planless and opportunistic quality to the way many job change decisions are made. If it is so common for careers to be constructed in such *ad hoc* and unpredictable ways, then perhaps we should look critically at conventional definitions and assumptions about what is 'a career'. We shall consider this theme at the end of the chapter.

From the factors associated with career types we can begin to appreciate some of the forces surrounding them. It is particularly interesting that specialists and generalists exhibit different patterns: generalists experience more satisfaction through fast upward goal directed movement, while specialists tend to make more radical moves in search for career fulfilment. The sex differences we have observed in managerial career types also are of some importance: it is evident that women's careers in management do not conform to the conventional male stereotype of targeted upward achievement, an issue we shall come back to in Chapter 9. Finally, amongst industrial and occupational factors, we have noted that size of organization has a powerful bearing upon career perceptions. In particular, again we have found middle sized companies are often the least satisfactory environments for managers: slow progression, little goal-directedness, careerlessness, plateauing, 'stuckness', and career dissatisfaction, are all especially evident in them.

Together these observations suggest that a complex and varying mixture of motives and constraints determines managerial job change and career directions. Expediency and idealism, normally thought of as opposing principles, seem to converge in the career choices people make. We have documented managers' needs for high order fulfilment and how they can trigger job change as a way of avoiding present frustrations and of finding greener grass on other hillsides. We have also noted that however much people might want or not want to undertake job moves they are dependent upon the facilitating and inhibiting effects of opportunity structures. In concrete terms this means that whether one is male or female, a specialist or a generalist, in one kind of organization or another, all determine which doors are open, which are closed, and which will give way if pushed.

These conclusions are derived from a 'careers' perspective, by examining the accounts people give of particular moves they have experienced.

Reasons and causes for job change

Three different sources of information help us to bring the origins of job change into closer focus. First, in the CDS-I we asked people to explain their last five job changes by nominating from a list of 16 options the primary and secondary reasons for each change. Second, in the CDS-II we asked people to say what life events they had experienced in the period between the CDS-I and CDS-II, which we were then able to relate to job changes they had encountered at the same time. Third, in the CDS-II we asked people through open-ended questioning to give accounts of the reasons for any job changes they had experienced between the CDS-I and CDS-II. Each of these sources gives a somewhat different but complementary picture of the causes of job change.

First, in the CDS-I we used a fixed list of reasons (developed from pilot interviews)[9] from which managers were asked to nominate the 'most important' and 'secondary' reason for each of their last five job changes. The use of a predetermined list was necessary for us to be able to gather standardized data on all five previous moves from the total sample. Table 4.4 shows reasons for job change in order of frequency, comparing results for men and women.[10]

The reasons could be said to fall into three broad types of motive force: circumstantial, avoidance, and future-oriented. It is clear that most managers explain their job changes as *future-oriented* – the top five ranking

Table 4.4 *Reasons for last job change*

	Males	Females
1 To do something more challenging and fulfilling	48%	42%
2 I saw it as a step toward career objectives	46%	46%
3 To change career direction	20%	18%
4 To improve my standard of living	19%	11%
5 To acquire new skills	11%	11%
6 I saw no future for me in my job	10%	10%
7 Things I disliked about my company/job	9%	10%
8 To move to a different location	9%	9%
9 Made redundant	7%	4%
10 Negative pressures from superiors	5%	5%
11 Pressure from domestic factors	3%	6%
12 To return to employment after being unemployed	4%	4%
13 End of contract	4%	3%
14 To enter employment from full-time education	1%	3%
15 For further education	1%	1%
16 For child rearing	0%	2%

(%'s total more than 100 because more than one reason could be given)
(*Source:* CDS-I, $N = 2,304$; main and secondary reasons for last job move)

reasons are all proactive positive moves towards desired futures. A much smaller number of reasons are *avoidance* moves: job changes to escape undesired circumstances. The remainder, only mentioned by a very small proportion of the sample, are *circumstantial*. However, if we cross-tabulate 'most important' and 'secondary' reasons, mixed motives become evident. For most managers a single job change springs from both future-oriented and circumstantial or avoidance reasons. We can also use the data to see whether men's and women's job change motives differ. But as Table 4.4 shows there is only one major sex differentiating item – 'to improve my standard of living' – which is twice as often a male as a female reason for job change, confirming our observation in Chapter 2 that material rewards are consistently more important for men than women.

But our assessment of these changes depends upon how comprehensive was the range of options we made available to managers. Although our list was devised as a result of pilot interviews with managers, it soon became clear from the free comment section of the questionnaire that our list had one important omission.[11] Many managers' job changes were enforced by structural changes in their organizations: 'shake-ups', mergers and reorganizations. In the CDS-II we were able to check on this directly, verifying the categories we had included in the CDS-I and identifying other possible omissions.

At Time 2 instead of a fixed list of options we asked people in a free response format, for up to three possible job changes they might have experienced between the Time 1 and Time 2, to tell us the following: 'What have been the reasons for each job change? Please describe both the circumstantial pressures/opportunities for each job change and your underlying motives and personal reasons for each change.' Content analysis of these free response data provided strong support for all the categories we had originally included, but it did also confirm that the reason 'restructuring of organizations or jobs', omitted from the CDS-I, is an important cause of job change. [12] In these CDS-II data we find two reasons for job change predominate: 'a step toward career objectives' (28% of all reasons) and 'restructuring of organizations or jobs' (26%). Moves 'to do something more challenging and fulfilling' comes a poor third (10%), while equal fourth come 'made redundant' and 'things I disliked about my company or job'. On this evidence, circumstantial and avoidance pressures may be rather more important than the first survey had indicated.

Independent confirmation of this is to be found in the CDS-II's 'Major Life Events' inventory, which asked people to say whether in the last year they had experienced events such as 'death of spouse', 'major personal injury', 'marriage' and so on. Most of these turn out to be comparatively rare events (see Table 2.2) and are unrelated to any experience of job change at the same time, but much more common and relevant to job change are those events which centre on the domain of work. One of these, 'business reorganization or major organizational change' was reported by fully a third of the total sample, and by almost half of those who changed jobs in the year between the two surveys. Another of the life events recorded, 'deterioration of relations' at work was reported by 15% of the total sample, but by 20% of those who changed jobs. The third and last of the work-related life events, 'Involuntary loss of job', was much less frequent, reported by only 8% of job changers. Further analysis allows us to see how these life events intersect with our three dimensions of job change.

By looking across the rows in Table 4.5 one can see if there is any apparent linkage between these events and the dimensions of job change. Where percentages are roughly equal in magnitude along a row in Table 4.5 this means that there is no specific link between an event and the type of move. Where there are disparities across the row percentages one can infer there is some linkage between events and types of move. So we can see in Table 4.5 that employer changes and downward status moves are more often linked with negative organizational pressures – 'deteriorating

Table 4.5 *Life events associated with job change types between CDS-I and CDS-II*

	Employer changers %	Downward status movers %	Upward status movers %	Function changers %
Deterioration of relations at work	23%	30%	16%	18%
Involuntary loss of job	22%	27%	6%	9%
Business reorganization or major organizational change	36%	33%	49%	48%
N =	149	38	216	298

% of movers experiencing events between CDS-I and CDS-II
(*Source:* CDS-II, Time 1 to Time 2 job changers; N = 411)

relations' and 'job loss' – than the other two types of move: functional or upward status change. These two latter move types are associated more with internal organizational pressures, in the form of business reorganizations.

This association of causes with types of job change is assessed more directly through the free response 'reasons' of the CDS-II. Table 4.6 shows how the most common and important reasons differ for the two most common move types: in- and out-spiralling.

It seems from Table 4.6 that the attributed causes of in and out-spiralling differ in important respects. The search for challenge and fulfilment emerges as a significantly more central motive for out- than in-spirallers, while in-spirallers seem to be working more to the 'logic' of a career plan with identifiable objectives. Out-spirallers are also more motivated by dissatisfactions – which could be taken to imply that they have a clearer sense of their own immediate needs, if not of their future objectives. In-spirallers are more likely to be finding their way up the ladder through company reorganizations. Reorganizations are an exit route from their organizations for only a few out-spirallers, but where they are one can assume they constitute a negative pressure. From the reports and comments of several managers it seems that quitting one's organization is often preferable to the role changes that may be enforced by company reorganization.

So, to summarize, we can see that job change is variously motivated. It

The causes of mobility

Table 4.6 *Main self-reported reasons for in-spiralling and out-spiralling moves*

	In-spiralling	Out-spiralling
A step toward career objectives	51%	26%
For more challenge/fulfilment	9%	22%
Restructuring of organization/job	22%	3%
Dissatisfactions with job/company	3%	17%
To start own business	0%	5%
Made redundant	0%	3%
Miscellaneous other reasons	15%	24%
	100%	100%
	(N = 89)	(N = 58)

(*Source:* CDS-II, Time 1 to Time 2 job changers)

would be tempting, but inadvisable to divide people and their reasons into two mutually exclusive groups of internally vs. externally motivated job changers. Such a division may be possible for some single instances of job change, separating, for example, redundancies and company restructuring from self-initiated job search and radical career change. But in most cases where people have specified more than one reason for change it is clear from the various intersections of motives and pressures that this kind of neat division is not sustainable. Moreover, any such distinction is made more elusive by the subjectivity of attribution (Brown, 1986). For example, people may be apt to describe themselves as self-motivated when they have actually done no more than respond positively to opportunities over which they have no control. Equally, one can find people who are able successfully to wrest control from the impersonal forces for change, turning crises into opportunities. Mixed motives abound. Perhaps one of the most common examples of this is where people change employers because of job dissatisfaction (Porter and Steers, 1973). Even when it is clear that external forces beyond the person's control are 'pushing' them out of the organization, there is no inconsistency in attributing to the person the exercise of choice; they choose by deciding when a threshold of dissatisfaction has been crossed and by thereafter initiating and directing the change process.

Yet looking across the range of move types a distinctive and important pattern has emerged. Out-spirallers are more immediately buffeted by their internalized values and interests – negative reactions to dissatisfactions and positive responses to felt needs and interests. In-spirallers are more the captives of imposed organizational contingencies – the impelling forces of organizational change and the imperative pull of future career goals and objectives. We have remarked that this could be said to embody two different motivational modes: out-spirallers operate in a more existentialist mode, and in-spirallers more in a rationalist mode; a contrast that is consistent with the factors we found to be associated with these two move types in the last chapter.

The meanings and messages we have received and documented from our various data sources on managerial careers converge in a convincing fashion to uncover some common and contrasting themes in managerial job change and career types. It is apparent that most managers are trying to assert some control over their choices and changes, but against a background of constraint and uncertainty; constraint from the structure of opportunities and pressures, and uncertainty about the changing nature of these environmental forces. This being so, then what is the relationship between individual instances of job change and longer-term career patterns? How much foreknowledge or control do managers have over job changes, and thus, by implication, how able are they to forge the links of individual job changes into the chains they call their careers? Our longitudinal data provided a unique opportunity to investigate this issue empirically.

Future uncertain – are careers mythical? [13]

The high rate of job changing, its often radical form, and the varied forces that give rise to it, together convey an image of turbulence in the upper strata of business and industry. It is evident that managers are trying to ride the tides of change by pursuing their needs for challenge and fulfilment in the face of opportunities, demands and pressures over which they have little control. Preparation for change is one important way in which one can survive in a turbulent environment, but a necessary part of preparation and choice is anticipation. We now want to see how good managers are at anticipating their own job change, and thereby address the question of whether the idea of career development through successive acts of choice is a myth which fails to acknowledge sufficiently the ungovernable structural determinants of careers. [14] Is the idea of a 'career' a comforting story we tell ourselves to make sense of work histories which in reality have been made up of rapid, random and unconnected changes? In the minds of managers themselves there is clearly some ambivalence on this issue, for as we saw earlier a significant number agreed their work histories had been 'planless', i.e. not really amounting to a mapped career; and that many had undertaken

Table 4.7 *'How likely are you to change jobs in the next 12 months?'*

	Very likely %	Quite likely %	Unlikely %	Very unlikely %
A Stay in the same post but major change in work duties and activities	13	22	27	39
B Move to another post within the company	7	12	29	52
C Be promoted	6	16	33	45
D Move to a different employer	10	11	19	60
E Be made redundant	4	5	29	63

(*Source:* CDS-I, $N = 2,103$)

successive radical changes in a continuing search for a better fit between themselves and work.

The two-phase design of the survey allows us to analyse this. In the CDS-I we asked managers to predict how likely they would be to experience a number of different kinds of job change over the coming year. A little over a year later, in the CDS-II, we were able to check the accuracy of their predictions. How good are managers at foreseeing even this temporally close next step in their work histories?

First let us look at what they expected at Time 1. Table 4.7 shows this.

The results confirm the volatility of managerial careers. Over one third of the sample expect some kind of functional change in the next year (item A). Employer change (D), promotion (C) and more radical in-company moves (B) are expected by roughly equal numbers (around a fifth expect each of these). Redundancy in the next year is expected by one in ten: a startlingly high proportion. However, expectations may bear an uneven relation to actual job changing behaviour. Now let us test some aspects of this relationship by comparing managers' expectations with their experience, as recorded in the CDS-II, a little over a year later, and find out whether or not they changed jobs in accordance with their predictions. We shall concentrate on three measures: 'any job change', 'promotions' (i.e. in-company upward moves), and 'employer change' (inter-company moves).[15]

Complete data on both expectations and subsequent actual mobility were available from around 900 managers, and the results of the comparison are shown in the bar charts of Figure 4.1.

The causes of mobility

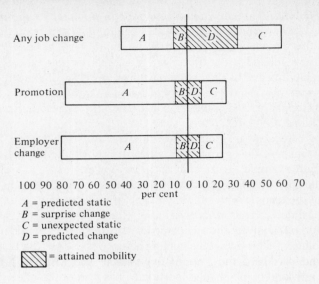

Any job change

Promotion

Employer change

100 90 80 70 60 50 40 30 20 10 0 10 20 30 40 50 60 70
per cent

A = predicted static
B = surprise change
C = unexpected static
D = predicted change

= attained mobility

Figure 4.1 Expected vs. attained mobility.
(*Source:* CDS-I and II, $N = 1,067$).

Each bar in Figure 4.1 represents 100% of the sample and is divided into four segments, A to D. The vertical line intersecting the bars divides those on the left side who said a job change was 'unlikely' or 'very unlikely' $(A + B)$ from those on the right hand side who said it was 'likely' or 'very likely' $(C + D)$. The shaded portion in the middle of each bar $(B + D)$ represents the proportion who actually experienced a job change of each type indicated. In this way the four segments represent: (A) those who correctly predicted that they would not change jobs over the next year ('predicted static'); (B) those who said they would not change but actually did ('surprise change'); (C) people who predicted that they would change jobs but actually did not ('unexpected static'); and (D) who correctly predicted they would change jobs ('predicted change').

Just comparing the size of the proportions to the right of the vertical $(C + D$ = expected change) with the size of the shaded proportions $(B + D$ = actual change), shows that people rather overestimate the likelihood of

90

mobility – 59% expected 'any change' but only 32% actually experienced any change, 22% expected promotion but only 14% experienced promotion; 20% expected employer change but only 10% experienced it. However, had we looked just at those who rated each change type as 'very likely' (i.e. excluding the 'likely' category) the proportions of expected and actual job change would have been very close on all three measures. If our analysis had stopped at this point, as is customary in many other surveys where predictions are matched with subsequent behaviour, such as when opinion polls forecasts are compared with election results, one might erroneously conclude that people are quite good at predicting their own behaviour. For example, 10% said they were 'very likely' to change employers and 10% did. The only problem with this is that it may not be the same 10% of the sample who say they expect to change who actually do change. And, indeed this is what we find.

Our longitudinal analysis shows managers have misplaced confidence in the predictability of their own job changing behaviour. Fewer than half the managers who predicted they would experience 'any change' actually experienced any kind of job change (portion D as a proportion of $C + D$ in Figure 4.1). The 'hit' rates for predictions of 'promotion' and 'employer change' are even worse. Only 28% of managers who expected promotion achieved it, and the proportion is identical for employer change. We find little improvement in prediction when we look at the other side of the coin: how many actual job changers had predicted their own mobility (portion D as a proportion of $B + D$ in Figure 4.1). Of those who experienced any kind of job change between the CDS-I and CDS-II, 26% had not been expecting this change when we asked them in the CDS-I; and fully 56% of those who achieved in-company promotions and 46% of managers who changed employer had failed to predict these moves one year or less before they occurred.

Yet if we apply statistical tests to these results we nonetheless find that the overall levels of hits and misses in managers' predictions are much better than would be achieved by chance.[16] This apparent paradox is easily explained. It is almost entirely due to the large group of 'predicted static' managers. Most of those who predicted they would *not* change jobs were correct – they did not change jobs. So it seems that mobile managers are very poor at predicting their own job changes, and only managers in stable, not to say stagnant, environments have an accurate view of their futures. Predictions of change are slightly more accurate for employer change than other types of change, presumably because employer moves are more under managers' unilateral control than are promotions and other changes. But the fact still remains that only a minority who expect to change organizations do so, even over as short a forecasting period as one year.

What does this tell us about managerial careers? If managers find it so difficult to predict job moves in the immediate future how much worse are they likely to be in previewing their careers over a longer period and what kinds of meaningful planning can the mobile manager undertake? Our data show that the only people who can plan with confidence are those in stable environments where any kind of change is unlikely. On the evidence of historical trends in job change (see Chapter 3), a small and shrinking number of managers are in this situation. The results of these analyses suggest that the growing unpredictability of organizational life and opportunity structures is poorly comprehended by those managers who are in the thick of it. There is little reason to share the confidence of many managers about how foreseeable is future mobility and consequently there are grounds for serious doubt about how well prepared they are for job change. At the same time, however, we should not forget that many managers are well prepared for radical changes in the sense of having confidence in the transferability of their skills (see Chapter 3). What they would seem to lack is the opportunity to anticipate the specific demands of future change, because of its unpredictability.

In Chapter 8 where we look at how managers view career development in their organizations, widespread inadequacies are perceived in the feedback they receive on their performance, and the degree to which prospects of advancement are felt to be based on 'luck' and 'politics'. Set alongside the findings we have been looking at here, these reflections on organizational career development are tantamount to an admission that managers neither understand nor can predict the forces that lead to mobility. Clearly there is more that senior managers, personnel specialists, performance appraisers, careers advisors and others with some responsibility for career development could do to lighten this darkness. Analysing the sources of career uncertainty could usefully form the agenda for the counselling and appraisal activities that are conducted with mobile managers in organizations.

Yet one should not entirely dismiss the planfulness of managerial careers or the reality of occupational choice. Rather our findings suggest that the notion of career, to be useful and relevant to managerial experience, needs to be redefined away from the stereotype of smooth continuous and planned development, an image that is promoted by the media, fiction, schools, professional associations, careers advisory services and paternalistic organizations. If we look at what managers actually experience, the notion of 'career' is best broadly defined to mean work histories.[17] For many, careers become fictitious if they are taken to connote personal 'strategic plans' or consistent thematic developments in working lives, and it would not be surprising if many managers, accepting the received wisdom of this fiction, feel some anxiety about why their own experience fails to conform to it. Similarly the notion of choice should not be equated solely with the realization of long held needs and desires, but should encompass the fluctuating reactions and wants which can emerge unexpectedly to produce sudden and unforeseen decisions. The trouble is that there is a mythology of careers and occupational choice in our society, fostered by the unfounded assumptions of educationalists, the wishful thinking of managers and the idealized imagery of recruiters and personnel specialists whose professional roles tend to reify the traditional notion of career. We would argue that this is mistaken. Managers and human resource specialists will gain rather than lose effective influence by coming to terms with the real uncertainty surrounding management careers. Only when the counsel of advisory professions is based upon accurate information and sound perceptions can it help people to prepare for change and deal with its challenge. Our next three chapters take us into this zone – evaluating the nature of the challenge of change, the task of adjustment, and the consequences that attend it.

Summary and conclusions

We have found that complex mixes of career perceptions are held by managers. It is not unusual to find people feeling simultaneously plateaued but satisfied, self-directed but planless, externally-directed but orderly in their career types, and so on. These are differentially related to career satisfactions and work histories. Conventional upward career paths seem to bring most contentment, whilst more radical and self-directed career patterns elicit more mixed sentiments. Externally-directed and impeded career types are more dissatisfied. We have also seen that there are quite different patterns of career types for men and women, for different occupations, statuses, company sizes and industrial areas. These point to the dualistic nature of career choice and the motivations underlying job change. For each of these groups there is a different blend of internal and external constraints and incentives. People are pulled by opportunities and images of the future; pushed by reactions to the past and the demands of the present; and all the time buffeted by the uncertainty surrounding these changes and forces. We have seen in the previous chapter that those who would succeed will often need to embrace radical job change, but in this chapter we have seen that those most exposed to radical change often have little prior warning of its advent. These findings have been further underlining the extent to which much directed choice in careers can only be exercised by managers seizing and exploiting the unpredicted moments of change and opportunity, or, to put it another way:

There is a tide in the affairs of men,
Which, taken at the flood, leads on to fortune;
Omitted, all the voyage of their life
Is bound in shallows, and in miseries.
On such a full sea are we now afloat;
And we must take the current where it serves,
Or lose our ventures.

(Brutus in *Julius Caeser*, IV, iii)

And as we have seen the fortune that managers seek is not purely materialistic. They are clearly ambitious but ambitious for what? Not for status alone, but for the challenging and creative work that is associated with high ranking roles. Our analyses in Chapters 2 and 3 have severely dented the image of the materialistic manager being lured from job to job by the bigger pay cheque, the plusher company car, and the fatter pension fund. We have also raised doubts about how realistic is the rationality of 'conventional' career development.

It would seem that many people are wedded to some very dubious assumptions about ladders of careers and stable patterns of managerial work. Many of our sample, well entrenched in middle-age, would still be unable to give a confident answer to the childhood question 'what are you going to be when you grow up?' Organizations are not pyramids, they are scattered encampments on a wide terrain of hills and valleys, and careers are not ladders, but stories about journeys and routes through and between these encampments. Some of these paths and stories are well trodden and well known, others are improvised and haphazard. Many have unclear beginnings and no obvious endings: they just peter out. Careers, as stories of these journeys, often get better with the telling. Logic, consistency and meaning are reassuringly accessible when one analyses the past, but become strangely elusive when one dispassionately appraises the present. Careers can be viewed as fictions about the past to help us feel good about the future. They are talismans, offering protection against the proximity of gaping uncertainties. They provide cognitive structures on to which our social identities can be anchored.

The practical implication of this is that mobile managers can be stronger if they remain open-minded but sceptical and prepared but flexible in the face of change. In the social arenas that lay the groundwork for job change and career development – schools, colleges, careers centres, recruitment offices, personnel departments and the like – the notion of career needs to be treated with more circumspect realism. These agents can best help people to help themselves by aiding their clients in the mapping of labour markets and opportunity structures, and by helping people build the self-confidence to quickly appraise and seize the varied and unbidden chances that may pass within their grasp.

It is clear that many of our respondents share our misgivings about the conventional fiction of career. At the same time we can recognize that the stories they have told of their work lives, like all the best stories, also contain truths about human capacities – tales of heroism, endurance, risks, disappointment and achievements. This brings us to the heart of the matter. To understand the meaning of career and the process of career development we need to understand the episodes that make up the story. We need to know how people experience job change – from anticipation through to outcomes. This is what we set out to explore in the chapters that follow.

5
Experiencing the Transition Cycle

If careers are journeys which begin at the point of entry into working life and end at retirement, then it would seem that researchers and personnel specialists have devoted their main efforts to the study of the starting points, destinations and major routes. Far less attention has been paid to the individual turning points and decisions that determine the direction of the journey. How these connections – job changes – are experienced has the power to shape the tangled course of careers, so insights into how people anticipate and respond to job changes has the potential to unlock our understanding of longer-term patterns of change. It is therefore our aim in this and the next chapter, to look at the process of changing jobs and its outcomes.

In Chapter 3 we saw how most managers can expect to change jobs at least once within any three year period and that most of these changes make radical new demands on their adaptive capacities. It would thus hardly be surprising if the process of job change were a major focus of managers' thoughts throughout their working lives. The very positive response to our interest in job change from the managers and organizations involved in our research confirms this. What has also become clear to us is how neglected a topic job change is in the management science media and in organizational practice. We have found that the notion of the Transition Cycle provides a useful starting point for thinking about the different challenges and problems encountered through the stages of this experience. Figure 5.1 shows the Transition Cycle, as it was described in Chapter 1 with an added consideration of outcomes. First, there is a period of anticipation or preparation during which the individual makes ready (or not) to undertake change, wondering about the new tasks and responsibilities and whether he or she will be able to cope with them successfully. One may also expect there to be anxiety over the impression one will make on one's new colleagues and boss.[1] Anxiety about one's performance is highly dependent upon self confidence, which in turn is partly contingent upon what sorts of previous experiences one can draw on. The amount of forewarning there is of a change sets the limits of time and resources one can use to develop new

96

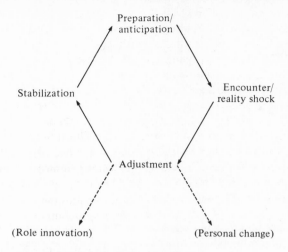

Figure 5.1 The cycle of work role transitions.

'scripts' and incorporate elements from previous learning. We have seen in Chapter 4 that the predictability of job moves and career changes is generally low. The preparation stage may therefore stimulate the individual attempt to find out more about the new job, or to take preparatory action, such as trying to increase skill levels in areas which are believed to be required in the new job. Both can help greatly to reduce anxiety, though the real underlying uncertainties may be harder to remove. Even one's new boss may lack a clear idea about one's duties.[2]

Second is the encounter or 'reality shock' period; the first days and weeks of the new job when the individual discovers how much dissimilarity there is between their previous experience, their anticipations, and the new reality. Surprise can be viewed as the hallmark of this period (Louis, 1980) and previous research has demonstrated that for people moving into new organizations the reality is usually very different from expectations (Richards, 1984; Arnold, 1985). This surprise typically is exacerbated by the inadequacy of the job previewing that is offered to prospective employees and the imagery that organizations tend to project to applicants in the recruitment process, i.e. selection often degenerates into a hard sales pitch designed to hook the person who is 'best' in some global sense rather than to secure the person best suited for the job. Indeed there is some research evidence that giving 'realistic job previews' can reduce the subsequent trauma of encounter and reduce the likelihood of early turnover (Premack and Wanous, 1985). The encounter stage is likely to be the most

97

acutely stressful phase of the cycle but also it is likely to be a time of great excitement, optimism, and discovery.

The third stage of the job change process is adjustment, when the individual engages the fundamental task of adapting to the new work environment. In Chapter 1 we identified two dimensions of the process of adjustment: the attitudes and behaviours of the incumbent are socialized to fit them to their new situations (Moore, 1969; Feldman, 1976), and the newcomer shapes the environment to meet her individual needs, talents and expectations (Schein, 1971b; Nicholson, 1984). These are equivalent to reactive and proactive coping strategies for achieving a good person–environment fit. In this chapter we will be focussing primarily on proactive adjustment or 'role innovation' (Schein, 1971b) – the process by which people mould the new role to meet their personal requirements; in the next chapter we shall concentrate on personal change as an outcome of reactive adjustment.

The emotional reactions stimulated by these processes can be expected, on the one hand, to include a sense of satisfaction at one's achieved innovations and successful adaptation and, on the other, to involve disillusionment and frustration at apparently irreducible person–environment misfitting. Negative reactions may be sufficient to lead the individual to quit without ever reaching the next stage, stabilization, by initiating job search strategies and escaping the role (Hirschmann, 1970; Dawis and Lofquist, 1984; Campion and Mitchell, 1986). Satisfactions are thus what hold many individuals in roles long enough to reach what we have called the stabilization stage, the state of 'settled connection' between people and roles (Hill and Trist, 1955). In this stage most of the adjustments made can be considered to be forms of self, role and environmental 'fine tuning'. However, under the conditions of high mobility which we have seen in this study are characteristic of managerial career paths, adjustment and stabilization can be viewed as tantamount to preparation for the onset of the next transition. Thus does the cycle continue.

In this chapter we shall be looking at the qualities of managers' experience at each stage of the cycle. What causes people most anxiety during the preparation phase? What kinds of surprise await them in the encounter phase? In the adjustment phase how much do managers attempt to role innovate and what circumstances favour this mode of adjustment?

Preparation/anticipation

This stage of the job Transition Cycle is particularly important because of its effects on later stages. For example, inflated expectations in the preparation stage are likely to bring a bitter harvest of disappointments in the encounter stage, which could continue to repercuss by impairing subsequent adjustment and result in dysfunctional forms of stabilization. Likewise excessive anxieties may inhibit proactive adjustment and give rise to various kinds of underachievement.

In a study of the present design it is only possible to investigate these anticipations retrospectively.[3] We asked managers about their transition anxiety as part of our general aim to evaluate the stressfulness of job change and to identify which aspects of change are viewed as especially threatening. In the CDS-I we asked the managers to reflect on how anxious they had felt prior to their last major job change (for most of them less than three years previously). They were asked to indicate the extent of their anxiety in relation to six specific aspects of their new jobs. The results, shown in Figure 5.2, show that anticipating job change is not generally stressful, though it must be borne in mind that these retrospective assessments are likely to be positively tempered by the fact that at the time of asking these anxieties were in the past for most of the sample, i.e. they had been mastered by subsequent adjustment to the reality. Therefore, it seems all the more important that we do take note of the small minorities (between 2% and 7%) who admit to having been 'very anxious' before their last job change. When we look at what aspects of new jobs people anticipate with anxiety, we find most worry about how well they will perform, and whether their contributions will be valued by influential people at work (corroborating findings from a smaller management sample reported by Marshall and Cooper, 1976). Least anxiety is felt about how well the new job will fit in with life outside work, and about future relationships with colleagues and bosses, though, as we shall see below, this confidence is often misplaced. One can interpret this as indicating that managers feel that they have the skills and abilities to handle relationships, but are more uncertain about the criteria that will be used to rate their task skills and personal qualities. Since most moves are upward in status these anxieties probably reflect a concern over achievement and the ability to meet net challenges successfully.

One might expect these concerns to be particularly potent for managers making the most radical and demanding job changes, those involving moves to new employers, and this is confirmed by our analysis. As Figure 5.2 shows, anxiety in every one of the areas we have considered is higher for employer changers than for other movers.[4] Sub-group analysis also reveals a major difference between the sexes in these feelings. Women experience higher pre-transition anxiety than men in all age groups, consistent with our observation (Chapters 2 and 8) that women managers are, on average, more tense, more unsure and less trusting than men at work. This is understandable when one considers that most women are anticipating the

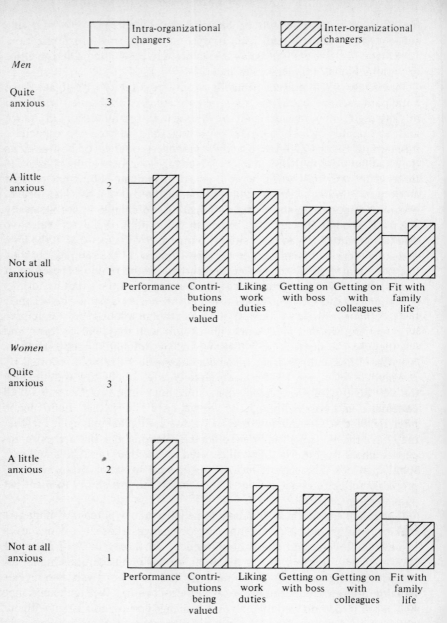

Figure 5.2 Mean levels of pre-transition anxiety.
(*Source:* Retrospective reports from CDS-I, *N* = 2,304).

double challenge of adjusting to change and gaining acceptance in male-dominated settings.

So it seems that the preparation phase of the Transition Cycle is marked by moderate but not high levels of tension, particularly by managers changing employers and by women.

Encounter

After the anticipatory first phase of the Transition Cycle how do managers react to the reality shock of the first hours, days, and weeks in the job? To discover exactly what kinds of surprises job changers encounter, we asked the managers in the CDS-II to indicate whether they had been surprised by what they had encountered in their new jobs. Respondents who replied to this question had changed jobs within the previous 15 months, so their recollections were reasonably fresh. They were asked to indicate whether they were 'very surprised', 'somewhat surprised' or 'not at all surprised' in relation to eight sources of surprise, which can be grouped into three general areas: work context, job content and self.[5]

The managers were also asked to report in a free response format, for each surprise, specifically what it was they had encountered which surprised them. Table 5.1 shows what proportion of managers expressed surprise in each of the eight areas, and what was the evaluative tone – positive, negative or neutral – of their reasons for surprise.[6]

Around 25% of the sample expressed surprise in each area, and 73% expressed surprise on at least one of these.[7] Thus, surprise is a fairly common short-term reaction to job change, even where the change takes place within a familiar organization, though it is apparent in Table 5.1 that surprise is much more marked among those who moved *between* organizations. So we see again that inter-organizational moves present a greater challenge to adjustment than other types of move.

Let us now look more closely at the experiential qualities of the encounter stage of the Transition Cycle by taking each of these areas in turn and summarizing how managers themselves described, in free response format, the reasons for their surprises.[8]

Looking first at *work context*, there is a preponderance of negative comments about the 'slowness' and apathetic general atmosphere of their new environments, while others mention lack of friendliness and tense formality in working relationships. Positive comments about work context convey an opposite image of surprised appreciation at the relaxed, easygoing and friendly character of the workplace. On training and learning opportunities the picture is less balanced: most surprises are negative. Organizations often appear not to be providing the training that managers

Table 5.1 *Sources of surprise*

	Inter-organizational changers ($N = 125$)	Intra-organizational changers ($N = 229$)
A *Work context*		
1 The general *atmosphere* or 'character' of the area you're working in	34%	24%
Reasons (negative–neutral–positive)	18–5–11	10–6–9
2 The *training* or learning opportunities you have received	27%	19%
Reasons (negative–neutral–positive)	17–9–6	8–4–7
3 The way *communications* and *decisions* are handled at higher levels	55%	36%
Reasons (negative–neutral–positive)	43–6–4	27–4–9
B *Job content*		
1 The nature of the *work* you're expected to do	25%	23%
Reasons (negative–neutral–positive)	7–13–5	5–10–5
2 What the *people* are like with whom you work	31%	23%
Reasons (negative–neutral–positive)	16–9–10	13–6–6
3 The type of *supervision* you receive	32%	24%
Reasons (negative–neutral–positive)	19–6–6	12–7–6
C *Self*		
1 Your own work *performance*	32%	24%
Reasons (negative–neutral–positive)	8–6–18	7–4–11
2 Your own *reactions* to and feelings about things	33%	25%
Reasons (negative–neutral–positive)	17–3–14	14–4–10
3 Your *lifestyle* outside work	26%	16%
Reasons (negative–neutral–positive)	10–2–14	7–5–3

(*Source:* CDS-I)

expect when they change jobs. The greatest area of surprise of any in the list centres on the quality of communications and decision making, and managers' appraisals of this are overwhelmingly and unremittingly negative. For example one said 'Decisions are arbitrary, often disorganized and late', and another that 'communications are typically bureaucratic'. The vast majority complain of operational inefficiency, fractured communications and autocratic decision-making.

Job content is also a major source of surprise, though here we find reactions are generally more positive. Many comment favourably on the amount of responsibility and independence they have been given, though some of the negative surprises are at finding their work *too* difficult. Finding the job lacking in interest is mentioned by only two respondents, perhaps indicating that high interest is an inherent quality of newness of role. Turning to the social aspects of job change, we can see in Table 5.1 that managers transferring jobs between organizations are more likely than intra-organizational movers to be unfavourably surprised by the people with whom they work, but more favourably surprised by their supervision. In their negative surprises at their new bosses most job changers complain of insufficient supervision, while others talk of incompetence. Only a minority express positive surprise at the scope they are allowed by bosses. Rather it seems that low profile supervision is interpreted as neglect. So overall one can conclude that neither managers who transfer within organizations nor those who move between organizations are well-prepared for the people or situations they will encounter.

Finally sizeable numbers of managers express surprise at *self*, i.e. toward their own reactions to their new situations, and these are by and large more equally balanced between positives and negatives than we have seen for work context and job content. Of the negatives, many feel unintegrated, that they are not coping well or enjoying their work. On the positive side an equal number are pleasantly surprised by how well they are coping and their awakened sense of their unique abilities and competences. Relatively few find their life styles outside work a source of surprise, though several complain of a lack of free time in their new jobs. As one manager expressed this: 'pressure due to under-staffing and having to learn the new job very quickly has resulted in a lot of late hours, and work at home – this causes family pressures.'

Two conclusions can be drawn from these findings. First, even when managers are transferring within their organizations, surprise is still a common reaction. Second, it is clear that negative surprises tend to outweigh the positive, and heavily so in some perceptions of people and environments. One can take this at face value as reflecting the commonplace deficiencies in organizational life, but the fact that they are a source of *surprise* also indicates that managers are often the victims of their own deficient or erroneous expectations; i.e. these can be seen as failings in anticipation and preparation on the part of individuals and of the organizations within or to which they move.

The model of the Transition Cycle would suggest that surprise and subsequent adjustment are related. Analysis reveals that among those expressing surprise about aspects of their new jobs (354 of the 404 job changers) there was a significant negative correlation[9] between degree of overall surprise and satisfaction with work life during the past year. In short, for almost all movers there are important and often difficult accommodations to be made during the early period of familiarization, before one can settle to the longer-term tasks of adjustment.

Our measures of 'surprise' concentrate on the experiential content of the early days and weeks in a new job. More general evaluations of this period were also derived from a series of questions asking managers to think back to their first three months in their present job and compare it on a number of dimensions with the job they held previously. Four of these asked about the positive features of 'authority', 'freedom', 'satisfaction' and 'challenge', and for around 70% comparisons were favourable: 'more' or 'much more' authority etc. in the new job.[10] Only 12–16% said they experienced less of these benefits, so it would seem that the short-term outcomes of job change are overwhelmingly positive. However, three other items on the same measure ask about negative experiences during encounter, allowing us to assess the prevalence of stresses during this period.[11] Table 5.2 summarizes the results.

It would appear that adjustment difficulties as represented in b) and c), although reasonably common, are not a problem for the majority, but that higher stress in the new job is much more widely reported. How is this to be reconciled with managers' evident satisfaction? The answer is twofold. One, stress and satisfaction are not mutually exclusive; two, stress effects can be short-lived and bearable. Combining these two observations leads to the conclusion that for many of the managers in our sample stresses are short-lived and bearable *because* of concurrent satisfactions in their new jobs. Indeed, it seems likely that managers actively welcome and seek out job changes that they know are going to offer the 'stresses' of increased challenge, authority and freedom.

We can verify this in two ways. First, we can test whether stress and satisfaction do correlate positively, and second, we can see how these reactions are related to different kinds of job change. The first of these tests strongly confirms that stress and satisfaction are very closely intertwined for most managers. The second analysis produces some unexpected and challenging findings.[12] The *most* stressful job changes are those which involve an upward status move and *no* change of employer. The *least* stressful are those where there *is* a change of employer, and where there is a downward status move. So stress seems unrelated to how radical is the type of move. How can this be explained? We need to set these results in the context of other findings. In particular we report later in this chapter that downward status moves have undeniable negative consequences for psychological adjustment, which suggests that the absence of stress during the settling-in period should not be taken to indicate satisfactory

Table 5.2 *Sources of stress in the first three months of settling-in*

Compared to my previous job I felt my new job had:	More	Same amount	Less
	%	%	%
a) Stress in the new job	55	21	24
b) Difficulties fitting in work demands of the new job with family life	30	45	25
c) Difficulties fitting in work demands with social and recreational life	30	47	23

(*Source:* CDS-I, $N = 2,233$)

adjustment; and the converse, that the presence of stress during the settling-in period often is not a harbinger of lasting difficulties for the person. In Chapter 6 we report that greatest satisfactions are experienced in moves which are simultaneously upward status and employer changing, and as we have seen it is upward moves that are associated with stress in the encounter phase. So it would seem that stress and satisfaction are almost synonymous for many of our recorded job changes, but escaping to a new organization where this does not involve an upward status shift is the move most likely to bring satisfaction without the stress. This seems to indicate a 'honeymoon' effect in moves to new organizations: perhaps because managers are less burdened with immediate role demands than when they change jobs in their current organization.

It seems therefore that the reported stresses and difficulties of short-term adaptation to job change cannot be simply taken at face value: they go hand in hand with all the main benefits of job changing. Stress-coping is an integral part of a desirable and rewarding experience. The experience of mastering new environments, whilst challenging and difficult, brings its own intrinsic satisfactions to people who are primarily motivated by their need for growth.

Adjustment

Work role transitions require people to adjust to new roles and social relations (Moreland and Levine, 1983). As we have argued this adjustment can involve two contrasting processes. First, it involves reactive change in the individual, ranging from minor alterations in daily routines and habits, to major developments in relationships and self-image. Second, adjustment

105

may involve moulding the new role to suit the requirements of the mover, ranging from minor initiatives such as variations in work schedules, to more dramatic role innovations such as changes in the main goals of organizational work. Often work role transitions also require major adjustments outside the work sphere, especially within family life where job change entails geographical relocation (Pinder, 1977; Brett and Werbel, 1978; Pinder and Das, 1978; Brett, 1980). Even in less radical moves some alterations in family or social relationships are to be expected. The outcomes of the adjustment process can have far-reaching significance.

One of us (Nicholson, 1984) has theorized about outcomes of work role transitions arguing that people's modes of adjustment can be predicted from a knowledge of three sets of factors: (1) new role requirements; (2) personal dispositions (from past socialization and current motives); (3) organizational induction and socialization practices. Figure 5.3 shows the general model that is proposed.

The two major predicted outcomes of transitions are: personal change (the individual adapting herself to fit the new job or organization) and role innovation (the individual moulding the role to suit herself). Combining these two outcome dimensions generates four distinctive adjustment modes: [13]

Replication

This is where there is little change in the individual and little moulding of the new role. An example might be the case of the production manager who moves to a new line which is little different from the previous setting and where there is negligible opportunity to vary current practice. Here we would expect little change in the individual and little change to the new role. [14]

Absorption

Here there is very little moulding of the new role but significant personal change is experienced by the individual. A typical example might be the young graduate entering industry for the first time with no previous work experience and no well-practised skills; the person does not attempt any major innovations in the role, but does undergo significant identity development in adapting to his or her new environment.

Determination

This is the converse of absorption where the transition involves little personal change but does result in significant role innovation. Such a case

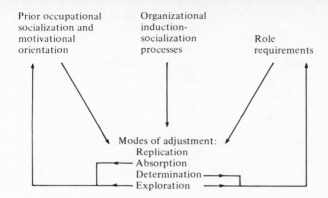

Figure 5.3 Determinants and outcomes in the theory of work role transitions. (*Source:* Nicholson, 1984).

might be a confident and purposeful technical specialist who transfers skills to the new setting with a clear determination [15] to make significant alteration to his or her new environment without having to concede change in his or her professional identity.

Exploration

The last outcome refers to those situations in which both the role and the individual are changed through the process of adjustment. An example of this could be the generalist manager who 'spirals' into a higher status and functionally novel role. Through role innovations the newcomer 'makes her mark', as well as undergoing personal change to accommodate the new meanings and values of a different position in a new sub-culture.

Nicholson predicts that two dimensions of role requirements are of prime importance in determining these outcomes. The first is job novelty. High novelty of job demands will predispose the individual to undergo personal change, as new skills and perspectives are acquired to meet the demands of new circumstances. The second dimension is discretion, or latitude in role performance. The greater the discretion in the new role, the more will the individual be predisposed towards role innovation. [16] High discretion in a new role does not of course preclude high or low job novelty since these two dimensions or roles are conceptually independent. Integrating these dimensions and their predictors yields four proposed configurations of job change and outcomes, as shown in Figure 5.4.

107

Role requirements	Outcomes	
Low job discretion + ⟶ Low job novelty	Replication	(Low personal change + Low role innovation)
Low job discretion + ⟶ High job novelty	Absorption	(High personal change + Low role innovation)
High job discretion + ⟶ Low job novelty	Determination	(Low personal change + High role innovation)
High job discretion + ⟶ High job novelty	Exploration	(High personal change + **High role innovation**)

Figure 5.4 Nicholson's theory of work role transitions: 1 – Role requirements, personal change and role innovation. (*Source:* Nicholson, 1984).

The second set of predictors of adjustment outcomes that concern us here are personal predispositions. The theory suggests that two dimensions may be especially linked with the outcomes of work role transitions: desire for control and desire for feedback.[17] People with high desires for control over their environments are more likely to be drawn to role innovation as a mode of adjustment than those with low desires for control. Desire for control is therefore the personal counterpart or complement of job discretion: high levels of both are associated with role innovation as an adjustment strategy. On the other dimension people with high desires for feedback will be attuned and responsive to the influences, communications and needs of others, and to the perceived demand characteristics of the work situation. For example, praise and criticism are more likely to induce personal change amongst people with high than low needs for feedback. So need for feedback is the conceptual complement of job novelty, since both favour personal change as a mode of adjustment to job change. (As with outcomes, these two dimensions are conceived as independent of one another.) Figure 5.5 summarizes these predicted relationships. The third set of predictors of adjustment outcomes in Figure 5.3, organizational socialization and induction, develop the ideas of Van Maanen and Schein but it is beyond the scope of this study to examine these here.[18] However to investigate the first two sets of factors, role requirements and personal dispositions, we can look at our data on self-perceptions and job characteristics to test the theory's predictions about who will role innovate and who will undergo personal change. In the remainder of this chapter we shall look at the first of these outcome dimensions, role innovation. In the next chapter we shall consider the alternative adjustment outcome, personal change.

Personality dispositions		Outcomes
Low need for control + Low need for feedback	⟶	Replication
Low need for control + High need for feedback	⟶	Absorption
High need for control + Low need for feedback	⟶	Determination
High need for control + High need for feedback	⟶	Exploration

Figure 5.5 Nicholson's theory of work role transitions: 2 – Personal dispositions, personal change and role innovation (*Source:* Nicholson, 1984).

Role innovation

In the CDS-I role innovation was measured by asking managers to rate the extent to which they carried out their present jobs differently from the people who did the job before them or from other current equivalent job holders. They were asked to do so on four dimensions of role innovation: setting work targets or objectives; deciding the methods used to achieve these objectives; deciding the order in which different parts of the job are done; and choosing who to deal with in order to carry out work duties.[19] Table 5.3 shows the overall levels of role innovation that were reported by managers. It is apparent that moderate to high levels of this adjustment strategy are commonplace. We can further identify what kinds of managers are most likely to role innovate by looking at other individual difference measures.

We find that age, status and managerial role type are all independently linked with innovation. Older people regardless of their status, are more likely to be role innovators, but there is no systematic relationship between role innovation and either general educational qualifications or specific professional qualifications.[20] Higher status managers are more likely to report being role innovators (regardless of their age), and generalist managers more likely to innovate than functional specialists (controlling for age and status).

Now let us move to test some of our theoretically derived predictions about the factors that facilitate role innovation, starting with discretion. In order to measure discretion in the CDS-I, managers were asked to indicate how much freedom they had in their present jobs compared to their previous jobs on five dimensions which combine to provide a robust measure of discretion.[21] There is, as predicted, a positive and significant relationship

Table 5.3 *Reported role innovation following last job change*
'... how you approach your job, compared with how other people have done or currently do this job in your organization'

Area of role innovation	Much the same %	Somewhat differently %	Very differently %
Setting work targets/objectives	18	44	38
Deciding methods used to achieve objectives/targets	15	46	39
Deciding the order in which different parts of the job are done	23	44	33
Choosing whom you deal with in order to carry out work duties	32	38	30

(*Source:* CDS-I, $N = 1,493$, excluding newly created job movers, see Chapter 7)

between discretion and role innovation with high levels of discretion associated with high levels of role innovation.[22]

Among the environmental factors which are associated with role innovation at work, organization size is particularly interesting. Smaller organizations (though not the smallest) are the settings most conducive to role innovation, as shown in Figure 5.6. One may infer that the decrease in innovation, with increasing size is due to administrative and bureaucratic systems in larger enterprises which enforce standardization and routinization, and thereby inhibit innovation (Mintzberg, 1979). This is confirmed when we examine the relationship between size of organizations and job discretion. It is negative: large organizations offer managers least discretion. It seems that the smaller the organization, the less clearly delineated are managerial roles.

Finally, an additional finding of interest and importance is that high role innovators are more likely than low innovators to report having experienced personal change as a result of their last job change.[23] This indicates, in the terminology of the theory of work role transitions, that 'exploration' is more common as an adjustment mode than pure 'determination'.

Since so many diverse factors predict role innovation, it is important to try to disentangle them. Because, for example, age and status are both good predictors of innovation, we need to know if older managers are not higher innovators simply because they are also high status, or vice versa. We can

110

Table 5.4 *Predictors of role innovation*

Individual characteristics:
Age
High Status
Dominance
Creativity
Need for growth
Situational factors:
Discretion
Predictable work environment
Opportunities for growth

(*Source:* CDS-I, N = 2,304)

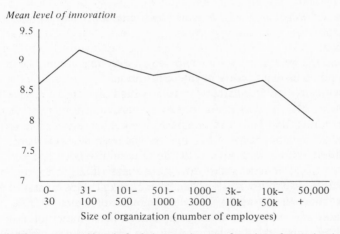

Figure 5.6 Mean reported level of role innovation as a function of organization size. (*Source:* CDS-I, N = 2,304).

apply statistical techniques to assess the effects of each of these factors independently.[24] Table 5.4 shows the results of this analysis and confirms that reported levels of role innovation are predicted independently by dominance, creativity, and need for growth. Factors in the work environment predicting role innovation are jobs that are high in both discretion and status, but low in predictability.

The two stage design of the investigation allows us to check our findings longitudinally,[25] confirming some of these relationships. In particular high role innovators, who again we find to be high in self-confidence and needs for growth, at Time 2, were more likely than others to have moved into new roles of high discretion and low predictability. Longitudinal analysis also enables us to look at what predicts *increases* in job changers' levels of reported role innovation,[26] and here too we find this occurs among growth driven confident managers and is associated with increases in job discretion and decreases in predictability at work. If these are the conditions conducive to managerial role innovation, then they have implications for placement policies, job design and organizational socialization.

So far we have defined role innovation in terms of its effects, but one can take a more differentiated view of it as an adjustment strategy by considering the different kinds of challenge that might face the would-be innovator. In particular, two quite different origins can be envisaged. On the one hand are what might be termed 'converters': managers who are changing the ways in which their new roles are performed by carrying over well-practised methods from their previous roles, without any necessarily creative intent. On the other hand are what we shall call 'developers': role innovators whose new jobs are very different from their previous jobs and for whom there is less opportunity for the transfer of experience. We empirically distinguished these groups by selecting out the 217 managers who had the maximum possible scores on our measure of role innovation and dividing them into two roughly equal groups on the basis of their reports of job novelty, we then tested for differences between them. One hundred and twelve who rated their new jobs relatively low in novelty we categorized as converters, and 105 who rated their jobs relatively high in novelty we classed as developers. We find a number of significant differences between these two groups. As expected the developers do indeed report a greater need to develop new skills than converters. They also report higher personal change following their last job move, and place greater importance on working with friendly and congenial colleagues.[27] This analysis illustrates one dimension of the complexity of the innovation process, and how behaviours which appear similar can have radically different origins and meaning.[28]

It is beyond the scope of this book to explore these complexities further but we can briefly comment on two other of our findings that have potentially far-reaching significance. The first is that people who report high levels of role innovation tend to have been more satisfied with their last job change. Here we encounter a problem of interpretation – role innovation could be linked with satisfaction in three ways: one, people may feel at liberty to role innovate because they are secure and happy in their work; two, environments in which it is possible to role innovate may tend to be more satisfying locations on a number of dimensions; and three people who successfully role innovate may have, in the process, made their environments more personally satisfying. There are indications in our findings to support all three of these explanations and, of course, they are not mutually exclusive. Further research is needed to clarify these relationships, but whichever holds true it does seem that there is an important link between innovation and quality of working life.

The second aspect of the results needing further research is the positive association we have found between high levels of innovation and self-reported personal change after job moves. This can be interpreted as giving support to the idea, discussed by Hall(1976) and Zurcher(1977) that some individuals are in a sense more 'Protean' or mutable; especially skilled at adapting both themselves and their environments to achieve a better fit. Personal change is the second main dimension of adjustment to job change we discussed in our theoretical review, and the fact that both role innovation and personal change can occur together strongly confirms our assumption that these are independent but not mutually exclusive dimensions. To better understand the nature of the adjustment phase of the Transition Cycle we need to look at personal change more closely. This is a major topic in itself, for the nature and forms of personal change in adult life are issues of some controversy in contemporary social science. We shall therefore look at this area separately in the next chapter.

However, we can briefly anticipate the main findings that relate to our thinking about the Transition Cycle. As we shall see, of the two modes of adjustment – role innovation and personal change – role innovation is associated with the greatest satisfaction. Personal change seems more often to be a response to anxiety. People adjust their attitudes, values and dispositions to fit situations in which they feel uncertain and we shall elaborate on this and other aspects of personal change in the next chapter.

Before we proceed to look at the stabilization phase, a brief comment should be made about our measure of role innovation, upon which much of our preceding discussion has hinged. What reliance can one place upon retrospective self-reports? We have already argued that in some ways this method takes us closest to the phenomenological reality of role innovation, since often only the role holder is in a position to make the judgement that is called for. However, in many situations one might wish for this to be corroborated by independent observers. In a separate study (West, 1986) we have assessed the validity of our self-reported method of measuring role innovation, and found it to be strongly associated with supervisors' ratings of job performance. This does not mean that our measure does not contain sources of perceptual bias, but it does lend some confidence to our assumption that managers' reported innovation has some foundation in objective as well as subjective reality.

Stabilization

For many people the stabilization phase of the work role Transition Cycle marks the beginning of the next cycle. In Chapters 1 and 3 we considered how frequently job changes occur for managers, and we have noted that many managers may barely complete the process of adjustment before they are off into another cycle of change and adjustment. The stabilization phase is, for some, a time of consolidation, marking the dissipation of surprise and adjustment, and the establishment of settled routines. For others this final stage is never reached. Job search strategies are already being initiated and the person is planning new career moves or anticipating impending organization changes. For many, as we have observed in Chapter 4, the impetus for the next job change arises without warning. Moreover, as we shall see in Chapter 8, managers have little opportunity to control the pace and continuity of movement through the cycle. Our results in this area also fit with our reflections in Chapter 2 that the stereotype of management as a stable and homogeneous occupational group cannot be sustained by empirical research. Our findings support those who argue for greater attention to individual differences (Jones, 1983; Brousseau, 1983) and moreover imply that any research on management is likely to be studying – whether wittingly or unwittingly – a population in transition. Stabilization is the exception, not the rule.

Summary and implications

This chapter has been structured around the four stages of the work role Transition Cycle: preparation/anticipation, encounter, adjustment and stabilization, and we have reached a number of conclusions about each of them. Taking preparation first, in the previous chapter we inferred that inasmuch as satisfactory preparation for job change requires some anticipation, managers are ill-prepared for transitions. It would not be surprising therefore if the preparation stage of the work role Transition Cycle was a time of some stress, but from managers' recollections of how they felt before their last job change we have seen that it is neither a general nor a major source of anxiety. However, the chief concern of managers before a job change is how well they will perform in their new roles, and pre-transition anxiety is most widely reported by women and by managers about to change employers.

114

These fears seem to be largely unfounded, for when we come to look at the encounter stage, and managers' experiences of positive and negative surprise after recent job moves, their own performance is one of the few areas of generally positive experience. Otherwise, managers are confronted by an array of largely contextual disappointments, which is itself somewhat surprising since many are enacting job changes within familiar environments. Most dismay is felt about organizational inefficiencies and insufficiencies, such as training, communications and decision-making. This is a disturbing comment on the shortcomings of the modern organization, but, at the same time, is suggestive of inflated expectations and unfounded optimism being held by mobile managers. Even more alarming perhaps are managers' negative reactions to their new bosses and colleagues. Again it appears that managers are ill-prepared for change by their over-sanguine expectations that they will encounter enlightened human resource management in their new settings.

We have devoted most attention to the longer-term process of adjustment, and in particular, how managers try to mould their roles to achieve a good fit with their environments. This strategy is apparently very common, especially amongst generalist, older, and high status managers. A climate of high discretion is clearly conducive to role innovation, and this we have found to be more a feature of small than large organizations. We have also seen how individual differences in managers' personal dispositions are linked with role innovation. Confident and self-directed types are most likely to engage this mode of adjustment. However we have noted that role innovation can have different meanings for people. 'Developers', for whom role innovation involves the greater creative challenge of job novelty, differ in their psychological orientation from 'converters'.

We also commented on the links between role innovation and two other important experiences: satisfaction and personal change. Role innovators seem to reap benefits of work satisfactions, though the causal relationships are probably multidirectional. Personal change is also often positively linked with role innovation; in the terminology of Nicholson's theory of work role transitions, 'exploration' is a more common mode of adjustment than 'determination' or 'absorption'. The predictors of these outcomes are also consistent with propositions derived from this theory.

Finally, there is little that we can say about the stabilization stage over and above our observations in Chapter 2 about the nature of managerial work. Our focus in this chapter has been primarily on the processes of change though it does appear from this perspective that past researchers in the field of management may have too readily assumed stabilized and settled connections between managers and their work roles. One may also conclude that role innovation, as an important and widespread managerial behaviour, has not received the attention it merits from scholars in organization behaviour. There are signs of a growing wave of interest in the topic, but much of this is pitched at the macro level of organizational performance rather than at how individuals discharge work roles innovatively (West, Farr and King, 1986). The other main dimension of adjustment we have discussed, personal change, has received far more concentrated attention, and in the next chapter we shall evaluate what our research can contribute to this issue.

6

Outcomes of job change

If transitions are turning points then clearly some are more redirecting than others. At one extreme, transitions can be the changes that keep one on a steady course, like the adjustments a driver has to make to keep on the road or the budgetry changes a household initiates to maintain a steady state in the quality of life. Alternatively transitions may be junctures at which the entire balance and direction of the life-course shifts. Our interest veers toward the latter, though it is important to recognize that such far reaching effects may not always be immediately visible to the person undergoing the change. Fundamental life changes may initially only be apprehended as small movements; the significance of a change may not be appreciated for some time; successive minor developments may accumulate into major new branches of growth, and so only be perceptible as turning points when one is looking back over a lengthy period of time.

The theory of transitions we considered in Chapter 5 illustrates how a number of different outcomes may flow from the adjustment process, and we have seen how role innovation is a fairly constant adaptive strategy in managers' work lives. But we have also seen how the job changes managers experience are, more often than not, radical in the altered situations they represent and the new demands they make. It is common for the job changer to have to adapt simultaneously to new organizational settings, the responsibility of altered status, the demand to practice new skills, and involvement in a range of new relationships. The theory of transitions we have considered (Nicholson, 1984) proposed that adjustment to novelty acts as a stimulus for personal change. This connects the study of job change with one of the most important issues in social science – the nature of adult development. What kinds of personal development can be envisaged as a result of job change? Our view is broad, embracing both the minor and the fundamental parameters of identity. It can be supposed, for example, that through job change people may acquire any or all of the following: new behaviours and habits, different ways of relating to other people, fresh attitudes and values, altered intellectual or cognitive capacities, and reformed personality traits or dispositions.

It was beyond the scope of our study to look at all of these, and our method commits us to caution in the attempt, for two reasons: one, we must rely upon self-report data, and two, we can only measure change over a short time span, though we are able to supplement this with retrospective reports of personal development.

In this chapter we will first examine the complex question of personal change as it has been represented in the literature, and then we shall consider how much personal change was exhibited by our sample, using various criteria. Our results present an image of simultaneous change and stability: throughout all of the life and work changes managers experience, they retain a fairly high degree of psychological constancy, but at the same time many systematic changes are visible.

The next step is to try to explain these changes. This we do by looking at both life events and job mobility as possible causes. A number of different analyses are used to unravel these. We shall be showing that personal change is a constant if not dramatic process for people, whether or not they move jobs, but the *nature* of the change is affected by whether people have or have not moved between jobs. In other words, change begets change, and stability begets change too. These findings have a direct bearing on the study of adult development, as well as practical implications for how transitions might be used by human resource management systems to promote well-being and effectiveness in organizations.

Finally, we conclude the chapter by looking at one type of job change which has consistently negative personal implications: downward status job mobility. In the next chapter we shall look briefly at one other type of mobility that has almost completely opposite causes and effects: moves into newly created jobs.

Personal change

Before we recount what our study has to say about personal change as an outcome of adjustment to transitions, let us briefly consider how personal change has been generally viewed by scholars. There seem to be four schools of thought debating the nature of identity change over the adult life-span.

First, there are those researchers who emphasize the endurance over time of well-formed and differentiated psychic structures. According to this view, in-born temperamental differences and traits established through early life experience, lay the foundation for the full range of human types we can see around us, and these types retain their basic characteristics through the adult life-span. It is mainly behavioural scientists from the psychometric tradition, attempting to define and accurately measure individual differences,

118

who espouse this view.[1] They generally point to the high statistical reliabilities of measured traits derived from large data sets and sophisticated personality inventories to sustain their case for stability (Costa and McCrae, 1980).

The second group of scholars would complain that the measurement methods used by the first group are predisposed towards invariance, and that important changes in identity are overlooked or even suppressed by the psychometrician's techniques of scale development. These scholars, coming largely from social psychology, see identity as a dynamic process, evolving continually to incorporate and shed elements from the shifting field of symbolic and personal relationships.[2] They see our sense of self as inseparable from the statuses we occupy, the roles we fulfil, and the interactions we undertake. They conclude that methods of inquiry cannot comprehend the subtlety and dynamism of human personality unless they depart from conventional quantitative paradigms (Mischel, 1968; Harré and Secord, 1972).

A third group of writers takes the view that identity undergoes cyclical or phasic change over the life cycle. The pace of change is uneven and punctuated by irreversible transitions. These are linked with people's changing awareness of their own mortality, with culturally demarcated boundaries in the central role relationships to which social identity is anchored, and with the accumulation of experience and knowledge. These scholars agree that the form personal change takes may vary, but they are chiefly interested in extracting from this variety the major themes that recur. This biographical approach has wide appeal, from biologically oriented psychologists looking for species general patterns (Erikson, 1950) to more popular writers who find in human lives clusters of themes and familiar stories (Sheehy, 1976).

Fourth and finally are social scientists, both sociologists and psychologists, who generally accept the idea of personality change over the lifespan, but without any strong commitment to particular theories which specify the extent or nature of change. This is a long-standing empiricist tradition (Liebermann, 1956; Newcomb, 1958) of attempting to identify which facets of identity do show measurable change, and what causal factors are associated with such change. It is broadly within this tradition that scholars have linked changes in people's values, intellectual functioning and sense of self-direction to the kinds of demands to which they are repeatedly exposed in their jobs (Mortimer and Simmons, 1978; Kohn and Schooler, 1983; Brousseau, 1983).

Our position is closest to the last of these insofar as our approach to theory and method is eclectic, but without being atheoretical. We hypothesize that personal change is one important adjustment outcome of job change, but with no *a priori* commitment to the mutability or otherwise of any particular facets of identity. These developments we expect to be contingent upon individual differences and environmental circumstances. Our two stage design with repeated measures gives us an opportunity to investigate factors associated with personal change empirically, though with the major qualification that we can only do this over the short time span of just over a year. Nonetheless, it may be argued that this period is sufficient to reveal major change among a small number of respondents, and for others to uncover the small changes which may be the beginnings of larger and longer-term changes, with a norm of stability amongst the remainder.

So let us start by evaluating just how much personal change there was between Time 1 and Time 2 for our sample. Even this is not a simple question to answer, because there are many types of change and criteria for measuring it. Drawing upon the exemplary work of Mortimer *et al.* (1982) we shall consider four main ways of measuring change.

Type 1 – Structural change

This denotes change in the structure and organization of personality. This would be revealed by, for example, personality instruments at one point in time yielding a clear structure of psychological traits which is not replicated at a later time, i.e. because the structure of identity has changed. This can be regarded as the least likely or rather the most fundamental type of personal change. We have examined this in two ways. First, we investigated the statistical structure of our scales at Time 1 and Time 2,[3] an analysis which confirmed the structural integrity of the internal relationships of our measures at both times. The second method was to see if the different dimensions on which individuals were measured related to each other in the same way at both times. This too revealed high structural invariance. There is a close match in the interrelationships of scales at Time 1 and Time 2.[4] These findings are not unexpected, for it would be difficult to explain how or why the general structure of identity should change over so short a time.

Type 2 – Normative change

This denotes differences over time in people's attributes relative to one another, i.e. normative change would be registered where person A was higher than person B on some factor at Time 1 but was lower than person B on the same factor at Time 2. Normative change is measured by correlating Time 1 with Time 2 scores. Our results from this analysis are similar to the findings of Mortimer *et al.* over a much longer time period, which in itself

120

suggests that normative change is not conspicuously time based – changes in people's relative levels on psychological constructs are as likely to occur over a short as a long period. For our five main psychological measures (adjustment, dominance, predictability, growth, and rewards) these relationships are all highly significant (0.46 to 0.66).[5] But even this range leaves a lot of variation unexplained, i.e. although Time 1 scores are strong predictors of Time 2 scores, there is still a good deal of normative change, especially in need for predictability, the lowest of these correlations.

Type 3 – Directional level change

This is perhaps what we are most inclined to think of as constituting personal change: increases or decreases over time in the aggregate 'centre of gravity' of a sample's scores on a scale. Level change measures the direction of shifts overall, so that half the sample increasing and the other half decreasing on the same factor would cancel each other out by this criterion. Therefore one would expect to find level change where a sample (or a substantial subset of sample) in common had experience of some change influence in the intervening period. So here we might expect, for example, directional change between Time 1 and Time 2 to result from the aggregate increase in status we have seen was experienced by our management sample (i.e. there were many more upward than downward movers). So if we find significant directional level change this may indicate that there has been some shared experience, event or process in the life of the sample over time. We assessed level change on all our repeated measures. Table 6.1 shows the results, for self-descriptions (work preferences and self-concept) and for job characteristics. The latter are presented to help us infer how much level change in personal dispositions may be associated with similar shifts in work characteristics over time.

First, the general scale results show a decline in managers' need for growth, and in their adjustment and dominance. Individual items amplify this, especially in the area of general psychological well-being, where we can see there has been a notable decline over the year in people's feelings of fulfilment, confidence and similar factors. Because these downward trends were from fairly high starting points at Time 1 our sample are still on the whole quite fulfilled and confident people at Time 2, but significantly less so than they were at Time 1. In their work preferences there are also clear shifts: greater value is placed upon 'hygiene' factors (location, fringe benefits), and less on more personal concerns (advancement, quality of senior management). How are these changes to be explained? We can look at parallel changes in job descriptions from Time 1 to 2 to see if there is some linkage with them. There is some sign of this, for example, in the

Table 6.1 *Directional level change in self-descriptions, work preferences and work characteristics over time*

Scale	Change
Self-rating measures	
Need for predictability	ns
Need for growth	↓ *
Need for rewards	ns
Adjustment	↓ **
Dominance	↓ *
Job characteristic measures	
Work predictability	↓ *
Work growth opportunities	ns
Work rewards	ns
Work preference items showing significant change	
(important–unimportant)	
A job where I can get feedback on how I am doing	↓ ***
The quality of senior management	↓ **
Work where individual accomplishment is appreciated	↓ ***
Opportunity for advancement	↓ *
Fringe benefits	↑ *
Job characteristic items showing significant change	
(good–poor)	
Opportunity for advancement	↓ ***
Location	↑ ***
Fringe benefits	↑ ***
Belonging to an organization that is highly regarded	↑ ***
Quality of senior management	↓ **
A job where I get feedback on how I am doing	↑ *
A job which allows me to make a contribution to society	↑ *
Work where individual accomplishment is appreciated	↑ *
Self-description items showing significant change	
Ambitious → Unambitious ***	
Fulfilled → Frustrated ***	
Happy → Sad ***	
Confident → Unsure ***	
Relaxed → Tense **	
Trusting → Suspicious **	
Sociable → Reserved *	
Contented with myself → Discontented with myself *	

*** $p < 0.001$; ** $p < 0.01$; * $p < 0.05$
(*Source:* CDS- I to II repeated measures, $N = 1,100$)

finding that people's ratings of their senior management and opportunities for advancement decline in both sets of measures: in how much people valued these benefits and how much their jobs provided them, i.e. as we observed in Chapter 2, people care less about what they get less of. But this is not true of all work needs; for example, feedback and recognition of accomplishment became *more* important to people as these two factors were experienced less in jobs.

So it appears from these data that there is a fair amount of level change taking place over this short time span.[6] The causes are not self-evident. We shall shortly be looking for these specifically, by showing not only that job change is implicated as a cause of this change, but also that job immobility is associated with change, albeit change of quite a different character. Before we examine effects on level change of job mobility and immobility we shall first consider another set of predictors: life events. The reader may recall that people were asked what life events had befallen them between the two surveys (CDS-I and CDS-II). A number of these events are associated with personal change between the two surveys, independently of whether or not they had changed jobs.[7] There are too many individual results to report in detail here, but some of the most interesting and readily interpretable can be picked out.

Managers experiencing divorce between the two surveys are more likely to be frustrated, sad and discontented with themselves at Time 2 than they were at Time 1. Money problems are associated with a drop on our adjustment scale. People moving house have a reduced need for predictability at work and are more likely to describe themselves as 'liking uncertainty'. Pregnancy (of self or spouse) is associated with an increase in the rated importance of a job that fits in with life outside work, while children leaving home is associated with a decrease in this same factor. In short, life events outside work impinge significantly on work needs and values.

But in considering these level changes in work preferences and self-perceptions there remains an unanswered question about whether they are just transient shifts over a short period of time in response to environmental conditions, or whether they are the small beginnings of more important changes in identity. It is difficult to draw confident conclusions on this matter from empirical change data of the kind we have here. Indeed, in one respect it would be equally difficult with data from a longer time span, for one could still not be sure that measured changes were not temporary or reversible. So some other criterion for change is needed here. We would wish to argue that there is no absolute or reliable benchmark for the 'importance' of identity change, but there is an alternative criterion that should be given serious consideration, people's own account of personal change they have undergone. This is our fourth and final measure of change.[8]

Type 4: Self-assessed change

All the previous methods of measuring personal change have been unobtrusive. They operate on the assumption that it would be difficult for the person to 'fake' change data by exerting conscious control over the results, for to do so people would need to have accurate memory of all their Time 1 responses when answering the same questions at Time 2 over one year later. The scientific goal of this comparative method is to achieve a detached and objective measure of change. There is nothing wrong with this so long as it is not seen as the only valid criterion. It is also valuable to pay attention to peoples own global judgements of how much they have changed, for two reasons. First, it allows people to consider and report on changes over time, above and beyond the content areas represented by our measures. Second, it accords due recognition to how people judge themselves to have changed, regardless of whether this registers on other more detached measurement methods. After all, if you feel you have changed, this may have more behavioural significance for you and others around you than shifts on measures of unknown relevance or importance to you and your circumstances.

We do not erect this as a superior or more important criterion than the others we have looked at, but we do want to reject the psychometrician's tendency to devalue the 'subjectivity' of all measures that are not externally and 'reliably' derived. How a person evaluates the changes they have experienced and how they believe their identity has adapted and grown has important meaning. It helps to capture how an individual interprets the way their present is connected with their past. This logic gives self-assessed change the power of causal agency, i.e. how a person construes themselves in the present encapsulates the values, ideals, motives and beliefs that set their bearings for future directions (Gergen, 1980).

The ideal way to capture this kind of change is probably through clinical interviews or other semi-structured methods. This approach was not open to us here, but experience in a parallel study showed that people are able to summarize their perceptions quite effectively through simple self-report scales.[9] Here we asked the question: 'Do you think that adjusting to your present job has changed *you* in any way?' Answers were on a series of 'not at all' to 'a great deal' (5 point) scales.

This form of questioning consciously aims to capture change attributed to job mobility, for we felt it would be easier for respondents to think of change within the specific context of work adjustment than in purely abstract terms.

We asked them to assess their personal change in four domains: personality, values, career goals, and attitudes. From the literature on individual psychology one might expect this to be the rank order of their mutability: i.e. 'personality' the least changeable, and 'attitudes' the most mutable (Ziller, 1976). As Table 6.2 shows, this is not the case.

The differences between these scales are not due to the fact that we were asking for personal change that is attributable to work adjustment. Similar results have been obtained from an independent sample where self-reported change was not linked with job mobility in the question format.[10] It would seem that these results present something of a challenge to the psychological orthodoxy that sees personality as a stable configuration and attitudes as continually adaptive to social environments. Here we find the opposite. Attitudes, defined in our questioning as 'the things I like and dislike', seem to capture fairly settled orientations to the world. Personality, defined as 'what sort of person I am', emerges as more akin to the Jungian notion of 'persona', i.e. the mutable face we present to the world, than to the psychometrician's construct of personality. Viewed in this way one can see a compelling logic to the findings. As one's social world changes so does one's presented self, but one's tastes and likes are more deeply embedded in temperament, transcending particular settings and interactions.

This opens up an interesting area for debate about the relationship between the theories of academic psychology and the everyday understandings of lay people. Psychologists are good at measuring and defining stable aspects of human functioning, and indeed, many of their measurement techniques are predisposed to capture enduring dispositions. This has encouraged theoretical psychology to conceive of identity and personality in ways that emphasize structure and consistency, but which under-rate the responsiveness of self to environment and its proactive potential for creating change. On the evidence of these findings, we can reach different conclusions about personal change from these two standpoints. Our results have shown some change by orthodox measurement criteria but even though many differences over time were statistically significant, their magnitude in terms of measurable scale points is very small indeed.[11] In contrast, when one looks at self-assessments of personal change much more radical shifts are reported. It is thus important when we look at the causes of personal change to employ more than one criterion, as we shall now do when we look at the effects of job mobility on personal change.

Job mobility and personal change

First we shall take self-reported change as a criterion, since it is here that we may expect the most clear-cut findings.[12] Table 6.3 shows how the

Table 6.2 *Extent of self-assessed personal change following last job change*

	No change %	A little/ moderate change %	Quite a lot/ a great deal of change %
Career plans (my plans about my future)	24	37	39
Personality (what sort of person I am)	30	42	28
Values (what is important to me in life)	37	37	26
Attitudes (things I like and dislike)	40	37	26

(*Source:* CDS-I, $N = 2,261$)

dimensions of personal change are linked with the three dimensions of job mobility.[13]

Table 6.3 reveals no relationship between functional mobility and self-assessed change of any kind. Employer moves are strongly linked with changes in career goals, attitudes and values but not with changes in personality. This supplies further evidence that employer change is the most critical dimension of job change, in terms of causes and outcomes. The pattern for status change is quite the opposite: it is associated only with personality change but not with changes in attitudes, values and career goals. This result extends the logic of our earlier explanation of self-assessed change. Employer moves typically entail simultaneous radical shifts in one's boss and colleagues, type of work, place of work, and outside life. Changes of residence are also likely.[14] It is hardly surprising that people have a strong subjective sense of personal change in response to such radical novelty and that most of this personal change will only be recognized by the individual herself, since most or all her working colleagues are new and will have had no previous knowledge of her. Status change involves the exact opposite. It is more publicly noted by colleagues since it signals a changed relationship with them, i.e. many upward status moves turn former colleagues into subordinates. Both parties will be aware of the new relationship between them, and a sense of changed personality, i.e. how one presents oneself publicly, might be expected under these

126

Table 6.3 *Self-assessed personal change in relation to three dimensions of job mobility*

	Mobility dimensions		
Self-reported change	Function change	Employer change	Status change
Values	ns	**	ns
Attitudes	ns	**	ns
Career goals	ns	**	ns
Personality	ns	ns	**

** Significantly greater personal change amongst movers than amongst non-movers ($p < 0.01$)
ns No statistically significant differences between movers and non-movers
(*Source:* CDS-I, $N = 2,304$)

circumstances to change. Changes of function involve neither of these critical accompaniments of status and employer changes, and this would account for the absence of any linkage between function mobility and personal change.

So it would seem that how much people feel they have changed is connected in clear and explicable ways with the kinds of mobility they experience. What other causes might be identified? In our theoretical analysis in Chapter 5 we have identified two main groups of factors that may encourage or inhibit personal change: individual personality characteristics, and work situational characteristics (especially role requirements). Table 6.4 summarizes which of these emerge as significant predictors of self-assessed personal change.[15]

Table 6.4 shows (as we also found for innovation in the last chapter), that these two groups of factors, personal dispositions and role requirements, are indeed important independent predictors of personal change. First, looking at personal dispositions, we find that managers with high self-assessed personal change also report having been more anxious before their last job moves, and to have higher needs for growth at work. But they do not seem to need more predictability in their work environments, as one might have expected from the theory that personal change is a product of high desires for feedback (Nicholson, 1984, see Chapter 5). Second, looking at role requirements, managers who report high personal change see major differences between their new jobs and their previous jobs (in tasks, skills

Table 6.4 *Predictors of personal change following a work role transition*

Individual characteristics	Pre-transitional anxiety
	Need for growth
Situational factors	Job discretion
	Job predictability (–)

(*Source:* CDS-I, $N = 2,304$)

and methods). Our theoretical prediction that job novelty determines personal change is therefore supported. Managers reporting high personal change also see their new jobs as higher in discretion and lower in predictability than do managers reporting low levels of personal change.

So it appears that self-reported change is related to a range of environmental, experiential and personal factors, and in ways that are readily interpretable. A much harder task is to try to predict the small amounts of directional level change we were able to measure between Time 1 and Time 2. We undertook this task in a number of ways. First we generated a 'total change' measure for each person, aggregating all the self-descriptive measures on which we could measure change over time, and then looking at what Time 1 factors were associated with this aggregate change index. We found no clear predictors, apart from one important exception: pre-transition anxiety. This means that the magnitude of total personal change is independent of types of job move, job characteristics and other factors, but those people who reported in the CDS-I having been anxious about their last job change recorded the greatest total change after Time 1. This is interpretable within the theory of work role transitions (Nicholson, 1984) which proposes that desire for feedback induces change (because people with high desires for feedback are motivated to conform to external demands, cf. Witkin, 1978) and we would suggest that this desire may be stimulated by anxiety.

This connection between anxiety and personal change has recurred throughout our analyses and seems to be of some theoretical and practical importance. In theoretical terms it constitutes a potentially important mediating link between the environment and individual adjustment. In practical terms it also offers insights into how the change process may be influenced by strategies that affect the level of anxiety experienced by job changers. These implications are not necessarily benign. For example, if you want people to conform then make them anxious; if you want them to innovate give them support. But this finding apart, our strategy of creating an index of total personal change seems to have been unproductive. This is not surprising given the indications of earlier findings that change differs considerably in magnitude on different dimensions and measurement criteria. So we undertook a series of analyses separating out different components of change. At the same time, instead of trying to predict the *magnitude* of change we used methods that identify which change factors are associated with different kinds of job mobility.

Job changers versus non-changers

Our first comparison is between two groups: those who changed jobs between Time 1 and Time 2 and those who did not. Table 6.5 shows the results from statistical procedures that identify which factors best discriminate between groups, and assess these effects independently of one another.[16] This analysis reveals a number of differences between job changers and 'immobiles'. First it shows that job changers do not seem to be 'change prone types' since they have had no greater history of frequent moves before the time of the CDS-I than non-changers. However, we can see that they are likely to be younger, to have been functional specialists at the time of the CDS-I, and to see themselves as creative. The picture which emerges from how they describe the jobs they held before their most recent change is one of low predictability and low discretion, and sited in unsatisfactory locations. It is perhaps particularly because of this restricted job scope that job changers were evidently less able to role innovate in their previous jobs. It seems likely that many of the job changers were motivated to seek out and accept mobility because of job frustrations – frustrations which were successfully removed by moving to a new job. This is implied by the finding that job changers are more likely than the immobiles to have a positive view of career opportunities and future growth in their new organizations.

But, perhaps the best way of learning about the effects of job mobility (or immobility) is to follow managers over time and examine measurable differences from before to after job moves on identical scales. This generated results which are both striking and instructive. Table 6.6 shows them.

It seems that managers who did *not* change jobs between the two surveys *decreased* in their adjustment and gave less favourable ratings on all our measures of work characteristics. Why should this be? Very few researchers have looked at the effects of *job* longevity independently of length of service, and those that have, fail to agree about its effects. Katz (1978) recorded increases in job satisfaction with tenure, but Kemp and Cook (1983) found no significant effects. Our results present a different picture to either of these blue-collar samples: for the managers in the present

Table 6.5 *Significant differences between those who changed jobs and those who did not change jobs between the CDS-I and the CDS-II*

	Job changers vs Immobiles ($N = 402$) ($N = 665$)
Biographical and individual variables	
Age	<
Creative (self-concept)	>
Role innovation in CDS-I	<
Career variables	
Employer change prior to CDS-I	<
Status	<
Career opps. in present organization perceived as influenced by previous career experience	>
Career opps. in present organization perceived as influenced by own performance	>
Present and previous roles	
CDS-I role predictability	<
CDS-I role discretion	<
CDS-I job location	<
Organizational culture	
Crisis oriented	>
Rapid growth	>

> Job changers higher/greater than immobiles
< Immobiles higher/greater than job changers
(*Source:* CDS-I and II)

study job longevity seems to *reduce* opportunities for growth and the acquisition of skills. One may speculate that this indicates that even after a short period in the same job they begin to feel a sense of stagnation, as if becoming increasingly aware of job limitations. We have referred already to how managers seem to be driven principally by needs for growth – more so than by material wants. There is the suggestion in these results that these needs engender a continual search for change and challenge; familiarity breeds contempt for jobs that have become well-practised.

This interpretation is supported when we examine the pattern of change recorded for people who did move jobs, as shown in Table 6.6. For these people it is apparent that job change heralds multiple benefits and a sense of personal development. Their ratings of work increase, particularly in

130

Table 6.6 *Changes in self-concepts, work preferences and work characteristics from CDS-I to CDS-II**

	Job change	No change	Out-spiral	In-spiral	Employer change	Function change	Status up	Status =	Status down
Self-concept									
Adjustment		↓↓↓	↑↑		↑		↑		↓↓
Dominance			↑			↑			
Work preferences									
Need for growth			↑						
Need for predictability									
Need for material rewards									
Work characteristics									
Growth opportunities	↑↑	↓↓↓	↑↑↑	↑	↑↑↑	↑↑↑	↑↑↑		↑
Predictability	↑	↑			↑		↑↑		
Material rewards					↑	↑			
Skills									
Used	↑		↑↑		↑		↑↑		
Needed	↓↓						↑		↑

↑ = Significant increase in scores $p < 0.05$; ↑↑ = $p < 0.01$; ↑↑↑ = $p < 0.001$
↓ = Significant decrease in scores $p < 0.05$; ↓↓ = $p < 0.01$; ↓↓↓ = $p < 0.001$

* *Source:* Based on matched sample t-tests (two-tailed), $N = 1,067$

Table 6.7 *Changes in work characteristics, work preferences and self-concepts for Time 1 to Time 2 job changers versus immobiles*

	Job changers ($N = 402$)	vs	Immobiles ($N = 665$)
Work characteristics			
Opportunities for growth	>>>		
Material rewards	>		
Predictability at work	>>>		
Work preferences			
Need for growth			ns
Need for predictability			ns
Need for material rewards			ns
Self-concepts			
Adjustment			ns
Dominance			ns

>   Job changers show higher positive change than immobiles ($p < 0.05$)
>>> Job changers show higher positive change than immobiles ($p < 0.001$)
ns   No significant differences
(*Source:* Combined CDS-I and II data)

opportunities for growth, and they have a heightened sense of being able to use previously acquired skills in their new situation. Before we accept this interpretation we need to dispose of the alternative explanation that it is simply due to the fact that the non-changers were happier with their jobs at the time of the first survey. Table 6.5 does indeed show that non-changers were more contented with their work at Time 1 in the CDS-I, but this does not account for these contrasting trends in change scores. For Table 6.7 shows that even when we take account of the initial differences between the mobiles and immobiles, the mobiles' ratings of job characteristics move strongly in a positive direction while all the immobiles' record negative shifts.[17] So the pattern is clear and consistent: jobs get better for movers and worse for non-movers. This implies that job changing is not just a periodic event which has no systematic effect upon managers' careers and the quality of their working lives; it plays an important role in fostering a continuing sense of development. It is as though job change demands adjustment which in turn creates new opportunities for personal growth. Indeed, one may infer that the deleterious shift in the work experience of non-changers denotes a causal cycle in which managers experience satisfaction

Table 6.8 *Time 1 to Time 2 intra- versus inter-organizational job movers compared on Time 1 work preferences and work characteristics*

	Intra-organizational movers (N = 252)	vs	Inter-organizational movers (N = 150)
Work preferences			
Need for growth		ns	
Need for predictability		ns	
Need for material rewards	>		
Work characteristics			
Growth opportunities	>>		
Material rewards	>		
Predictability	>>		
Self-concept			
Adjustment		ns	
Dominance		ns	

>   Intra-organizational movers significantly greater than inter-organizational movers ($p < 0.05$)

>>   Intra-organizational movers significantly greater than inter-organizational movers ($p < 0.01$)

ns   No significant differences

(*Source:* CDS-I and II combined data set)

early in their jobs, which thereafter declines until dissatisfaction and opportunity trigger a restart to the mobility cycle.

So far in this analysis we have looked at job change as an undifferentiated phenomenon. Now let us look at different forms of job mobility by considering the three major dimensions of employer, status and function change, and also by contrasting the two most common move types: in-spiralling and out-spiralling. Through various analyses we can see how they relate to the antecedents and outcomes of change.

First in Table 6.8 we contrast job moves within and between organizations, looking at job changes which occurred in the interval between the two surveys.[18]

The table shows that inter-organizational movers were more dissatisfied with the jobs they left than intra-organizational movers, consistent with our observation in Chapter 4 that managers who change employer are, more often than other job changers, 'pushed' out by dissatisfactions.

Outcomes of job change

Table 6.9 *Time 1 to Time 2 changes in self-concepts, work characteristics and work preferences associated with intra- versus inter-organizational job mobility*

	Intra-organizational movers ($N = 252$)	vs	Inter-organizational movers ($N = 150$)
Work preferences			
Need for growth		ns	
Need for predictability		ns	
Need for material rewards		ns	
Work characteristics			
Growth opportunities			<
Material rewards			<
Predictability		ns	
Self-concept			
Adjustment		ns	
Dominance		ns	

< Inter-organizational movers show greater positive change than intra-organizational movers ($p < 0.05$)
(*Source:* CDS-I and II combined data)

Table 6.6 showed that employer changes are experienced generally as beneficial, bringing improvements in assessed work characteristics as well as enhanced psychological adjustment. We can now extend this analysis by incorporating measured changes in self-concept and ratings of work characteristics. Table 6.9 shows the results.[19]

We see that it is employer changers who record the consistently greater positive change, confirming that these shifts into more rewarding work are not simply an artifact of initial group differences. This result gives further support to the positive image of employer changing we found in Chapter 3; moving to a new organization tends to confer not only benefits of improved chances of future status attainment but also yields immediate psychological and material benefits.

In Table 6.6 we can also see that upward status moves are associated with increases in psychological adjustment and with improved ratings of work characteristics. Because of this, similar effects are recorded for both in- and out-spiralling (i.e. upward) moves, though because of the additional benefits of employer movement the effects are stronger and more diverse for

134

out- than in-spirallers. In every case, opportunities for growth appear to improve and in some cases material rewards are also rated more favourably. Opportunities to deploy previously acquired skills increase too, reflecting managers' sense of positive ability to cope with new tasks and responsibilities. Taken together, these findings enlarge and strengthen our earlier observations of the benefits of out-spiralling. Moving onwards, upwards and outwards across organizations appears to spur the need for more growth opportunities and at the same time to satisfy these needs. It is as if facing the challenge of radical job change creates an appetite for further similar opportunities.

The picture is more neutral for functional and lateral status movers in Table 6.6. Neither group shows so many manifest benefits from their moves, and indeed the function changers actually seem to decline somewhat on the self-concept measure of dominance. But even for function changers some benefits do seem to accrue from change, in the form of increased ratings of job growth opportunities. Again it is important to note that our analysis excludes the possibility of this being simply due to pre-existing differences between groups. Rather it is another manifestation of the pattern we find emerging repeatedly throughout this study. Job changes, for this heterogeneous population of managers, represents much more of a growth opportunity than a threatening obstacle. Positive challenge rather than dysfunctional stress is the hallmark of managerial mobility. Indeed, it seems that the greatest psychological and career penalties are incurred through *failure to move*.

Yet there is one highly negative pattern of change in Table 6.6 which we have not yet discussed. Downward status movers show major decrements over time in their psychological adjustment and their ratings of work characteristics. The pattern is unequivocal. On almost every standardized measure which was repeated in the two surveys – work characteristics, work needs, and self-concept– managers moving downward in status show significant negative shifts in ratings. The only exception is in need for predictability, a factor which in any case has equivocal value for managers. So the overall pattern suggests that these are undesirable and unhappy moves. Consider the following case, typical of many we extracted from the record.

Mr C is a married man of 56 with two children, one of whom is still at school. Prior to the CDS-II he had a lengthy period of unemployment before taking a job as a training officer in education. This move was to a new employer, a new function, and involved a downward status shift. The reason Mr C gave for the move was: 'The closure of the publicity and marketing business. There were nil opportunities and taking this job became an absolute financial necessity.'

He describes his misgivings about the new job:

> The people show a lack of decision-making and job indif-
> ference. There's no room for progress, flair, ideas, no profit
> motive. The atmosphere of the place is like a closed shop, and
> there's a servile non-productive attitude . . . but it's not worth
> rocking the boat. It's impossible to progress, offer sound advice
> or reason with authority because it's the sure way to the exit
> door. I have no recognizable lifestyle as previously known. The
> salary is too low.

This unfortunate case is no exception amongst the downward status
movers. The depressing pattern is confirmed when we look at the much
larger CDS-I sample, comparing with the rest of the sample those whose
last move had been downward. The downward status movers were
generally older than other job changers, and were now in jobs which they
rated in less favourable terms on a number of dimensions.

Analysing the *prior* jobs and self-ratings of downward status movers
shows the negativity to be a persistent phenomenon. At Time 1, people who
subsequently moved down in status were not only in worse jobs but scored
lower in adjustment and dominance before the move. Table 6.10 shows
these results.[20]

Growth needs again emerge significantly, with downward movers rating
them lower in importance than other movers. Two explanations may
account for this and our evidence provides some support for both of them.
First, the lack of growth opportunities people encounter after downward
status moves may lead to a decline in their growth needs, following the logic
of earlier findings that needs adjust to job circumstances. Consistent with
this is the finding that downward status movers described their previous
jobs as much lower in growth opportunities than other movers. The second
explanation is that through selection processes (self-selection or
organizational selection) people with low growth needs tend to be more
easily drawn into downward status moves. Findings in Table 6.10 support
this too: downward movers had lower growth needs than other movers
before their job changes. So it would seem that low needs for growth may be
both a cause and an effect of downward status moves. It is not difficult to see
that this could constitute a downward spiralling vicious cycle of deteriorating jobs and personal dispositions, equal and opposite to the positive cycle
of challenge, growth and success we have inferred from analogous findings
with other types of job move. The net result would be to create two diverging
populations of managers, a sizeable group on a success spiral, and a small
minority on a failure spiral, with a third more stable group in between
these two.

Table 6.10 *Time 1 to Time 2 downward status vs other movers compared in self-concept, work characteristics and work preferences scores at Time 1*

	Downward movers (N = 30)	vs	Other movers (N = 369)
Self-concept			
Adjustment			<<<
Dominance			<
Work characteristics			
Opportunities for growth and development			<<<
Predictability			<<<
Opportunities for material rewards			<<<
Work preferences			
Need for growth and development			<
Need for predictability		ns	
Need for material rewards		ns	

< Downward movers score lower than other movers ($p < 0.05$) <<< ($p < 0.001$)
(*Source:* CDS-I and II combined data set)

Finally, we also determined from other analyses,[21] that these negative effects of downward status moves are not attributable to any experience of joblessness between moves. So overall the results strongly suggest that downward status moves pose a real threat to managers' psychological adjustment. In recent times much attention has rightly been given to the problems of the unemployed, but our results underline the view of some observers that finding work of *any* kind does not necessarily represent a successful outcome for the jobless professional (Kaufman, 1982; Fineman, 1983).

Summary and conclusion

This research relates to the study of lifespan development in two ways. First, it contributes to debate about the nature and extent of personal change in adult life. Second, it looks at an issue that has been largely neglected by lifespan developmentalists, how personal change is related to the experience of job mobility, as well as to other life events.

Our contribution to the first of these issues augments the similar results from previous research in several respects, though with the important qualification that we have only studied change directly over a short time span. We have seen, for example, evidence of high structural stability in self-concept and very modest signs of level change. However, these latter shifts clearly indicate that even within small slices of the adult lifespan people do change significantly in how they see themselves. These discontinuities may be part of much longer and larger patterns of change which are inaccessible to our methods. More an issue of controversy is the interpretation of normative change, alterations in the *relative* levels of people on self-concept measures. Previous researchers (Mortimer *et al.*, 1982) have tended to conclude that relationships of similar magnitude to ours denote stability. Two points may be made about this. One is that there seems to be no greater stability on this index over the short period measured in our study than has been found over the much longer periods in other research. The second point is that in either case the data could be said to exhibit high degrees of *in*stability, for in both our and other research, people's self-ratings on self-concept measures are only moderately predictive of their ratings on the same measures in either the short or long-term future. One may infer that this means people are constantly changing in many different ways, many of which reverse or cancel out changes from previous times. The full import of such changes can probably only be articulated by case study methods, rather than by survey designs which aggregate and hence tend to obscure individuals' idiosyncratic patterns of change. We also departed from the customary methods of measuring change by taking self-assessments, and these showed that people are quite definite in their judgements about the personal changes they have undergone. Our findings with this method cast a different light on the psychological orthodoxy that attitudes are unstable and personality dispositions are stable aspects of identity. We would suggest that people's view of what sort of person they are is subject to change through environmental adjustment processes, while attitudinal orientations are more deeply rooted in stable individual differences.

This interpretation is supported and enlarged when we turn to look at the causes of personal change. The job changes that epitomize changed social relations, i.e. status changes, are linked with personality change, while changes involving major environmental relocations, i.e. employer changes, are linked with attitude and other change.

We have seen that both self-assessed change and directly measured longitudinal change are associated with a number of predictors and outcomes in important ways. Some support has emerged for predictions from the theory of work role transitions (Nicholson, 1984) that job novelty and state anxiety stimulate adjustment through personal change. Although we did not find much significant measured *level* change accompanying these altered circumstances, it could be argued that personal development is more likely to be a longer-term outcome than we were able to measure directly, and our self-assessed change data would support this proposition.[22] We have also gained an appreciation of the motivational theme of much job change. People tend to move out of jobs where they feel there is restricted scope for growth, and tend to reap immediate benefits of improved work characteristics in their new roles. This is especially true for employer moves; status or function changes alone fail to deliver the same benefits. The regrettable exception to this pattern of neutral or positive outcomes is downward status movement, which seems to yield immediate equal and opposite effects to the most beneficial moves. We found clear indications that downward moves are deleterious to the mental health and quality of managers' lives.

We have suggested that the causes and effects of job change may be cyclical with personal change mediating between them. This is consistent with our model of the Transition Cycle: through constant recursion each effect can constitute a cause for the form and content of future change. We also arrive at a picture of the culture of management in which immobility is much more of a problem than job change. From our earlier analyses one can see managers as inhabiting a world of constant change, in which their diverse labour markets offer the promise of personal growth for those who are prepared to exploit opportunities for career mobility. Failure to take the risk of radical job change may hasten career frustrations and foreclosed options.

7

The cutting edge of change – the case of newly created jobs[1]

Innovation is a more immediate and visible mode of adjustment to mobility than is personal change, as we have seen in the preceding two chapters. Role innovation is widely reported by managers as a way of coming to terms with new jobs, while personal change is harder to detect. Our interpretation of these data is that role innovation is inherent in many managerial roles – situational adjustments are constantly required to maintain performance. It is also inherent in managerial motives, for we have seen how people are much more strongly drawn to challenge and achievement than they are toward the satisfactions of security and stability. Personal change is also widely reported but our direct measures show only small shifts in the immediate post job change period. This suggests that personal change has quite a different rhythm and pace to innovation. Innovation is immediate and direct, whereas personal change is time-lagged, incremental and cumulative.

This analysis is tantamount to a model of personal and social systems. Personal systems are anchors in the tides of change, but they shift their position over time to accommodate environmental evolution. Innovation is a direct form of exploration and creative adjustment within the immediate domain, a response that is evoked by the turbulence and uncertainty of contemporaneous environmental demands and ambiguities.

The phenomenon of newly created jobs provides an opportunity to look at these processes more closely. Newly created jobs are roles where the incumbent has access to neither predecessors nor precedent in the new situation to guide them, roles where there has been no previous incumbent and there are no other visible equivalent job holders to serve as models. We have devoted this chapter to these jobs for two reasons. First, because they are astonishingly common; they are of considerable social importance yet there is no extant literature on them. Second, because they are the embodiment of innovation; in newly created jobs the individual is inevitably a pioneer, presented with responsibility for constructing the basic parameters of their own performance.

Newly created jobs are the cutting edge of change in two ways: through their origins and in their effects. Their causes lie in processes of structural change in organizations and in society more widely, borne of the need of some organizations for fluid and flexible roles; they also are a product of the propensity of some individuals to create new roles to suit their needs and skills. In their effects, newly created jobs encourage innovative behaviours as a natural mode of adjustment to the pervasive ambiguity of roles without guidelines. Newly created jobs represent new beginnings, and how they are performed can have long-term and far reaching effects for both job holders and their environments. For the individual, success in pioneer roles is likely to be identity-enhancing, and for the organization it may presage the beginnings of significant and lasting developments if it stimulates the growth of new functions and roles as offshoots from the thriving new stem.

We shall start by looking at the nature of newly created jobs, how common they are and from whence they originate. Subsequently, we shall consider their psychological and behavioural impact. At this point though we must admit they are a phenomenon to which we had not given any thought when designing and conducting the CDS-I investigation, but which our first analyses instantly revealed to be a startlingly common and potentially highly important feature of managerial life. Amazingly for such a ubiquitous organizational phenomenon, the management literature has nothing to tell us about newly created jobs. The only reference we could find to them is in Alvin Toffler's *Future Shock* (1970) where he refers to a survey carried out in the mid 1960s by *Fortune* magazine of 1,003 young executives employed in major American corporations which found that 'fully one out of three held a job that simply had not existed until he stepped into it' (p. 105).

We made our similar discovery fortuitously. In the CDS-I our scale of role innovation questions asked managers to compare the way they performed the jobs with how their predecessors discharged the role or with how other people perform similar jobs elsewhere in the organization. Respondents were allowed two 'get out' categories, N/A and D/K, with the instruction 'If you are the first person to do the job use the N/A column. Only if you have *no* idea how it was done before you, use the D/K column.' We had expected small numbers to score in either category. Sure enough, there were only a few D/K responses (around 8%) but it was somewhat surprising to find that *fully one third of the total CDS-I sample scored every item of the scale in the N/A category.* Could it be true that one third of all job changes were moves into newly created jobs, or were people just scoring the N/A category because for some other reason they couldn't make the comparison or follow the instructions? The difference between the D/K and N/A percentages (8% versus 33%) would be difficult to explain by either reasoning. So in the CDS-II we set out to check that these really were newly created jobs by including a prominently displayed box for people to score in order to answer yes to the direct question 'Was this a newly created job?' The result was even more extreme than in the first survey – fully 52% ticked the box. Where do these jobs come from? The CDS-II contains more free response data than the CDS-I – on reasons for job change, occupations and industries, and general comments about careers. Using these data we compiled case records of every move into a newly created job that occurred between the CDS-I and II – 225 people in all were involved – and analysed the circumstances surrounding each of these changes to discover their origins.[2]

Of these some 42 provided insufficient information to tell us anything about the jobs or where they came from, but the remaining 183 shed considerable light on the phenomenon – to the authors' knowledge providing the first documentary evidence on the subject (apart from Toffler's observation, mentioned above).

Our analysis reveals there are three broad types of origin to newly created jobs, each of which could be said to represent an important aspect of the innovation process. First there are roles of *intrinsic novelty*. Innovation is inherent in many jobs because to create and shape the parameters of performance is the very essence of the job. Such roles are often well-known and much sought after; they can be mobile functions within the community of work, such as the roles of some consultants, entertainers, or researchers; or they can be institutionally embedded, like the jobs of many teachers and trainers, planners and public relations professionals. For many such positions, how other similarly titled and visible role-holders perform has low relevance to the demands of their own situations. The high discretion and unique challenges facing many chief executives or managers in small organizations fall into this category. Some 43% of all our cases of newly created jobs come in this group, though it should be noted that this kind of intrinsic novelty is also a feature of our other two main categories, for it is an overarching theme in all newly created jobs.

The second group comprises jobs which have been created within organizational structures, *roles resulting from organizational change*. Forty-six per cent of newly created jobs originate in this way. If the jobs in the first category represent those roles for which there is an established need for novelty in the world of business and industry, then in this second category are those for which the need has newly arisen, and thus they reflect the rate and form of change in organizations. These then constitute the visible surface of environmental evolution and turbulence. There are several sub-varieties in this category of newly created jobs. Some are component parts of entirely new organizational structures; others are add-ons to well-established structures. Many are formed through reorganizations that alter

142

and recombine existing roles. All these could be called structural innovations. There are also much more localized structural origins to newly created jobs, where there has been a highly circumscribed or restricted alteration to the functions within a managerial role.

The third category of newly created jobs is *self-created roles*, accounting for 11% of the cases we examined. These represent the furthest extreme of role innovation, and it is therefore not surprising that they are relatively uncommon compared with the other categories. Here individuals, through their independent agency, have established roles where there were none before. Moves into self-employment form the majority of these cases, though in a few instances individuals have had the will and the power to create new roles within an established organization. It should be noted though that even where newly created jobs are the result of individual choice and effort, they do not always take their starting point from a willing decision. Many people set out to create new roles as a response to some initial external compulsion, such as being made redundant. This has been noted by many writers in the literature on job loss and unemployment: self-created roles are one of the most fruitful adaptive strategies of people who lose their jobs (Dyer, 1973; Kaufman, 1982); such people have been aptly named 'good copers' (Fryer and Payne, 1984).

These three types of newly created jobs could be said to embody three dimensions to innovation. First, intrinsic novelty represents the *products* of innovation, where we recognize innovation because of the effect it has on the environment. Second, roles resulting from structural change represent innovation as organizational *process*; innovation is a necessary part of the mutual adjustment of dynamic systems. As such it may often not be seen primarily as innovation, but regarded as something that facilitates a range of much more routine and established tasks. The third type, self-created roles, represent the creative *motives* and skills of innovation. What the person establishes may be commonplace in the community of work, but to the person performing the role it represents a radically new departure and a significant extension of themselves and their capabilities.

Let us now look in more detail at these varieties through a systematic subdivision of newly created jobs, with brief case examples to illustrate each.

Group I: Intrinsic novelty (43% cases)

Highly unstructured occupations (27 cases)
Examples include consultants, some training managers, logistical and corporate planners, researchers, lecturers and people in publicity.

Case example: Mr A is married with four children all at school. He is one level from the top of a charity organization with 30 employees. His job involves research and publishing and he says he took it because 'my previous company was moving to "Xtown" where for family reasons I did not wish to go. I was independently approached and offered a new job.' He reports 'never having worked harder than since taking up this role'.

Contract or sub-contract work (4 cases)

Case example: Mr B, a married man of 32, was made redundant, experienced a major deterioration in financial state, changed his place of residence and was subsequently employed by an agency offering freelance engineering employment – 'my motives were to maintain some income, stay in the industry, have a job whilst seeking a permanent post'.

Senior or top jobs where role entails new responsibilities (23 cases)

In these situations the new occupant in a sense embodies new responsibilities which they create to fit their skills and interests. Examples include many partnerships and directorships.

Case example: Mr C is in general works management in a manufacturing company. He is one level from the top and his last move involved a change of employer (going into partnership), an upward status shift and a functional change. He moved because of 'personal motivation to work for myself – the opportunity to join a friend in partnership – the possibility to mould my own future'.

'Fluid' roles in very small organizations (12 cases)

Case example: Mrs D was unemployed and looking for paid employment at the time of the CDS-I. Her partner was self-employed and she reports a major deterioration in financial state between the two surveys. She is now practice manager in a medical practice with less than 30 employees. She describes the move as a downward shift in status and on self-concept scales is sad and discontented with herself.

One-off or new projects (15 cases)

Case example: Mr E is in telecommunications four levels from the top of a large company. His most recent job move followed an 'opportunity to return to my home base to lead a computer centre project involving the implementation of a large software package, the creation of a new computer centre and a new organization for materials management'.

144

Group II: Jobs created by organizational change (46% cases)

Structural:

Merging of functions following rationalization (11 cases)

Case example: Mrs F is a married woman of 44 with one child, working in financial control, costing, and internal services of a public utility at local level. Her move to a newly created job followed the merging of two local districts. 'I obtained the post for the combined district.'

Cosmetic or political reorganization (1 case)

Case example: Mr G is in project management in the purchasing area. He is a functional specialist in the motor manufacturing industry. He gave as the reason for his move to a newly created job the 'office needed to achieve a political goal'.

New job arises as element in newly formed subunit (18 cases)

Case example: Mrs H, a single woman of 52 with no children, is employed in personnel in the retail industry. The organization has between 10,000 and 50,000 employees. She was asked to move to the new job (which was similar to her old job) as a result of expansion of the business and creation of a new department – 'initially requiring a great deal of organizing and hard work'.

Company taken over, new job in new structure (4 cases)

Case example: Mr I is a married man of 35 with two children. He is working in marketing and sales of computer software and hardware in a company with between 100 and 500 employees. He is two levels from the top. His job move involved an upward status shift, a change of employer and a change of residence. He gave the following reason for his move: 'Market and new product introduction required that resources not available at the previous company had to be found if the business was to remain in the country. Another company took control and I moved with the business.'

Person joins newly formed organization (4 cases)

Case example: Mr J is a married man of 49 with three children. He recently changed jobs to move to a newly specialist computer company in which his previous company had a minority interest. 'I accepted the post of Chairman as an exciting challenge in high technology.'

Internal reorganization creates new posts and functions (30 cases)
Case example: Mrs K is a buyer in the retail industry in a company with between 10,000 and 50,000 employees. She is five levels from the top. 'Restructuring of the various buying departments has given me the opportunity
to develop a completely new range of merchandise not normally associated
with the company.'

Localized:

Boss or other adds to or alters responsibilities (11 cases)
Case example: Mrs L is a consultant in a computer software company. Her
job move involved upward status shift and function change. 'A position
arose internally which suited my skills and I got involved first indirectly and
then directly as it appeared that I was the best person to do the job. It's not
what I was trained for but it fits my skills perfectly. It was a very lucky co-
incidence that brought me to it.'

*Jobs created by cascaded responsibilities from a top vacancy (1
case)*
Case example: Mr M, a married man of 52 with three children, is in personnel
in manufacturing industry. He is two levels from the top of a company with
between 10,000 and 50,000 employees. His most recent job change
included an upward move in status. 'Reorganization of functions caused
through a change in the function of my job superior and the reallocation of
the activities of the personnel organization.'

Absent boss enables subordinate to absorb part of duties (2 cases)
Case example: Mr N, aged 56, is in financial control of the marketing and
administrative department of a manufacturing organization (size 3–100
employees). His last move was upward in status and involved a function
change. 'Nothing official, just a general acceptance that the Managing
Director is away more and more and that greater responsibility is left with
me. It's a natural development both for me and the other people
involved.'

Group III: Self-created roles (11% cases)

Voluntary quitting for self-employment (7 cases)
Case example: Mrs O had no children at the time of CDS-I but at Time 2
was working freelance in arts sponsorship having left her full-time salaried

146

position to have a child. 'I left my last position to have a child and did not consider the job worth going back to. I had spent a frustrating and occasionally humiliating nine months with the company which left me thinking that I should start to operate on a freelance basis.'

Involuntary quitting for self-employment (7 cases)
Case example: Mr P is a married man of 40 with two children at school. He indicated a deterioration of relations at work between CDS-I and CDS-II, the involuntary loss of his job and a major deterioration in his financial state. He is now self-employed, responsible for running 'our small company' – size less than 30 employees. He had a period of two months unemployment before he became self-employed. 'I was dismissed because of irregularities by subordinate staff, of which I was totally unaware until I discovered their actions. I now look forward to the challenge of steering and building this business.'

Role innovation in employment – creating own job (6 cases)
Case example: Mrs Q, 48, is married with three children and is a lecturer in education. Her move involved a change in function. 'I included a new course within my teaching duties. I researched and developed this short course because I felt there was a local need for it. I believe it added variety to my work.'

Let us briefly try to evaluate what this analysis tells us about the origins of newly created jobs. From Group I we see that newly created jobs are integral elements in the structure of certain kinds of organizations and occupations. For a range of occupations, novelty is part of the job specification. Each task breaks new ground, and useful precedents and comparisons cannot be identified by job holders. It is interesting to note that this is a characteristic of many roles in small organizations. In larger companies well-defined roles are more often accepted and standardized elements of the structure (Mintzberg, 1979), but in very small companies, the organization of work and the distribution of responsibility are much more fluid and *ad hoc*. The small company manager is likely to find herself rapidly switching between new and unfamiliar tasks, or temporarily having to blend familiar elements from various tasks into a novel synthesis. The scope for this kind of innovation undoubtedly contributes considerably to the excitement and challenge of life in very small organizations.

Group II newly created jobs are very different. They are outcomes of common change processes in larger organizations. Here we see newly created jobs emerging from upheavals and revolutions that simultaneously affect a wide range of operations and organizational areas. Yet we should

147

remember that even quite extensive structural changes can in reality be more cosmetic than fundamental, though only one of our respondents actually articulated this thought. In most instances, whole families of new functions are created at the same time, and in some cases newly created jobs are but facets of completely new born organizations. At the other extreme are highly localized changes – a new job is created without there being any wider surrounding reorganization, though of course this does not preclude the possibility of far-reaching changes developing at a later stage from these small beginnings.[3]

Group III are the real pioneers amongst newly created job holders – people who move into self-created jobs – and in many ways they are the most interesting. They are people who have taken individual initiatives and built new jobs where none existed previously. The stimulus is sometimes enforced, as when the redundant manager decides to set up on his/her own rather than try to gain re-entry to the conventional managerial labour market. Others voluntarily have turned their backs on the perfidies of organizational life, whilst another small group have by force of will and effort created new roles within their organizations.

Putting the four groups together all can be seen as pioneers in one way or another. Some are so by accident or because of forces beyond their control, while others have driven themselves to the edge of change. All are facing demands on a scale quite different to other job changers. By comparing newly created job holders with conventional job holders (in both the CDS-I and II) some of these different demands can be identified more closely, along with their circumstantial causes and possible outcomes.

Excluding the sub-group who entered self-employment,[4] we analysed the characteristics of the organizations and jobs of newly created job holders.[5] This confirms that newly created jobs arise under different circumstances to other forms of job changing. They are more often to be found in small than large organizations – twice as many newly created job changers move into companies of less than 30 employees than other job changers. Newly created jobs are also unevenly distributed across organizational types; they are especially prevalent in the new service category (such as consultancy and market research organizations), and particularly uncommon in the government group. They are significantly more common in the private than public sector: 70% of moves to newly created jobs are in the private sector compared with only 61% of other job changes. In view of this organization-type patterning it is especially interesting to find that they are not associated with particular *occupational* types. This is important for it demonstrates that highly unstructured roles and the absence of constraining precedents are to be found right across the range of occupational categories of management we have encompassed.

In the CDS-II we also asked managers to describe the 'culture' of their organizations through a series of scales. These are discussed in detail in Chapter 8, but we can see here how these measures reaffirm the distinctive character of the organizations, if not the occupations, in which newly created jobs arise.[6] Their organizations are much more likely to be described as 'innovation oriented: dominated by a need to develop new items and products' and less likely to be seen as 'rules oriented: dominated by concern with administration through policies and procedures'. Moreover, not only are they less bureaucratic and more innovative but they are also more economically surgent, for newly created job movers are more likely than other movers to predict that their current organizations will experience growth in the next five years (by the criteria of sales, budget or manpower increases).

So, to summarize it seems that newly created jobs are in the most volatile and surgent areas of business and are an incipient stimulus to innovation. They are a common feature of managerial life, equally prevalent in all the job areas of management, but at the same time unevenly distributed across areas of business and types of organization.

There are also psychological differences between newly created job movers and other job changers, in their motives, experiences and outcomes. We now turn to these by considering who moves into newly created jobs. Analysis of individual difference factors shows them to be more likely to be female, highly educated, professionally qualified, and with longer job tenure than other job movers.[7] In the CDS-II we also found that newly created job movers have above average needs for growth and a greater concern for material rewards.[8] Of particular interest too is that people who moved into newly created jobs between the two surveys were more likely than other job movers to describe their *previous* jobs as having had high levels of freedom and discretion, and to report that they were able to enact a high degree of role innovation in these jobs.[9]

This raises the question of whether the experience of high job discretion and role innovation create the motives which predispose people to move into newly created jobs. If successful proactive adjustment to challenging roles heightens people's growth needs, then they may subsequently be motivated to seek out or accept the most extreme manifestations of role discretion, newly created jobs. But there is an alternative explanation: newly created jobs may be a characteristic feature of some management and labour markets and types of organizational cultures, in which both high discretion roles and managerial populations with high needs for growth are particularly common.

Our results support both interpretations. Analyses of job characteristics in both the CDS-I and the CDS-II[10] suggest that newly created jobs are perceived, relative to other jobs, to be high in discretion but low in predictability, with few sources of guidance on how the role should be performed. We also find that people with high growth needs who have previously been high role innovators tend to move into newly created jobs. Moreover, as we have seen, these jobs tend to occur in organizations characterized by growth opportunities, surgency and freedom.

Does personal change also follow from moving into newly created jobs? The answer appears to be that newly created job movers exhibit no more personal change than other job movers, but they do change in different ways. Managers who moved into newly created jobs between the surveys showed a much greater increase in needs for growth than other job changers, and this despite the fact that newly created job movers had higher growth needs than other movers at Time 1.[11] This corroborates our conclusion in the previous chapter that needs change to match the characteristics of the jobs – as needs are fulfilled in the new job, managers become more aware of how important these needs are to them.

Examination of these data also reveal that the magnitude of newly created job movers' personal change depends partly upon the characteristics of who makes these moves in the first place. Table 7.1 shows that managers moving into newly created jobs who report high personal change tend to be less well adjusted and more anxious than those who report low personal change. They also find less stability and satisfaction in their jobs. This seems to suggest that for certain personality types, such as insecure or anxious individuals, moving into the uncertainty which is characteristic of newly created jobs, can prove rather too much of a challenge, while people with a high tolerance for unpredictability fare better.

This suggestion is reinforced by our finding that not everyone who moves into a newly created job is satisfied by the experience. Managers who experience low satisfaction tend to have been more anxious prior to the job change and perceive their jobs as offering relatively low levels of discretion and predictability. These managers are therefore confronted by a combination of low predictability and low discretion, i.e. an uncertain environment without the autonomy to exercise control over it – a combination with great potency to induce frustration and dissatisfaction.

We have established in previous chapters that employer changing is probably the most critical dimension of job change, therefore we extended these analyses to test whether it has equal significance for moves to newly created jobs. One might expect so, for clearly inter-organizational moves to newly created jobs are particularly radical, involving both novelty for the organization and for the individual. Table 7.2 shows that managers making moves to newly created jobs in new organizations report high anxiety prior to the job move, high personal change subsequent to it, and high expec-

Table 7.1 *High versus low personal change among newly created job movers*

	High personal change	vs	Low personal change
Individual variables			
CDS-I: Self-concept adjustment			<
Pre-transition anxiety	>		
CDS-II: Need for material rewards	>		
Present and previous roles			
CDS-I: Job discretion			<
Predictability at work			<
Job novelty	>		
CDS-II: Predictability at work			<
Opportunities for growth	>		
Job discretion	>		
Role innovation at CDS-I	>		
Career variables			
CDS-I: Post-transition satisfaction			<
Employer changes (out of 5)	>		
CDS-II: Career satisfaction			<
Organizational variables			
CDS-I: External career influences (luck, politics, impersonal corporate decisions, prejudice)	>		
CDS-II: Rapid future growth expected			<

> High personal change movers higher/greater scores than low personal change movers.

< Low personal change movers higher/greater scores than high personal change movers.

(*Source:* CDS-I, $N = 313$; 125 high personal change and 188 low personal change
CDS-II, $N = 151$; 82 high personal change and 69 low personal change)

tations of future mobility. So it seems that moves to newly created jobs which involve a change of employer are among the most radical of job moves in their demands on individuals. They are anxiety provoking and lead to high levels of personal change, even for managers who describe themselves as confident and controlling. It is also noteworthy that managers

151

moving into new jobs across organizations are more likely to anticipate an imminent further inter-organizational move. This may indicate that career paths from newly created jobs are not planned or clearly way-marked within organizations generally. It could also be the case that they tend to be found in volatile organizational environments where previously trodden career paths forward are not visible.

Newly created jobs have Janus-like light and dark faces. On the positive side they present opportunities for growth, exploration and job satisfaction. On the negative side they can present an overload of simultaneous novelty and change. In Chapter 1 we noted that models of job change have generally adopted a stress-coping perspective but even looking at the negative side to newly created jobs our findings suggest that undesirable outcomes may be avoided where there is freedom to explore and create the new role in a climate of feedback and support. Proactive growth models seem to be more appropriate generally than reactive stress-coping models for our understanding of the outcomes of job moves in general and for moves to newly created jobs.

If, as seems confirmed here, newly created jobs represent the cutting edge of change within organizations, it is essential that those who have responsibility for introducing, managing or modifying them are sensitive to their unique demands and challenges. Providing supports and tailoring resources to facilitate passage through the transition is needed to help ensure valued and lasting outcomes for both the individual and the organization. Newly created jobs are common and important phenomena in work environments, embodying both change and ambiguity. They have importance as challenges for individuals, opening up opportunities for personal growth and development. Our analyses have suggested that a dynamic relationship between organizational change and personal change lies at the heart of these phenomena. Organizational change produces changes in people and jobs, and as people change and move jobs they are motivated to effect changes in their organizations.

Moves into self-employment

Until now we have excluded from the discussion of newly created jobs those cases where managers left their organizations to become self-employed. This was because the newly self-employed are in many ways a very different group from others moving into newly created jobs. This difference manifests itself not least in the relationship between work and family life. Moves into self-employment are often joint ventures by both partners in a marriage. In the first survey we found that 39% of the self-employed also describe their spouses as self-employed, whereas only 7% of the remainder

Table 7.2 *A comparison of inter- and intra-organizational movers into newly created jobs*

	Inter-organizational movers	vs	Intra-organizational movers
Individual variables			
Pre-transition anxiety	>		
Self-concept dominance	>		
Post-transition personal change	>		
Present role			
Job novelty	>		
Career variables			
Likelihood of inter-organizational move	>		
Likelihood of intra-organizational move			<
Organizational variables			
Organization size			<
External career influences (luck, politics, impersonal corporate decisions, prejudice)			<
Rule-oriented organization culture			<

>   Inter-organizational movers higher/greater scores than intra-organizational movers.

<   Intra-organizational movers higher/greater scores than inter-organizational movers.

(*Source:* CDS-I, $N = 359$; 174 intra- and 185 inter-organizational movers
CDS-II, $N = 168$; 59 intra- and 109 inter-organizational movers)

of newly created job movers have self-employed spouses. Allied to this, we also find that the self-employed report greater satisfaction with the fit between their work lives and their lives outside work than do other newly created job movers. The two groups also differ in other respects. They come from different occupations and organizational types: movers into self-employment in the CDS-I are more likely to be in advertising, consultancy, market research, other professional services and less likely to be in manufacturing industry.

The picture we receive of the self-employed from the CDS-I is of self-directed individuals who have experienced marked changes in their lives

Table 7.3 *A comparison of self-employed and other newly created job movers*

	Self-employed vs (N = 101)	Other newly created job movers (N = 597)
Individual variables		
Post-transition personal change	>	
Need for predictability		<
Need for material rewards		<
Present role		
Job discretion	>	
Fit with life outside work	>	
Opportunities for growth	>	
Organizational variables		
Internal career influence (job performance)	>	

> Self-employed higher/greater scores than other newly created job movers
< Other newly created job movers higher/greater scores than self-employed
(*Source:* CDS-I, N = 698; 101 self-employed movers and 597 other newly created job movers)

through radical transition into situations high in scope, opportunity and with better opportunities for integration with non-work life. In short we get a very positive image of self-employment as more challenging and satisfying potentially than their previous roles in the employment of others. The results of these analyses are shown in Table 7.3.[12]

Only 20 managers moved into self-employment in the interval between the two surveys, insufficient for controlled statistical comparison with other newly created job movers. But it is of interest that of the 20 people moving into self-employment, eight reported on the life-events scale that they had involuntarily lost their jobs in the preceding year and six reported a major deterioration in their financial state. This suggests that the move into self-employment is very often a response to externally imposed circumstances.

With this group of 20 it is also possible to see how they changed between the two surveys in their self descriptions, work preferences and perceived job characteristics.[13] Like their CDS-I counterparts, they saw their new jobs as offering much better opportunities for growth and more job discretion. Their work needs also changed. They became less concerned with pre-

Table 7.4 *Changes in work needs and work characteristics for managers moving into self-employment between the surveys*

Work preferences		
Need for growth	ns	
Need for predictability		↓
Work characteristics		
Need for material rewards		↓
Growth opportunities	↑↑↑	
Predictability	ns	
Material rewards	ns	
Self-concept		
Adjustment	ns	
Dominance	ns	

↓   Significant decline in work needs/descriptions ($p < 0.05$)
↑↑↑ Significant increase in work needs/descriptions ($p < 0.001$)
(*Source:* CDS-I to CDS-II change data, $N = 20$)

dictability and material rewards, as shown in Table 7.4. Does this reflect a real change in the nature of the work, or a change in the individual's needs resulting in a better fit with the nature of work? On the reasoning that transitions to self-employment tend to represent moves to less predictable environments where material rewards are less guaranteed, one can infer that this change in motivational orientation is a genuine psychological accommodation to changed circumstances.

An alternative explanation is that the manager moving from a predictable to an unpredictable working situation may enjoy the new variety and the challenge of uncertainty, and this in turn triggers a revision of work needs. Similarly the increased opportunities for accomplishment, challenge, creativity, improved knowledge and skills and the like which come with a move into self-employment, may cause the individual to reappraise and devalue material rewards at work as a reaction to their enhanced experience of intrinsic rewards (Deci, 1975). This may also explain our finding that the self-employed score significantly higher than other newly created job movers on organizational commitment and job involvement.[14]

These findings may help to extend our understanding of entrepreneurial behaviour more widely. They confirm the image of the entrepreneur as a highly innovative individual who creates opportunities for herself in order to find practical expression for growth needs. The jobs of the self-employed are described as high in discretion and in opportunities for accomplishment, advancement, creativity, challenge. At the same time the self-employed have high commitment to their work, and see themselves as in control of their careers. Interestingly too, they find a good fit between their family and working lives – suggesting that they are able to achieve high levels of control by integrating growth and social/emotional needs across the work and non-work spheres. Managers moving into self-employment therefore seem to be people who seek control over their own destinies, who can tolerate unpredictability, and who have a high desire to create environments within which they can satisfy their growth needs. This latter desire is also more important to them than desires for material rewards, contrary to the common supposition that people move into self-employment purely out of material considerations.

Conclusion

Our examination of newly created job movers, and our concentrated attention on inter-organizational mobility and moves into self-employment, points to the importance of growth opportunities, challenge and exploration in the working lives of managers. Newly created jobs do seem to justify our characterizing them as located at the cutting edge of change, both in existing organizations and in the economy more widely. Understanding their causes and consequences provides clues about the dynamics of radical change processes in organizations. Moreover, charting the psychological antecedents and consequences of transitions into newly created jobs confirms the entrepreneurial energy latent within both organizations and individuals. Our findings suggest this energy can be released and constructively directed if appropriate facilitating conditions and safeguards are present. The opportunity to harness that energy for the benefit of both individuals and organizations is perhaps optimal at the point of job change. At a more general level, this also illustrates how studying the phenomenon of job change has considerable potential for enhancing our understanding of individual work lives, because, in contrast to the broader notion of the career, it is a visible event which can be precisely defined, observed and analysed.

8

Organizational career development – the management experience

No matter how hard managers try to achieve some self-control over their career paths, however radical their career moves, and whatever success they feel they experience, they do so within the confines of the very real but uneven constraints imposed by circumstances and opportunities. Managers' occupational and organizational environments are an important influence on the process of job change. We have seen evidence of this in preceding chapters, showing how career paths and adjustment processes differ widely across occupational and organizational types. We now want to look more closely at these types, and, through the eyes of the managers, examine the different qualities of career experience that are to be found in them.

In so doing it is our aim to complement an extensive literature on career development in management. Within this literature there is an abundance of rich case study reports and numerous prescriptive handbooks on how organizational careers should be managed by human resource specialists. Career development is also big business for management consultants offering guidance on personal and organizational development. Yet there is very little to be found in writings on the subject that tells us how managers experience career development or how much organizations are practising what the management scientists are preaching.

There could be said to be four distinctive themes in career development, each involving different agents, techniques and outcomes. They are: matching people to jobs, facilitating work adjustment, developing perform- ance, and managing the future. The first of these, matching people to jobs, is the domain of recruitment and placement systems. We have little to say from this study about how this is achieved, though the uncertainty we have found surrounding management mobility suggests that, from the manager's point of view at least, it is often not a long-considered or planful process. The literature on how to make effective selection decisions is large, informative and full of sound advice. Nonetheless it would seem that organizations more often than not achieve the worst of all worlds in a pretence to scientific precision using techniques that yield 'measures' of doubtful validity, unknown reliability, and untested relevance to their or the candidates' needs (Lewis, 1985).

157

The second theme, bringing about good work adjustment, is the province of supervisory, control, feedback and reward systems. Again, there is much in the literature and in the field of management training which communicates laudable ideals and well-designed methods for achieving them. However, within these writings relatively scant emphasis is placed upon the special requirements of the newcomer and how supervisory/control systems should adapt to their developing needs over time. In short, this is too often designated as belonging to the separate province of training, rather than conceived as an integral part of more general career development.

The third theme, developing performance, is the chief concern of those systems which assess and attempt to enhance the utilization of individual capabilities. Appraisal/assessment methods, linked with promotion systems, bear the main responsibility for this task. Again it would seem that organizational practice often falls short of the prescribed ideal, in terms of measurement methods, modes of application and the management of outcomes (Fletcher and Williams, 1985).

The fourth theme, managing the future, involves those systems aimed at building tomorrow's organizational excellence through longer-term development activities, such as career counselling and planning, mentoring, and culture-management. These are the activities in which currently there is fastest growing interest in the literature (Kilmann *et al.*, 1985; Hickman and Silva, 1985; Clutterbuck, 1985).

The reader may note a resemblance between these four themes and the four stages of the Transition Cycle, discussed in Chapters 1 and 5. This is intentional, for these four themes, approximating to the stages of preparation, encounter, adjustment, and stabilization-preparation, can be conceived similarly as interdependent elements of a recursive career development process. Pouring organizational resources into one or more of these four areas whilst neglecting the others is likely to be self-defeating. Success in one area needs to be built upon by subsequent career development activities. For example, it is no good operating highly sophisticated recruitment procedures if you just then throw new recruits into the deep end of organizational waters without support or guidance to ensure they are going to be willing or able to do what is wanted of them.

Our study, with its large and heterogeneous sample of middle to senior managers, provides a rare opportunity to actually find out how career development is being experienced. An important feature of this is that we are able to make general statements about both the diverse and shared features of many types of managerial roles and organizations by looking at a broad and mixed managerial population.[1]

This is not a study of organizations, and therefore is not an objective or comprehensive survey of organizational practice. Rather this is a review of how managers *perceive* the way their career experience and development is managed by their organizations. The size of the sample, and the knowledge we have of their roles, statuses and industries, means that we can evaluate systematic influences on these perceptions. From this we can, with due caution, make inferences about how qualities of career development vary as a function of personal and contextual factors.

We shall be drawing on data from both the CDS-I and II to describe four important aspects of managers' experiences: the demands of their roles and the qualities of their performance, the kinds of feedback and learning they receive, the organizational career policies and practices to which they are subject, and finally the general climate and culture of their organizations.

Qualities of managerial jobs

The CDS-II contained a 15-item self-assessment scale. It asked managers to say how important were 15 different tasks or demands in their jobs, and then to rate their own performance on them. Table 8.1 shows the results.[2]

It is hardly surprising that all these highly positively worded qualities are rated as 'important', though there is sufficient variation in responses to tell us something about the priorities managers attach to various aspects of their work. It is noteworthy, perhaps, that communications, and the ability to control tasks and relationships are highly rated, but that attending to the needs of their subordinates is less valued. It is a pity we did not ask them about how they would value these qualities in their *own* bosses, or that we could not ask their subordinates to rate what priorities they would wish their bosses (our respondents) to value. It is fairly safe to surmise that we would have seen a reversal of these values. In the role of subordinate, one's boss's ability to respond well to criticism, delegate, evaluate objectively and so on would probably be accorded more importance than the boss's communication skills or ability to set priorities. Indeed, some confirmation of this has already been seen in Chapter 2 where it was plain that our sample do care a great deal about the feedback and recognition they receive from their superiors. In short, is there a hint of some double standards here? Do managers fail to see that what they want from their bosses might also be equally desirable in their own job performance? We cannot answer the question directly here, but other writers have affirmed the existence of this kind of logical dualism in managerial self-assessment (Argyris and Schon, 1974). But we did ask managers to rate their own performance on these fifteen attributes. The results, summarized by the rank order given in the last column of Table 8.1, show that managers generally assign a favourable

Table 8.1 *Managers' ratings of importance and performance on 15 job demands*

	Importance	Own performance
	% scoring 'very important' (3-point scale) %	Rank order of self-ratings (7-point scale) %
1 Communicating effectively	92	4
2 Recognizing priorities	83	1
3 Completing assignments	82	2
4 Keep individuals informed	71	6
6 Keeping up to date	69	12
5 Maintaining positive relations	71	7
7 Attacking problems logically	68	5
8 Treating subordinates fairly	64	3
9 Stimulating subordinates	62	12
10 Seeking knowledge	55	10
11 Generating ideas	55	8
12 Evaluating people objectively	54	10
13 Delegating effectively	52	14
14 Helping subordinates	48	9
15 Responding well to criticism	41	59

(*Source:* CDS-II, $N = 1,064$)

rating to their performance in those areas they consider to be most important in their jobs. This similarity of rankings between importance and performance lends further weight to our observation that our sample of managers do not always treat their subordinates the way they might like to be treated themselves by their own bosses. However, a few discrepancies between these importance and performance rankings merit brief comment. For example, managers are not as good at communicating as they might like to be, but feel more confident about their more directly task-based duties. They are also less assiduous in 'keeping up to date' than they feel they should be, but rather better at 'treating subordinates fairly'.

Do these activities differ in importance for different kinds of managers? This we can test, and Table 8.2 shows the results.[3]

The importance of these job demands, and performance on them, seems to be much more a function of the type of manager than of the industry or job area they come from. In particular specialists appear more task oriented, and generalists more person oriented, though there are a couple of exceptions.

The same kind of analysis can be performed on scales and items from the CDS-I to see if job qualities differ across occupational and organizational characteristics. The results are shown in Table 8.3.

Most of these qualities are clearly positive in value, though predictability is perhaps more questionable: predictability may not always be a positively valued job characteristic. As if to underline this, job predictability is more in evidence in the ratings of managers from the public than the private sector. Elsewhere the most outstanding finding is in relation to job status where one can unequivocally say that 'high is beautiful'. Managers in the private sector also seem to have more scope in their jobs, and are happier about their bosses while older managers also tend to be more positive generally. There are few specific job area or industry group effects.

At the bottom of Table 8.3 can be seen the results of similar analyses on measures of organizational commitment.[4] There are three components to commitment (see Cook *et al.*, 1981): identification with the values of one's organization, loyalty, or commitment to staying with the organization, and effort – how prepared one is to give one's best energies and performance to the organization. The results show a continuation of the consistent pattern we have just seen for type and status. High status generalists have higher commitment on all three components, suggesting that specialists give higher priority to professional commitments. The size effect is of particular interest, since it confirms the important disjunction between medium sized and other companies we have noted previously.[5] Managers feel more commitment to giving their best effort to small companies, but in medium sized companies they identify less with the organization's values and are less inclined to stick with their organization in the face of competing opportunities (two of the three loyalty scale items pose this dilemma), i.e. another sign that career development in medium organizations is least satisfactory.

These results suggest how job experiences may be linked with mobility and performance. An important element in the link between work experience and mobility is the kind of feedback one receives on performance, opportunities to learn, and how adjustment to work is managed. We shall now look at these support systems.

161

Table 8.2 *Factors positively associated with job demands and performance*

	Age	Sex	Type	Status	Sector	Size	Job area	Industry group
1 Communicating effectively	—	—	High-status specialists	—	Public	—	—	—
2 Recognizing priorities	—	—	Generalists	—	—	—	—	—
3 Completing assignments	—	—	—	—	—	—	—	—
4 Keeping individuals informed	—	—	—	—	Large private and medium public	—	—	—
5 Maintaining positive relations	—	—	—	—	—	—	—	—
6 Keeping up to date	—	Female	Specialists	—	—	Small and large	—	—
7 Attacking problems logically	—	Male	—	—	Private	—	—	—
8 Treating subordinates fairly	Older	—	Generalists	—	—	—	—	—
9 Seeking knowledge	—	Female	Specialists	—	—	—	—	—
10 Stimulating subordinates	—	Male	Generalists and mid-status specialists	—	—	—	—	—

11 Generating ideas	Middle	—	—	—	Private	—	—
12 Evaluating people effectively	—	—	Generalists and high-status specialists	—	—	—
13 Delegating effectively	—	Male	Generalists	—	—	—
14 Helping subordinates	Older	—	Specialists	—	—	—
15 Responding well to criticism	—	Female	Specialists	—	—	—
* Performance	Older	—	Generalists	—	—	—

* Total scale score, aggregating performance self-ratings on these 15 job aspects

— = No relationship with factors

(*Source:* CDS-II, $N = 1,082$)

Table 8.3 *Factors positively associated with job qualities and commitment*

	Age	Sex	Type	Status	Sector	Size	Job area	Industry group
Job qualities								
Opportunities for growth and development	—	—	—	High	—	Small	Mgt-services, administration, (low: technical services)	—
Predictability	Older	Female	Generalists	High	Public	Middle	—	Commerce (low: government)
Discretion	Younger males & mid-age females	—	—	High	Private	Small	—	—
Quality of senior management	Older	—	Generalists	High	Private	Small & large	Males in administration, females in human relations	—
Job satisfaction	Older	—	—	High	—	Small	—	—
Commitment								
Identification	—	—	Generalists	High	—	Small & large	—	New services (low:industrial, government)
Loyalty	Older females & young & old males	—	Generalists	High	—	Small & large	—	—
Effort	Older	—	Generalists	High	—	Small	—	—

— = No relationship with factors

(Source: Job qualities, GDS I, N = 3,204; commitment, GDS II, N = 1,067)

Feedback and learning

First, we can look back to three of the questionnaire items that were briefly mentioned in Chapter 2, which measure the general level of responsiveness managers perceive in their work environments. Table 8.4 shows how these perceptions are affected by our main factors.[6]

Again, it is high status managers who fare best. Although no-one would begrudge them this support, it could be argued that they are the people who least need it, or rather that junior managers need it more. This balance of support in their favour is, as we shall see, achieved through their greater access to specific sources of feedback. The table also shows that feedback is more available in the new service group of industries than others, and more in private than in public enterprises. Industries in the government sector seem to be conforming to some of the bleaker stereotypes that are applied to them, though opportunities for learning do seem to escape this pattern. However we see again that medium sized companies come out worst on this measure. Small organizations give greatest recognition of accomplishment.[7]

In both the CDS-I and CDS-II we asked more specifically about if and how people get feedback on their performance. Table 8.5 summarizes the general findings, and these do not paint a very rosy picture of the amount of directed or intentional feedback and support managers are getting. *Almost two thirds have never received any kind of formal appraisal of their performance.* Any feedback they have received has been informal. This might compensate for the absence of formal systems if informal feedback were given consistently, but our question only asks 'have you had *any*', not how much. Table 8.6 answers this question, drawing on CDS-II questions asking how much feedback managers received from various sources.[8]

The table confirms that around two thirds of superiors do give some support but it also shows that for most this is at best 'moderate'. Only a quarter receive consistent feedback. Nor do colleagues fill this gap. Most feedback comes from directly task related sources: clients, customers and contacts, or concrete job indicators. Indeed, for many managers the latter is their only major source of feedback and even if they feel satisfied about this, it is a less than ideal situation. However responsive one's work environment is, it is important to have external reference points for comparison, encouragement and guidance. This is primarily a boss's job, and on this evidence most of our managers' bosses aren't doing this part of their jobs.

Table 8.7 looks at how these sources vary across our main factors. Amongst biographical variables there is an indication that women receive, and perhaps seek,[9] more interpersonal feedback than men, otherwise it is

Table 8.4 *Factors positively associated with feedback and learning*

	Age	Sex	Type	Status	Sector	Size	Job area	Industry group
Work where individual accomplishment is appreciated	Older	—	—	High	Private	Small	—	New services (low: government)
A job where I get feedback on how I am doing	—	—	—	High	Private	—	Administration (low: tech. servs. and education)	New services (low: government)
Opportunity to improve knowledge and skills	—	Female	—	High	—	Small & large	Males in education females in tech. servs.	Commerce (low: industrial)

(*Source:* CDS-I, *N* = 2,304)

Table 8.5 *Sources of feedback on performance*

Have you had any feedback from the following sources on how well your superiors think you are doing in your present job?	Yes %	No %
Formal appraisal system	38	62
Informal communications from boss	79	21
Other sources	60	40

(*Source:* CDS-I, $N = 2,061$)

the occupational and organizational factors that tell the most interesting story.

There seems to be a clear distinction between the different kinds of feedback that high and low status managers receive. Lower status managers are more dependent upon their superiors or appraisal systems (presumably operated by superiors), while higher status managers are able to rely more upon direct job experiences. Middle ranking managers make more use of colleagues than either high or low status managers. This implies an interesting set of contrasts between qualities of managerial experience at different organizational levels. Top management have the most direct control over their output; middle managers are human resource functionaries, operating as crucial intermediaries between higher and lower levels; junior managers are more administrators of downward flowing power and directives. This corresponds closely with Katz and Kahn's (1980) systems analysis of managerial roles.

There are some sector effects, with appraisals and job indicators more available in the private than public sector, but there are different effects for size. In large organizations experience of formal feedback is greater, while in small enterprises job indicators are more useful. These results indicate the effects of bureaucracy in large organizations. Managers in big enterprises are more remote from the tangible outputs of work or the clients by whom their effectiveness might be measured, and indeed they have their performance assessed more by criteria which are established internally through the managerial hierarchy. This also supplies an explanation for some of the evident discontents with career development in middle sized organizations, where both sorts of feedback are deficient.

A varied picture is given by the job area and industry group findings. Two features are worth particular mention: the low level of various sources of

Table 8.6 *'How much feedback do you get in your job from . . .?'*

	A great deal/ quite a lot %	Moderate %	Little or none %
Superiors	23	44	32
Colleagues	24	54	22
Clients, customers, contacts	33	45	23
Job indicators (i.e. visible results/output)	50	36	14

(*Source:* CDS-II, $N = 1,031$)

feedback in the government group, and the relative absence of appraisal systems in the new service group. The latter is not surprising when one considers the fact that appraisals are found in larger and more bureaucratic enterprises, but this makes their low frequency in the government organizations all the more remarkable. State sector organizations seem to have the double negative of bureaucratic forms and poor human resource management systems.

Some of these differences in support and feedback are amplified when we look at the sources of help people say they received during the period they were adjusting to their current jobs, i.e. within a few months of joining. In both surveys, at Time 1 and Time 2, managers were questioned about this. In the CDS-I we asked a general question about who or what 'were useful during the first few months of your present job in letting you know what was required of you'. In the CDS-II we asked more specific questions about how useful were various sources and agents in helping newcomers acquire three different sorts of information especially needed to achieve fast and effective adjustment: (1) standards of performance, (2) procedures, methods and equipment, and (3) the attitudes, motives and relationships of people in the organization. The general responses to these questions are summarized in Tables 8.8 and 8.9.[10]

These two tables tell the same story, but in somewhat different ways. Table 8.8 shows that informal and interpersonal agencies are found to be more useful than formal sources during the settling-in period. Indeed, it is disturbing to note that barely a quarter of managers found company literature and training useful in their early learning. And one cannot feel too confident about how adequately informal sources compensate for this

Table 8.7 *Factors positively associated with sources of feedback*

	Age	Sex	Type	Status	Sector	Size	Job area	Industry group
CDS-I								
Appraisal	Younger	—	Specialists	Low	—	Large	Human relations (low: administration, finance)	Commerce (low: new services, government)
Informal from boss	—	—	—	Low	Public	—	—	—
Other sources	—	Female	—	—	Public	—	—	—
CDS-II								
Superiors	—	—	—	—	—	—	Finance (low: tech. servs., education)	Trad. services (low: government)
Colleagues	—	Female	—	Middle	—	—	—	—
Clients etc.	—	Female	—	High	—	Small	Education (low: finance)	—
Job indicators	Middle	—	Generalists	High	Small private and large public	—	Sales, line (low: human relations)	Industrial (low: government)

— = No relationship with factors
(*Source:* CDS-I and II, *N* = 2,063 and 950)

Table 8.8 *Sources of learning for adjustment to job changes*

'During the first few months in your present job, how useful were each of the following in letting you know what was required of you?'	Extremely or Moderately useful		Of little or use	Not at all useful
		%		%
Immediate boss		68		32
A particular colleague		60		40
Colleagues in general		55		45
Subordinates		47		53
External professional skills courses		41		59
Company literature, written job specifications and rules		27		73
In-company training		24		76

(*Source:* CDS-I, *N* = 2,073)

deficiency. A third of all our managers found their bosses 'of little use' or worse. Even less help is given by colleagues and subordinates.

Table 8.9 allows us to be more specific about who or what helps for which types of early learning. Note that here our analysis is restricted to people who have very recently changed jobs, so these reflections are fresh in their minds, and, for many, were still being experienced at the time of the survey. The results show that one source of learning is valued above all other – on-the-job experience – but again there is cause for concern about deficiencies in other areas. Of these recent job changers 40–50% find their bosses 'not very useful' in *any* of the three learning areas. Previous job holders or other concurrent job holders are of negligible use and, one suspects, often not accessible – remember, that around 50% of the Time 2 job changing sample were in newly created jobs, i.e. without predecessors or precedents to guide them (see Chapter 7). Colleagues and subordinates seem to have more to teach our sample than their bosses, even on such concrete matters as standards and methods, and, interestingly, it is in the much more abstract area of organizational politics and interpersonal relations that colleagues' help is especially highly rated. As Louis *et al.* (1983) and Feldman and Brett (1983) have noted, in these areas informal agents are likely to be more

Table 8.9 *Usefulness of learning sources after a recent job change*

	Very useful %	Not very useful %
A For learning about *standards of performance*		
On the job experience	58	8
Immediate boss	27	41
Other colleagues	16	33
Previous job holder or colleague currently doing the same job	16	63
Subordinates	13	47
Formal training/job description	11	67
B For learning about *procedures, methods and equipment*		
On the job experience	57	10
Other colleagues	19	35
Immediate boss	19	50
Previous job holder or colleagues currently doing the same job	19	35
Subordinates	16	47
Formal training/job description	12	69
C For learning about the *attitudes, motives and relationships* of people in the organization		
On the job experiences	57	12
Other colleagues	25	24
Immediate boss	26	41
Subordinates	20	40
Previous job holder or colleague currently doing the same job	17	56
Formal training/job description	6	78

(*Source:* CDS-II sub-sample who changed jobs between Time 1 and Time 2, $N = 381$)

important sources of learning for people who have changed employer than for in-company transfers. Empirical tests on our data here provide some corroboration of this.[11] Finally, the contribution of formal training or job descriptions to any of these areas of learning is miserly. The results suggest that most organizations display an almost contemptuous neglect of the provision of formal aids to learning and adjustment. It looks very much as if in most organizations, thinking about managerial training does not go beyond the 'strategy' of throwing managers into the deep end to learn by themselves (Mangham and Silver, 1986). This may produce adequate, and, on occasions, even excellent performance, but it leaves much to chance, is unlikely to establish a climate of attentiveness to career needs, and does nothing to help establish either loyalty or controlled adjustment to performance requirements.

Now let us look at how these sources vary across our major dimensions. Table 8.10 shows the results for the CDS-I measures.

These results complement similar analyses we have described earlier.[12] Once more we see that it is generally low status managers in large organizations who find various external aids most helpful in settling into their jobs. Does this mean these groups receive especially favourable treatment? Or is it that they are more assiduous in appealing to these sources for assistance in the settling-in process, while senior managers are more reluctant to seek or accept help? In short, females, low status managers and people in large companies have the greatest need of this kind of support, and they initiate and make more use of these external aids. From this conclusion one would expect high status managers and managers in small companies to have the benefit of more help and guidance in adjustment from intrinsic work factors, such as on-the-job experiences. We were able to test and partially confirm this on the CDS-II data: we find job indicators are rated as more helpful by managers in small companies, but there are no clear cut status effects.[13]

So in summary, the picture we have of feedback and learning is mixed. The bad news is that organizations seem to be grossly neglecting to offer the support that managers need to let them know how they are doing and help them adjust to job demands. The good news seems to be that in various ways managers go out and solicit the help they want, and derive direct positive learning experiences from the jobs that they do. Most feedback on performance is reported by managers in the traditional rather than the newer functional areas and industries, and at junior rather than senior levels.[14] External sources of feedback are most used in large organizations, but job indicators are more accessible in small companies. On a number of indicators we find state-owned or run organizations give low feedback.

Organizational careers policies and practice

Here we shall look at what managers think governs their career prospects within their organizations. We saw in Chapter 2 that managers are generally optimistic about their career prospects, but what do they have to do to realise them? In the CDS-I and CDS-II we asked a series of questions aimed at revealing this. Managers were asked to assess how much their career opportunities were influenced by a number of factors such as

172

Table 8.10 *Factors positively associated with sources of learning*

	Age	Sex	Type	Status	Sector	Size	Job area	Industry group
Immediate boss	–	–	–	Low	Private	–	Line (low: tech. servs.)	–
A particular colleague	–	Female	Specialists	High & low	–	–	–	–
Colleagues in general	Younger & older	Female	–	–	Public	Large	–	–
Subordinates	–	–	Generalists	–	–	Large	Line (low: finance, education)	Government (low: commerce)
Company literature, job specifications etc.	Older	–	–	Low	–	Large	Males in line, females in education	Industrial (low: commerce)
In-company training	Younger & older	–	–	Low	–	Large	–	–
External professional skills courses	–	Female	–	–	–	–	–	Government (low: commerce)

— = No relationship with factors
(*Source:* CDS-I, N = 2,073)

'performance', 'politics', or 'luck'. These can be interpreted as revealing how much control managers feel they are able to exert over their organizational careers. Clearly perceptions vary widely on this dimension. Table 8.11 summarizes the general findings. [15]

Again, the news is mixed. One may take some comfort from the fact that most managers confidently believe their job performance is the single most important influence on their career success. There might also seem to be some natural justice in the fact that past career experience is the second ranked influence, though of course this does present a Catch-22 dilemma for managers. They need to have had the benefit of good career opportunities in the past to be confident of getting good openings in the future, so how does one start on the right track? Well, the less favourable answer to this question supplied by these data is that managers also see career opportunities as pretty much of a lottery, for 'politics' and 'luck' are both accorded considerable weight. This implies that getting a good early career break is of the utmost importance to subsequent career development (cf. Veiga, 1983). Formal qualifications are seen as important by only a minority, and 'corporate planning' does not seem to be at all widely recognized as a controlling influence. It is striking that tenure and seniority have even less importance – not a result one might have expected in British management just a few decades ago.

Finally, one might be tempted to express some relief that 'prejudice' is seen as insignificant for all but a minority. But, and this is a big but, this item was included specifically to gauge whether women feel discriminated against in their managerial career development. There is a huge sex difference on this item. Most of those who give affirmative answers to this factor are indeed women. A third of the women managers in the sample say prejudice has a moderate or greater influence on career prospects; only 8% of the men give equivalent responses. Is this *prima facie* evidence of actual prejudice? There are sufficient highly convincing first hand accounts in the free comment section of the surveys (see Alban-Metcalfe, 1984) to suggest that sex discrimination is real enough. We shall return to this issue in the next chapter. Now let us look at how these career influences are affected by our major dimensions of individual differences and organizational circumstances. The results, shown in Table 8.12, build upon the picture that is accumulating from our previous analyses. [16]

It seems that women not only feel prejudice plays a greater part in their career fortunes than it does for men but they also seem more bounded by the bureaucratic constraints of impersonal corporate career systems (length of service and corporate planning). Yet even so, women are more optimistic about their opportunities for advancement and the value that is placed on their work by influential people in their organizations. This can be seen as

174

Table 8.11 *Perceived influences on career opportunities*

'What do you think influences your career opportunities in your present	A great deal	or	Quite a lot	Little	or	Not at all
	%			%		
1 Individual performance: how well I perform in my job	76			11		
2 Career experience: having had the correct type and sequence of jobs	67			15		
3 Organizational politics: knowing and influencing the right people	61			18		
4 Luck: being in the right place when opportunities arise	55			22		
5 Formal qualifications: having specific academic/professional certificates or training	37			33		
6 Corporate planning: impersonal decisions made at higher levels	33			44		
7 Length of service: depending upon seniority and time in the job	23			47		
8 Prejudice: belonging to a group that is discriminated against	12			77		

(*Source:* items 1, 3, 4, 6, 8, CDS-I, $N = 2,222$;
        items 2, 5, 7, CDS-II, $N = 1,020$)

another indication that women in management develop motives and beliefs which provide the psychological impetus to overcome the barriers they find unequally stacked in their paths.

Status and size effects are pervasive in Table 8.12. High status managers have greater confidence that job performance will be rewarded – clearly a self-enhancing perception, for it implies a belief that they have got to their present positions by virtue of their talents rather than through more capricious or exterior influences. This seems an unrealistically rosy picture of organizational career progression for it is evident that low status managers are more cynical and inclined to attribute career success to luck, politics and all the other exterior influences in the scale. There is also an interesting division between how specialists and generalists view the role of past career experience. It seems that high status generalists share this view,

Table 8.12 *Factors positively associated with perceived career influences*

Industry group	Age	Sex	Type	Status	Sector	Size	Size	Job area Industry group
1 Performance	Young	—	Generalists	High	Private	Small	Line, sales, management serv. (low: education)	New serv. (low: government)
2 Experience	Older	—	High status specialists Low status generalists		—	Large	—	—
3 Politics	Young	—	—	Low	—	Large	—	—
4 Luck	—	—	—	Low	—	Large	Tech. services (low: finance)	—
5 Qualifications	Older	—	Specialists	Low	—	Large	Education (low: sales)	Government (low: trad. serv.)
6 Corporate planning	—	Female	—	Low	—	Large	—	Commerce (low: new services)
7 Length of service	—	Female	—	Low	—	Middle	—	Commerce, government (low: trad. serv.)
8 Prejudice	—	Female	—	Low	—	Middle & large	—	—
A Opportunities for advancement	Young	Female	—	High	Small private and large public	—	—	—
B How much influential people at work value one's contribution	Older	Female male	—	High	Small private and large public	—	—	—

suggesting that they are looking forward with some optimism to their future careers.

The results for size indicate that managers see themselves as having greatest control over their own destinies in small companies. The consistency of the results is overwhelming. In larger organizations, exterior influences are seen as much more significant. There are also some noteworthy effects for sector. Job performance is accorded greater weight in private sector companies, but on the last two items (A and B) there is a highly interesting replicated finding linking size with sector. Opportunities for advancement and feeling valued are greatest in small private and large public enterprises, again implying the presence of blockages in middle sized enterprises.

Finally, there are some job area and industry group effects. The latter are especially noteworthy. Again it is in the new service organizations where life looks best and government the worst for the self-directed manager. Performance is seen as most influential by the new service managers and the three bureaucratic criteria are rated as least important. This pattern is almost exactly reversed for managers in the government group of organizations.

So, in summary, we see that managers are generally positive about the influence of performance on career chances, but are also aware of the importance of more impersonal and uncontrollable forces. But there are wide ranging and important differences in how managers see these influences. Women, it seems, feel more subject to external control, especially the discriminatory judgements of superiors. Managers of low status, in large organizations and in State enterprises all tend to feel similarly powerless in their careers. But at the same time not all of these groups are pessimistic about their career opportunities. Women, notably, have positive perceptions of their future careers.

These differential perceptions could be seen as reflecting some quite distinct types of organizational culture. Our next section throws further light on this.

Organizational culture

What is an organizational culture? The notion of culture is broad and imprecise, necessarily so to capture the more abstract qualities of institutional and social experience. It may be defined to encompass the shared values, beliefs and customary ways of behaving in any social system (Frost *et al.*, 1985; Schein, 1985). It is the almost indefinable quality of 'difference' that one notices on moving from one organization to another, however superficially similar they may be in their business methods or market position. To some degree, everything we have said so far about the differences in perceptions of managers from different types of organizations has been telling us about organizational cultures. We are not going to try to give definitive descriptions of cultures here, but to try to examine more directly some of the characteristics which are commonly associated with major cultural difference between organizations. A number of items in the CDS-II were designed for this purpose.[17] The general results are shown in Table 8.13.[18]

Table 8.13 *Cultural dimensions of organizations*

My organization is . . .	Very much like this or	Quite like this	Not really like this or	Not at all like this
	%		%	
1 Cost oriented: dominated by its need to produce goods and services efficiently and competitively	71		23	
2 Market oriented: dominated by its need to change quickly in response to its environment	58		38	
3 Leader oriented: dominated by the personality(ies) of character of its chief executive(s)	57		33	
4 Security oriented: dominated by its need to maintain its position and/or status	57		31	
5 Innovation oriented: dominated by its need to develop new items and products	48		42	
6 Rules oriented: dominated by its concern with administration through policies and procedures	46		46	
7 People oriented: dominated by its concern with employees' welfare and team spirit	41		48	
8 Crisis oriented: dominated by its concern with power and conflict resolution	28		60	

(*Source:* CDS-II, *N* = 1,022)

The general experience managers have of their organizations is consistent with stereotyped conceptions of business and industry as hard-nosed and fast-moving. Our sample's organizations seem to be driven by market forces and strong personalities. Innovation and security are moderately valued, but concern for people receives lowly emphasis, a value that is no doubt displaced by the more economic business values. Conflict is the least dominant principle.

We also asked managers to describe whether their organizations had been growing or contracting over recent years, and how they saw their future growth or decline. Table 8.14 summarizes their answers.

A generally optimistic vision of British business is suggested by this two to one majority reporting growth over decline, both past and future. But these generalities conceal wide differences in the views of managers of different types and industries. Table 8.15 shows how they vary across our analytical dimensions.[19]

How are we to interpret these findings? Do they reflect objective differences between organizational types or are they just the perceptual biasses of different types of managers? Of course both can be true together – managers' characteristics and perceptions are not divisible from the kinds of organizations they inhabit. Yet, it is striking that in Table 8.15 it is the industry group results that are the strongest and most consistent.[20] Sure enough, there are also clear effects by status, but the industry group effects are entirely independent of status and size. The almost complete absence of

Table 8.14 *Perceptions of past and future organizational growth**

	During the past five years my organization has had: %	During the next five years my organization will probably have: %
Rapid growth	27	21
Some growth	37	45
Static	12	13
Some decline	17	16
Major decline	7	5

* Growth and decline defined as 'increases or falls in sales, budgets, number of employees'
(*Source:* CDS-II, $N = 1,007$)

179

Table 8.15 *Factors positively associated with dimensions of organization culture*

	Age	Sex	Type	Status	Sector	Size	Job area	Industry group
1 Cost oriented	—	Male	—	—	Private	Large	Line (low: education)	Trad. serv. > industrial > commerce > new serv. > government
2 Market oriented	—	—	—	High	Private	Small	Sales (low: education)	Trad. serv. > industrial > new serv. > primary > government
3 Leader oriented	—	—	—	High	—	Small	Human relations (low: tech. serv.)	Trad. serv. & industrial > new serv. > government > commerce
4 Security oriented	—	—	Specialists	Low	—	—	—	Commerce > trad. serv. & government > primary > new services
5 Innovation oriented	—	Male	—	—	Private	Large	Line (low: finance)	Industrial > commerce > new serv. > trad. serv. > government
6 Rules oriented	—	—	—	Low	Public	Large	Education (low: all others)	Government > commerce > trad. serv. > industrial > new serv.
7 People oriented	—	—	Generalists	High	—	Large	Human relations (low: tech. serv.)	Commerce > trad. serv. > new serv. > industrial > government
8 Crisis oriented	—	—	—	Low	Public	Large	—	Government > trad. serv. > commerce > industrial > new serv.

Past growth	Younger	—	—	High	—	Small	—	Commerce > new serv. > trad. serv. > industrial > government
Future growth	Younger	Male	Generalists	High	—	Small	Finance, sales (low: education)	Commerce > new serv. > trad. serv. > industrial > government

— = No relationship with factors
(*Source:* CDS-II, $N = 1{,}022$)

age, sex and type associations lends weight to the argument that these responses reflect more than just the idiosyncratic views of different types of manager; they are telling us about real differences between organizational types. Because of this in the last column 8 of Table 8.15 we have shown the rank order of all five industry groups on these items.

Some summary statements can be made about each of the industry groups, for from this analysis they would seem to have distinctive cultural profiles. *Traditional services* are strongly led fighters in the market-place with a high internal involvement in power and conflict issues. Enterprises in the *commerce* group are equally in the thick of a fight for survival, but with more bureaucratic than personal leadership, and making more use of innovation. However, their concern for personnel is the highest of any group and they also come out as the most successful of all groups in terms of growth. In the *industrial* group there is more concern for cost than market (i.e. more dependent on commodities and suppliers than on sales). They are strongly led and innovation oriented, with a low emphasis on bureaucratic rules. The *new services* are less market conscious, with a moderate emphasis on innovation and relative immunity from concerns about survival, which is consistent with managers' reports that organizations in this group have high growth. They also have the lowest concerns for rules. Finally, the *government* group presents a complete and unhappily bleak contrast. They are highly bureaucratic, dominated by crises with the lowest emphasis on innovation and market effectiveness. They show least concern for people and they are also the area of least growth.[21]

For the manager who wants a life of combative high pressure, commerce and traditional services are the place to be. Other areas, such as new services, offer more relaxed and expansive careers. But any manager (are there any?) who wants a static, rule-bound, conflictual environment, but free from the pressures of harsh business reality, should look to government owned or run enterprises. We must emphasize that we are making no kind of political statement here. One could wish the results otherwise, but the evidence for a sluggish and hemmed-in life in State enterprises is too strong to lightly dismiss. At the same time, we believe there is nothing inevitable about this. Not all State organizations do exhibit these tendencies or need to. The results also show that many of these problems are characteristic more generally of large organizations, whatever sector they are in,[22] but the results for government are independent of size on many of these items.[23] So on this reasoning, establishing small units in State enterprises would go some of the way to curing these ills, but not the whole way.

This completes our picture of occupational and organizational effects. We shall now summarize these results and consider what they imply for the quality of management careers and work experience.

182

Summary and conclusion

The managers have given us a fairly clear image of the organizational worlds they inhabit. Most confirm the impression of a fast-moving and hard-headed business reality. Involvements and satisfactions are generally high, but in this mêlée of activity there is less time and attention given to the managers' needs for feedback, support and guidance in career development. Most organizations are described as having a low concern for people, and indeed, as if to corroborate this, our managers themselves are more concerned with the cognitive tasks of job performance than the human tasks of developing their subordinates. It is therefore hardly surprising that they find themselves subjected to a similar neglect. Both are equally prisoners of the cultural norms of business. Structured and informal feedback are rarely received, and it seems that what little assistance and support organizations may attempt to give managers when they are settling into their new jobs is actually found to be of negligible practical value. Managers find more tangible feedback and valuable guidance in the more direct outcomes of their jobs, where they are fortunate enough to be in a position for these to be visible.

Consistent with this is how managers cling to the belief that their career opportunities are dependent upon their performance, but in the absence of external feedback how can they be sure? As if to underline this doubt most managers are well aware that also of high importance are organizational politicking and the luck of the draw in being in the right place at the right time. In short, managers fixate on the core of their jobs and how they perform them for reassurance about how they and their future destinies will be managed. But as we saw in Chapter 4, the control this gives them is illusory. With their eyes fixed firmly on their jobs managers have little vision or foresight about what changes lie ahead.

In terms of our introductory stage model of career development it would appear that after selection and job placement the adjustment process is left very much to chance by many organizations. Any help to be had in settling-in is through informal rather than organizationally controlled sources. Performance adjustment is mediated more by managers' individual work experience than well-designed feedback systems, and likewise future-directed career planning is not a common experience.

So much for the most general view. What we have also seen here is how experience varies across different kinds of settings and managerial types. Notable has been an extension to our earlier 'small and high is beautiful' theme. Being near the top of your organization or in a small, preferably private, company yields the best qualities of management experience in a climate of greatest informality. Differences of organizational culture are strongly linked with industry types, and one of the groups, government (local government, public services and utilities) is the subject of an uncomfortably converging series of negatives. They are rule bound, bureaucratic, no growth, yet secure environments in which direct job indicators on one's performance are rarely found: both feedback *on* performance and career opportunities *from* performance are largely absent.

We shall be summarizing biographical, occupational and organizational effects in the final chapter of this book, but before then we shall be giving concentrated attention to one major division in our sample that has been shown again in this chapter to be of importance. This is sex differences. We have seen in this chapter, as in many preceding chapters, a number of thought provoking differences in the reported experience of male and female managers. Of the most striking significance has been the widespread feeling among women that they are subject to discriminatory career opportunities, though this does not seem to dull their determined optimism about their futures.

In the next chapter we shall pull together all that we have observed about differences between male and female managers, add further findings from further investigation of the issue, and try to reach some summary conclusions about the experience of women in management.

9
Women in management

In preceding chapters we have seen how managerial work and careers could be described as a rewarding struggle. Frequent and radical job changes are often made, and for most people these provide psychological and material benefits. Yet we have also seen how the patterns and outcomes of change differ according to managers' circumstantial, biographical and psychological characteristics. One of these, gender, has been repeatedly identified as cutting across other dimensions and exerting a major influence on job change and its consequences. We are particularly fortunate here to be able to give this close attention through our access to a large sample of women managers,[1] probably the largest in any detailed survey of this kind in the literature. So now we shall pull together all our main findings on sex differences to try to answer some important questions about women in management. For example, is gender a critical variable in managerial experience, or is it only significant as a 'carrier variable', i.e. because it is linked with other significant factors, such as occupation or status. And how do women differ from men in their career situations and orientations?

Much has been written recently about women in employment. They have constituted a growing proportion of the labour force, and are increasingly represented in areas of employment that have been traditionally dominated by males. However, women do tend to be concentrated in particular sectors of the economy – principally in service occupations, and in lower level jobs in a variety of white-collar areas (Martin and Roberts, 1984; Beechey, 1986). Women's representation in management is also growing, rapidly in the USA according to the American census data (*USA Bureau of Labor Statistics*, 1980), and rather less rapidly in the UK, but growing nonetheless (Marshall, 1984; Davidson, 1985). However, they are still a small minority – 1 in 10 at junior to middle levels, and less than 1% in executive level managerial jobs. Judi Marshall's (1984) description of them as 'travellers in a male world' seems apt. Marshall studied the experience of 30 women in two areas where women are relatively numerous, retail trades and publishing, and concluded that women's approach to management was distinctively and importantly different from male norms. The only other detailed empirical focus on women managers in Britain has been the work of Davidson and Cooper (1983), documenting the stressors that are attendant upon their status as a minority group in organizations. There have also been a number of American studies of women in management and the professions (see Wortman, 1982), but these have tended to be rather limited in their focal areas of interest, sampling frames, sample sizes, or possibilities for gender comparison.

The present study enlarges upon previous research in several important respects. It provides the first detailed investigation of a large number of women managers, encompasses a wide range of career and work factors, and allows controlled comparison of women managers with their male counterparts. We shall be focussing on a number of issues. First, we shall look at how women differ from men in demographic and biographical factors. Second, we shall see whether their occupational and organizational situations differ from men's. Third, we shall examine how evident is the gender segregation of women in management. Finally, we shall overview our findings from a variety of other analyses to consider in what ways the work experiences, psychological profiles, career patterns and development of men and women differ.

Biographical

Before we attempt to evaluate sex differences we need to be sure we are comparing like with like. For in reality we do not have two samples, but six: the two sexes, $\times$ the two categories of BIM status plus a third 'other' category sampled through non-BIM sources. Table 9.1 shows this sampling frame.

The large number of women in this sample cannot, of course, be taken as evidence that women constitute a sizeable proportion of the managerial labour force. As we noted in Chapter 1, this large sample of women respondents was only achieved by a second mailing to all the 800 women Members and Fellows of the BIM, and the supplementary sampling of women from 'other' sources (women's professional associations and network groups). Indeed, one can immediately note that the small number of women Fellows in the final sample underlines how scarce women are at this elevated level (mainly board level executives).

In all subsequent analyses these groups are kept separate unless we have evidence that they do not differ significantly or we can apply other statistical controls. Because of its very small size, the group of 'other' men is dropped from all the analyses that follow.

Table 9.2 provides the first indication of important biographical differences between the sexes.

186

Women in management

Table 9.1 *CDS-I sampling frame*

	BIM Members	BIM Fellows	Other	Total
Men	993 (73%)	477 (92%)	28 (7%)	1498 (65%)
Women	371 (27%)	41 (8%)	394 (93%)	806 (35%)
	(100%)	(100%)	(100%)	2304 (100%)

(*Source:* CDS-I, $N = 2,304$)

The three groups of women do not differ much from each other, nor do the two male samples, but there is a clear difference between the sexes. Almost a third of the women are single but less than one in twenty of the men is single, and this is not due solely to the fact that the women tend to be younger (see 'average' in the bottom row of Table 9.2). Nor is this high proportion of single women a peculiarity of our sample. That it is a general phenomenon across the labour force is indicated by a recent large scale survey of women in all types of employment, conducted by the Office of Population and Census Surveys (Martin and Roberts, 1984), which also found 32% of women to be single. Is this due to women foregoing marriage in order to pursue their careers, or is it because a large number of women are kept out of the labour force by the unequal share of domestic responsibilities that falls on them in marriage? Of course, both may be true. Indeed, some women undoubtedly forego marriage *because* they can see how it restricts the careers of many other women. The higher incidence of divorce and separation among the women (also replicated in the OPCS survey) can be interpreted similarly.

The first is a statistical explanation. If we consider that a large proportion of the parent population of women is not available to be included in the statistics because they are full-time housewives, then it follows that other categories, single, divorced etc., will form a greater proportion of the remainder – a 'survivor' population of working women who are 'available' to be sampled. The second explanation is that it is probably true that divorce/separation is occupationally 'liberating' for childless women managers, and in many cases is caused by the role conflict of women's competing domestic and professional responsibilities. Of course these two explanations are not inconsistent with each other. It is precisely because of the greater strains of work on marriage and family that many women forego demanding professional careers. Independent corroboration of this sex difference in incidence of marriage breakdown is supplied by our

Table 9.2 *Marital status and age*

| | Women | | | Men | |
	BIM Members %	BIM Fellows %	Other %	BIM Members %	BIM Fellows %
Single	25	32	32	5	1
Divorced/separated	12	7	9	3	2
Widowed	1	2	4	1	0
Married	61	59	55	92	96
$N =$	371	41	394	993	477
Average age	39.5	48.3	37.9	45.6	50.1

(*Source*: CDS-I, $N = 2,276$)

longitudinal data from the CDS-II. The life events scale revealed that fully 7% of females experienced divorce or separation in the short interval between the two surveys (12–15 months), whereas only 2% of the males had this experience, despite the fact that more of the men were married in the first place!

One way of quantifying the scope for role conflict in marriage is to look at partner's occupation for the two sexes. Table 9.3 shows this comparison for married managers. (Since there were no differences between the two female and the two male samples these are not shown.) There is a clear and evident difference between the sexes.

It has been said that what every working woman needs is a wife. Table 9.3 shows that men have wives, women have working partners. From Table 9.3 we can see how different a choice marriage is for the two sexes. For men marriage provides a platform of support and security from which to launch their careers, while for women it is a competing demand and an obstacle (Langrish, 1981). Half the men have full-time housewives as partners, while less than one in ten of the women has a non-employed partner. Barely a quarter of the men have full-time working partners, but 90% of the women face the problem of coordinating their career demands with their partner's full-time work obligations.

Of course domestic responsibilites involve more than just the presence or absence of a spouse – though even where there are no children the unequal

Table 9.3 *Occupational status of partner for married female and male managers*

	Females %	Males %
In full-time employment	69	20
Self-employed	20	5
Employed on a fixed-term contract	1	1
In part-time employment	1	24
Looking for employment	3	3
Not looking for employment	1	45
Retired	5	3
$N = 468$		1395

(*Source:* CDS-I, married respondents only)

share of household duties does seem to be a hard-dying cultural norm – for it is responsibility for childcare that places the greatest non-work demands on couples, and around which centre some of the most manifest inequalities in the division of household labour. It would not be surprising therefore if women were prepared to forego the role of mother in the interests of their careers. Highly significant sex differences in family size statistics support this interpretation, as shown in Table 9.4 A and B.

The sex difference is huge and is not reduced by statistically controlling for age or status.[2] Almost half the married women are childless, but only one in ten of the men is, and when we restrict comparison to married managers who do have children (section B, of Table 9.4), it is striking that the women tend to have smaller families than the men. There is a strong suggestion here that married women are either foregoing or at least postponing the role of mother for the sake of their careers, and when they do have families they are limiting their family size to minimize competing role obligations. These explanations involve inference beyond the evidence directly available here, though we did find more specific confirmation of this in the comments volunteered by women in the free response section of the CDS-I, where many women described difficult choices and conflicts they have had to face and overcome in order to pursue their management careers (Alban-Metcalfe, 1984).

The last biographical factor we shall look at is education. Table 9.5

189

Table 9.4 *Family size*

	Females %	Males %
A *Married managers with and without children*		
No children	48	11
One or more children	52	89
$N=$	468	1395
B *Number of children for female and male* *managers with one or more children*		
One child	30	15
Two children	44	51
Three or more children	25	33
$N=$	243	1241

(*Source:* CDS-I, married respondents only)

shows that the women are, in general, more highly educated than the men.

Two thirds of the women have a first degree or higher qualification, whereas the men are more likely to have had a technical education (OND or HND) and to have some other professional qualification (such as a Diploma in Management Studies). This might suggest that men are more likely to be technical specialists in management than women, but as we shall see, the opposite is true – more women are technical specialists. So from this difference in education we may infer than men are more likely than women to move into general management from a technical educational base, while women tend to follow a more academic route (Ashridge, 1981). This may partly reflect an age-generation effect, and partly a social class difference. More male than female managers may come from working class backgrounds, and work their way through the ranks from technically based operative roles, while more women may be coming into management from middle class backgrounds by a more collegiate path (Lemkau, 1983).[3] This interpretation is consistent with the greater preponderance of men in blue-collar occupations and women in service and white-collar sectors (Beechey, 1986). If there is this kind of sex-role linkage between education and management careers, one might expect women to enter different

Table 9.5 *Educational qualifications*

	Females %	Males %
< 2 'O' levels	0	1
2 or more 'O' levels	11	13
ONC/OND	1	3
HNC/HND	4	17
'A' levels or equivalent	17	17
First degree	26	22
Postgraduate diploma	25	17
Higher degree	15	10
Other professional qualifications	26	36
$N =$	806	1498

(*Source:* CDS-I, $N = 2,304$)

spheres of management to the men. As we shall see, there is some evidence of this.

The results also suggest that women need higher qualifications to overcome selective gender barriers to management entry. So, taking all our biographical findings together, there is a strong case for saying that women face far greater obstacles in the career paths than men, in the shape of competing domestic commitments and restricted access to the traditional male routes to management. They help themselves to overcome these impediments by foregoing marriage or family and by obtaining higher educational qualifications than men. At the same time, the higher incidence of restricted family size and divorce amongst the women also prompts the thought that their unequal struggle entails greater sacrifices and psychological costs.

Occupational and organizational factors

We know that women are a long way from achieving numerical parity with men in management, but let us see first whether those that have entered the profession have achieved status equality with their male counterparts. Our measure of status is level from the top of one's organization. Since we know that organization size affects this measure – it is more difficult to be near the top of a large than a small organization – we need to be sure we are comparing like with like. Similarly, we need to be sure that the unequal representation of BIM Members, Fellows and other managers is taken into account since these groups are unequal in status. Table 9.6 shows the status levels for male and female managers in these different sample and size categories.

The results show that the women in the 'Other' category have consistently lower status than the men in all three size groups of organizations. As we have seen they are also younger, which together suggests that the 'Other women' are at earlier and more junior career levels than the BIM men or women. If we set the 'Other women' group to one side, and restrict our comparison to men and women of the same BIM membership grade there is clearly no sex difference in status,[4] and this holds within each of three organization size categories, and within each of the sub-samples of Members and Fellows. Nonetheless this could still conceal status differences in particular industries and occupations. Reanalysis of status differences within each of the eight job areas and five industry groups[5] demonstrated that there were no differences, except in one job area, administration. Only in this category, which broadly represents general office management, are women disadvantaged, probably due to their greater concentration in large organizations where this function is more common. So, even though women are a minority in management, especially in the upper reaches of board level representation (Fellows), we find them holding their own in terms of status attainment.

Now let us turn to look at the roles and industries in which women are found. Table 9.7 shows how many men and women described themselves as 'functional specialists' vs 'general managers'.

Here we do see a clear sex difference; in every sub-sample women are more likely to say they are functional specialists than men. It is also noticeable that the higher the status of the sample the more respondents of either sex are likely to describe themselves as general managers. The net result of this is that the proportion of generalists among women *Fellows* is on a par with the male *Members*. This suggests that women reach equivalent status to men through different, more specialized, routes, and men reach generalism more readily than women, a clear sign of an important gender difference in career patterns. We can identify possible areas of specialism by looking at job areas, shown in Table 9.8.

There is only moderate evidence of occupational segregation here. In two areas, human relations and education, women are relatively highly represented – confirming the observation of other writers that these are particularly gender-typed occupations (Hakim, 1979; Lockwood and Knowles, 1984; Martin and Roberts, 1984). And men are relatively more numerous in line management, supporting our earlier observation that men

Table 9.6 *Managerial status*

Company size:	Small			Medium			Large				
Sample:	BIM Members		Other	BIM Members		Other	BIM Members		Other	BIM Fellows	
	Men %	Women %	women %	Men %	Women %	women %	Men %	Women %	women %	Men %	Women %
Level											
1 top	40	45	27	4	3	1	1	0	3	27	31(11)
2	48	45	52	27	28	22	11	20	7	34	36(13)
3	9	6	17	34	35	23	22	20	12	20	19(7)
4	3	2	1	19	21	17	18	17	18	10	6(2)
5	0	1	0	9	8	19	16	13	9	5	6(2)
6	0	1	2	3	2	11	15	15	16	2	3(1)
7+	0	0	0	3	4	8	18	17	35	2	0
	N = 220	87	86	351	112	108	377	138	136	456	36

(*Source:* CDS-I, *N* = 2,276)

Table 9.7 *Role type*

	Women			Men	
	BIM Members %	BIM Fellows %	Other %	BIM Members %	BIM Fellows %
Functional specialist	54	44	69	44	21
General manager	45	56	31	55	79
$N =$	361	39	362	970	461

(*Source:* CDS-I, $N =$ 2,304)

predominate in the traditional industrial and commercial areas of management.

We can test this by also examining whether there is any tendency toward gender segregation in industrial groups. Table 9.9 shows this breakdown.

The chief difference is the greater proportion of women in the public sector, and of men in the industrial sector. But in the other three areas their relative representation is much the same. It must be remembered however that these do not signify their *numerical* strength since a random sampling within any of these industries or job areas would almost certainly reveal an overwhelming majority of male managers. We can look at this more directly by examining the sex composition of managers' current work situation, and from this make further comment on the degree of gender segregation to which women may be subject within occupations and organizations.

Gender segregation

We asked a series of questions of both males and females about the presence or absence of other males and females in their current work situation. Table 9.10 shows the results.

It is apparent that the women generally occupy male-dominated environments in that their bosses (A), colleagues (D), and same job title counterparts (F) are all more likely to be male than female. The prevalence of male bosses is particularly marked, and underlines how much women managers, whatever their status, have to work under the direction of the opposite sex. In their remarks on the free comment section of the CDS-I

194

Table 9.8 *Job area*

	Women			Men	
	BIM Members %	BIM Fellows %	Other %	BIM Members %	BIM Fellows %
Sales	12	7	14	17	10
Line	2	0	2	14	11
Finance	10	2	11	11	10
Human relations	20	10	18	8	8
Technical services	6	7	11	8	4
Management services	18	39	12	20	22
General management	15	29	11	15	29
Education	14	5	11	6	5
Other	3	0	10	1	1
$N =$	364	41	378	976	468

(*Source:* CDS-I, $N = 2,304$)

many women described this situation as one that they found difficult in the absence of available female role-models (Alban-Metcalfe, 1984). It is thus not surprising to find that women are far more likely than men to turn to another woman for help (B), though it would appear that only a minority are able to do so; most still have to call upon male assistance

If women are so evidently a gender minority, is there any evidence here that this means they are establishing footholds in male preserves? Items C and F certainly suggest this may be happening. First we can see that for all those who were able to identify a job predecessor (the 30% missing represent newly created jobs where there are no precedents, see Chapter 7) *fully 57% were entering jobs formerly held by men while on 4% of men were in an equivalent gender-role switch*. Item F tells the same story: women have twice as many male as female equivalent role occupants in their work settings.

However, there is some evidence of gender segregation here inasmuch as women are more likely than men to be working alongside women, a trend that is especially marked when we look at subordinates (E). It is only on this item that we get a same-sex crossover of the data – i.e. men supervising

Table 9.9 *Industry group*

	Women			Men	
	BIM Members %	BIM Fellows %	Other %	BIM Members %	BIM Fellows %
Industrial (e.g. manufacturing)	16	7	13	39	39
Traditional services (e.g. transport)	13	7	19	14	14
New services (e.g. consultancy)	17	29	18	12	15
Commerce (e.g. banking)	6	2	10	4	4
Government (e.g. utilities)	46	49	37	29	25
Other	2	5	3	1	2
$N =$	365	41	383	980	467

(*Source:* CDS-I, $N =$ 2,304)

more men than women, and women supervising more women than men. The most likely explanation for this is that many women's managerial roles are established by employers who feel the need to recruit women to manage female workforces, and resist recruiting women to manage male subordinates. It is also possible that women managers are more likely to employ women to work for them, and/or that men are less likely to apply for and accept jobs in which they would be working under women.

Nonetheless looking across all the results of Table 9.10 one can conclude that women are not in any absolute sense set apart in single sex ghettoes, away from the male-dominated world of managerial work, even if there are signs that some gender segregation may be occurring in certain areas of employment. To identify these more closely we can test for gender ratio differences on these items, looking separately at each of our job areas and industry groups. The results are shown in Tables 9.11 and 9.12.

These two tables are complicated and require some explanation. Each cell where there is an entry signifies a significant difference[6] between male

Table 9.10 *Gender ratios of managers' current work situation*

	Females (N = 806)	Males (N = 1,498)
A		
(My) Immediate boss is:		
Male	85%	98%
Female	15%	2%
B Colleague who has been most helpful in your present job is:		
Male	62%	87%
Female	38%	13%
(excluding 13% female and 9% male with missing data or scoring NA)		
C The person who did your job before you was:		
Male	57%	96%
Female	43%	4%
(excluding 30% female and 32% male with missing data or scoring NA)		
D How many current colleagues in your work section are:		
Male (average number)	8.5	14.3
% without any male colleagues	21%	19%
Female (average number)	7.2	6.4
% without any female colleagues	28%	36%
E How many of your immediate subordinates are:		
Male (average number)	3.4	9.0
% without any male subordinates	49%	20%
Female (average number)	6.1	3.9
% without any female subordinates	34%	38%
F Other people with same job title as you in your organization:		
Male (average number)	8.2	7.5
% without any male same job holders	54%	60%
Female (average number)	4.3	1.3
% without any female same job holders	64%	89%

NA = Not applicable
(*Source:* CDS-I, N = 2,304)

and female managers' sex ratios: i.e. their gender environment. So where an entry says 'more likely to be female' this means that women were more likely than men in this job area or industry group to have a female boss, helpful colleague or predecessor. Where it shows 'women have fewer' or 'women have more' this indicates that the women managers had

197

Table 9.11 *Within job area sex ratios*

	Sales	Finance	Human relations	Technical services	Management services	Administration	Education
Sex of boss	—	—	More likely to be female	—	—	More likely to be female	More likely to be female
Sex of helpful colleagues	—	—	—	—	—	More likely to be female	More likely to be female
Sex of predecessor	More likely to be female	—	More likely to be female	—	—	More likely to be female	More likely to be female
Number of male colleagues	Women have fewer	—	Women have fewer	Women have fewer	Women have fewer	Women have fewer	Women have fewer
Number of female colleagues	—	—	—	—	—	—	—
Number of male subordinates	Women have fewer	—	Women have fewer	Women have fewer	Women have fewer	Women have fewer	Women have fewer
Number of female subordinates	—	—	—	—	Women have fewer	—	Women have more
Number of male equivalent job holders	—	Women have more	—	—	—	—	—
Number of female equivalent job holders	Women have more	Women have more	—	—	Women have more	—	—
Male $N =$	217	160	115	94	298	297	84
Female $N =$	100	78	144	65	128	109	94

Table 9.12 *Within industry group sex ratios*

	Industrial	Traditional services	New services	Commerce	Government
Sex of boss	—	More likely to be female	More likely to be female	—	More likely to be female
Sex of helpful colleagues	More likely to be female	More likely to be female	More likely to be female	—	More likely to be female
Sex of predecessor	—	More likely to be female	More likely to be female	More likely to be female	More likely to be female
Number of male colleagues	—	—	Women have fewer	—	Women have fewer
Number of female colleagues	—	—	—	—	—
Number of female subordinates	fewer	fewer	fewer	—	Women have fewer
Number of male equivalents	—	—	Women have more	Women have fewer	Women have more
Number of female equivalents more	Women have more	Women have more	Women have more	—	Women have more
Male $N=$	567	200	198	80	406
Female $N=$	112	125	144	58	331

— = No relationship with industry group
(*Source:* CDS-I, $N = 2{,}304$)

significantly fewer/more male/female colleagues, subordinates, equivalent job holders etc. than men. For example, in column one, women in sales are no more or less likely than men to have a male or female boss, though they are more likely to have entered a job previously held by a woman. They do not differ from male managers in their number of female colleagues but they do have fewer male colleagues and subordinates, and are in environments where they work alongside more women equivalent job holders.

The simplest way to evaluate the extent of gender segregation from these Tables is by counting the number of column entries for any job area or industry group. So it is apparent that education is the most gender-typed job area, i.e. women are more likely to work with other women than are the male managers in education. And the least gender-typed area is Finance. Indeed, one of the cell entries in this job area – number of male equivalent job holders – is in the opposite direction to what one might expect; women in finance are *more* likely than men in finance to have *male* equivalent job holders. Scientific and technical management is the second least gender-typed occupation and administration the second most gender-typed. Table 9.12 shows equivalent analyses for industry group.

The most significant feature of this table is that the industry group with the highest concentration of women, government, is the most gender-typed, along with new services. The area with the smallest number of women managers, Industrial, is along with Commerce, the least gender-typed. One pessimistic interpretation of these findings is that it is only because women are a small almost 'token' force that they are in a position to work on equal terms with men. In the areas of principal growth in women's employment in management, namely the public sector and new industries, they are more likely to be working with other women. These two extremes could be a cause for pessimism if interpreted as evidence that women are caught between the devil and the deep blue sea of two alternative discriminatory trends in employment: tokenism and gender role-typing. Trend one is where a small number of women in an industry constitutes a token force, obviating or even impeding, the further growth of jobs for women (Kanter, 1977). Trend two is the tendency for developing concentrations of women in certain jobs and industries to cause these positions to become socially devalued, in the form of restricted organizational influence and inequitable material rewards (Barron and Norris, 1976; Hakim, 1979; Blau, 1984).

From our data we cannot comment directly on these trends, though we can look more generally at the quality of women managers' work experience and how, if at all, it differs from men's. So far, we have seen that women seem to have achieved equivalent status to men, but are few and far between in the very topmost reaches of management. We cannot say whether tokenism or gender role-typing are causes of this, though if women are achieving equality in the middle to senior levels, then there may be grounds for some optimism that they will increasingly break through the persisting discrimination barriers to reach the top echelons. We shall now turn to look at sex differences in career development and job conditions to investigate these questions further.

Here we shall overview sex differences in all the major areas that have concerned us in earlier chapters. However, as we have seen, in making such comparisons it is important that we compare like with like in terms of our sampling frame. In particular the sub-samples of BIM Members, BIM Fellows and women in the 'Other' category differ widely in status. So we have reanalysed sex differences on all our main measures to separate out sex from status. These are tabulated in Appendix 1 and we shall summarize the findings from each set of factors in terms of whether they indicate primarily sex or status differences.

First, on *biographical and demographic* factors we found there to be both major sex and status differences, but on the segregation and gender-typing measures we have seen more sex than status differences.

Next, looking at *career history* variables we also find more sex than status differences. Men have more upward status moves generally, but women have more employer changes, and, in particular, more out-spiralling moves. We noted in Chapters 3 and 4 that they have more changeable and self-directed careers than men. The self-description items on careers, reported in Table 4.3, suggested that women have rather different orientations to career moves than men. We argued then that their immediate, value-driven, opportunistic approach to job changing was more in keeping with the uncertainty surrounding managerial mobility than was the men's predominantly goal-directed, targeting approach. This is consistent with Marshall's (1984) assertion that women have different conceptions of careers and ambition to men. Our results certainly support part of this; they do have different career patterns and different reasons for job change. But although our analysis of work preferences and self-concepts does reveal important and wide ranging psychological differences between the sexes, as we shall see, they indicate that women are in general not less but *more* 'ambitious' than men.

In *work preferences* there are clear sex differences on two scales. Women consistently have higher needs for growth and lower needs for material reward than do men. There are also other indications of sex differences on the single item measures not included in these scales: women, especially those in the 'Other' category, care more about having congenial colleagues, a job that fits with life outside work, and which is in a good location. On the *self-concept* measures and items, we were able to contrast how managers rate themselves 'in general' and 'at work'. There are no evident sex differences on the adjustment or dominance scales, but on the remaining single item measures some further sex effects do emerge. Women are more likely than men to describe themselves as 'intellectual' and 'sociable' and less likely to 'keep feelings to myself'. It is of particular interest to note that several of these differences are reduced or disappear when we compare selves 'at work', implying that underlying sex differences in psychological dispositions are reduced by the socializing experience of work.

There are two items on the self-concept scales that deserve particular attention in this discussion. The first is 'show feelings readily' vs 'keep feelings to myself'. Women are more likely to show their feelings than to hide them in general, but at work they become more concealing, like their male counterparts. This finding reinforces the conclusions we drew in Chapters 2 and 8 that both women and men find their organizations lacking the support of well-designed human resource systems and consequently develop a watchful reserve. The second is 'ambitious' vs 'non-ambitious' where we find, contrary to Marshall's (1984) hypothesis, that women report themselves as slightly more ambitious than men both in work and in general. In an earlier analysis of this data (Alban-Metcalfe and Nicholson, 1984), in which only male and female members of the BIM were compared, a reversal by sex of the difference between self in general and self at work was found. Women in this sub-sample were more ambitious at work than in general, while men were less ambitious at work than in general. The question one should ask here, perhaps, is ambitious for what? If women have different work values and needs, then their ambition might be carrying them in quite different directions to men. If, as appears, they are more motivated by intrinsic factors (e.g. challenge) then it is conceivable that this lends women's ambition a more constant motivation force than men's whose greater focus on material rewards and particular career goals may generate less enduring or potent career motivation.[7]

Let us now turn to look at whether the perceived qualities of jobs and the experiences of job change differ for men and women. The differences we have noted in work preferences are not mirrored in differences in how they rate *job characteristics* (see Appendix 1) and what few differences there are seem to be as attributable to Status as they are to Sex. The high status Fellows, seem to have better jobs than their junior counterparts of either sex on most of these measures. Looking at *job change*, differences are more evident. Major differences occur on three scales: anxiety before last job move, satisfaction after last job move, and growth opportunities in present job. First, we can see that women are more anxious than men about their job moves – hardly surprising in view of the generally more radical nature of their moves, and the fact that women, much more than men, are entering environments dominated by the opposite sex. Women are also initially less satisfied than men in their new jobs, though they tend to find more growth opportunities. There is an apparent inconsistency here. Why are women less satisfied when they find the work more challenging?

One tentative explanation hinges on the importance of distinguishing the *content* from the *context* of managerial work since a job may be challenging in its content, but surrounded by unfavourable conditions – for example, in the way one is supervised, evaluated or related to. Individual item analysis from these scales supports this interpretation. Moreover, as we saw in Chapter 8 women have a more interpersonal orientation to job feedback, and seek out more help and support when settling into new jobs than do men. This might therefore explain why they are more attuned to deficiencies in the way their social adjustment is managed. Consistent with this are sex differences in the perceived *career influences* we looked at in Chapter 8 (see Table 8.12). Women are more likely than men to feel subject to impersonal criteria ('corporate planning' and 'length of service'), and at the same time much more likely to believe that they are discriminated against as a group ('prejudice'). Indeed, on this item they score significantly higher than men *in every one of our eight job areas and five industry group classifications*. Despite this they are generally more optimistic than men about their future career opportunities.

This is in keeping with the picture that has emerged of women having more mobile and radical careers than men and maintaining this pattern more continuously over the span of their working lives. An indirect sign of this is our finding that they have attained status equality within sub-samples, even though they are younger. Indeed, it is probably the case that the mechanistic and prejudicial criteria that women perceive as governing their future *within* their organizations is a contributory cause of their greater willingness to make radical job moves *out of* their organizations.

Before we summarize our overall conclusions about women in management it is important to consider one corollary explanation for sex differences that is widely held. This is that domestic responsibilities have an overriding impact on career paths and work experience and this accounts for more or less all of the differences between men and women managers. We have performed a series of further analyses on the data set to test this proposition: i.e. to separate sex from family situation. The results are complex[8] but the answer they give to the proposition is overwhelmingly negative. Sex and age effects have an overriding and independent significance. However, it is interesting to note that women with children have more rapid job changes and make more employer moves than single women or married women without children. This is the opposite to what one might expect, for earlier we argued strongly that domestic commitments were an impediment to women's managerial careers. However, there is another way of looking at this apparent contradiction, an explanation we have considered earlier in this chapter and in Chapter 2. If to have a family is an obstacle to women entering management, then those that do so may be exceptionally highly motivated to succeed. In other words they are a self-selected population of 'survivors'. Our data tentatively support this interpretation. Married women with children do tend to score high on dominance, adjustment, and need for growth, and one might predict from this that they also attain higher status managerial positions than other women. Our findings confirm that they do.

Conclusions

Any conclusions we draw about women in management are dependent upon how valid it is to generalize from our sample. First, in defence of the generality of our conclusions, it is evident that the size of this sample of women managers is unusually large, and drawn from every major job area and sector of employment. They match the men in their spread across these areas sufficiently to lend confidence to the comparisons we have been making. However, there remains the possibility of some bias from our primary use of a British Institute of Management sample to secure this diversity. The BIM is the major association for British male managers, but this is less true for women, who have a number of their own professional associations, some of which we used to double the size of our women's sample. For this reason two issues need to be considered. First it is important to evaluate differences between BIM and non-BIM women and second, we should try to consider in what ways motivation to join the BIM might differ for men and women. On the first of these issues, our analysis of inter-sample differences shows that neither the BIM nor the non-BIM women are demographically or psychologically exceptional. They are found in the same areas and industries and have broadly similar attitudes to each other. The only really clear difference is that the non-BIM women are younger and more junior, i.e. they are at an earlier career stage than the BIM women. The main fact of importance therefore is that women are probably under-represented in the BIM compared to their actual numbers in management generally, but they are one of the fastest growing sectors of the BIM membership.[9]

A corollary of this is that our profile of women managers, in terms of job areas, looks more like the male norm than is probably true of the real distribution of women in management. Another way of putting this is that there are, outside our sampling frame, large numbers of women in managerial jobs who would not perhaps call themselves 'managers' or consider applying for membership of any other of the management and professional associations we surveyed. For example, there are large concentrations of women in education, the health services, retail trades, catering, social services and other areas that are not highly represented in our sample. Where men are largely absent from such roles women may view their managerial status in a different light, and perhaps not think to proclaim their managerial identities by joining a general management association like the BIM.

So it seems that our sampling has entailed a bias towards the mainstream and male dominated areas of management. As such this bias makes our gender comparison all the more interesting and informative, for it carries the suggestion that some of the sex differences we have observed might have been greater still had we sampled more within the female dominated domains of managerial work. That being said, let us consider what are the main differences we have found. Eight general conclusions have emerged:

1 Women are to be found in all areas of management, but they are relatively scarce in the top echelons and at board level. Men overwhelmingly predominate in the top jobs.
2 There are some signs of gender segregation, by type of job area and industrial sector, but in many of the areas we sampled women are mainly working under or alongside men. However, we also have strong evidence here that women are increasingly entering male preserves and taking up jobs formerly occupied by men.
3 A career in management seems to mean sacrifices for women which are not equally demanded of men. The inequalities of the distribution of household labour mean that marriage and families are supportive structures for men, but obstacles for women. Consequently many women are foregoing marriage and family life for the sake of their careers.
4 Women are following different career paths to men. They are educated to a higher level and are occupying more specialist positions, at every level of the management hierarchy.
5 Women's career paths also differ from men's. In their patterns of job change they move faster between jobs and make more radical switches: typically employer-changing upward spiralling moves. They maintain this pattern more continuously throughout their careers than do men whose job moves become less radical as they age.
6 In keeping with their different career patterns and paths, women have different motives and attitudes to careers. They have higher growth needs, and are more self-directed and intrinsically motivated in career choices. Men are more materialistic, status oriented and goal-directed in their career orientations.
7 When we restrict our comparison to men and women of the same sub-sample (i.e. BIM Members), we find no differences in their managerial

status. The reason for this is probably a mixture of points 2–6 above. In other words, by travelling light, following specialist routes, making radical changes and trying to satisfy their needs for growth and development, women are not only finding their way to slots of equal status to men, but they are getting there earlier (remember, the women are significantly younger in every sub-sample).

8 Women are aware of the problems and challenges they face as 'travellers in a male world'. In particular they see themselves as discriminated against by organizational career policies. Perhaps this is one reason why they make the radical job moves that lead to the top. That way they are less subject to the prejudices of patriarchy, as they see it practised within organizations.

One overarching question remains. Does the future look bright for women in management? Will we see women entering male strongholds and achieving real influence, higher status levels, and managerial equality? Or are women condemned, on the one hand, to be perpetually under male domination through their restriction to a 'token' presence in key areas and industries, or, on the other hand, to be segregated into female ghettoes which subsequently become devalued?

These are early days for women in management, so it is probably unwise to come down firmly on either side of the optimism-pessimism divide we have drawn here. However, at this stage our results favour cautious optimism. Women are achieving equality, entering some of the bastions of male dominance, and achieving some footholds in the new and growing sectors of employment. To this extent, our results are telling a similar story to data on women in management that are emerging from the USA, where women have dramatically increased their representation in diverse areas over the last ten years or so (*USA Bureau of Labor Statistics*, 1980). The picture in Britain is much less clear cut, but we may be witnessing similar changes, at an historically later period and with less magnitude (Marshall, 1984), i.e. in this as in so many other areas, British society may be experiencing a 'slipstream' of cultural change from the New World to the Old.

Another way of trying to predict the future of women in management is by looking at the qualities of the environment in which change is occurring. Both our findings and evidence from other sources point to increasing volatility in the business world, the public sector, and, most importantly, managerial labour markets. The pace of mobility is continuing to quicken and the traditional notion of 'career' is being eroded by uncertainty. Radical job moves are being produced by revolutionary and evolutionary currents in society and by managers' unsatisfied needs for fulfilment, and in this context, women appear to be at the forefront of change. Their style and pattern of response is more in keeping with the climate of current times than men's. Of course the difference between the sexes' career development is not one of mutually exclusive types, but the distinctions are pronounced enough to justify the questions we have raised and the speculative answers we have offered.

If what we are seeing here is the beginning of a much bigger movement of women into management in the future, then, conceivably, many of the differences we have been describing may be slowly eroded by a process of convergence. Men may become more like women in attitudes and behaviour as their traditional norms become broken down by circumstantial forces and new values promulgated by female colleagues. On the other hand, in areas where women are able to establish a nominal presence approaching that of men, then the distinctiveness of their orientations could become sharper as they feel less constrained to conform to male cultural norms at work. In either event, though, we can predict that the growth of women's representation in the ranks of management will be a major force for change in organizational life.

10

Managerial job change – theory and practice

We chose to focus this investigation on a national sample of middle to top ranking managers for practical and theoretical reasons. First, managerial roles are growing in number, complexity and influence, and how they are discharged is of central importance to the health and wealth of society. Second, the variety and richness of their experience of change makes them ideally suited to testing and developing ideas about the relationships between the causes, processes and outcomes of transitions. These two premises embody the highly interdependent interests of practice and theory in the study of change.

It is also apparent that the issues of job change and career development at the heart of our study are of great personal importance to the managers we have surveyed. Much has been written about these topics in the management literature yet there has been a shortage of reliable and empirical data on them. We have sought to redress this deficiency, and at the same time to specify and substantiate the theoretical links between cause and effect in the Transition Cycle. In this final chapter we shall summarize the results of the research in three ways. We shall overview what we have learned about management in transition, then evaluate how this contributes to our theoretical knowledge about the transition process, and finally we shall consider the wider implications for theory and practice in a number of academic fields.

Management in transition

In Chapter 1 we reviewed the challenges facing modern management and set ourselves five objectives for this study. Now let us look back over these in the light of our findings.

The extent of change

Our initial portrayal of managers in the midst of change has been confirmed by what we have witnessed of their job mobility. Many are experiencing job changes with bewildering rapidity, while others are experiencing more measured and infrequent movement. But almost none is immobile. More important though than the rate of change is its radical character. More often than not job changes involve double or triple shifts of status, function and employer. These are not minor variations in the course of smoothly developing careers, but are genuinely radical alterations of roles and environments. We have recorded this in people's ratings of the changed demands they face and the amount of new learning required in initial adjustment, consistent with the truly dramatic switches of industry and occupational role titles we have seen that managers are commonly making. Those who change function are typically migrating between unrelated families of jobs, and those who change employers are characteristically making leaps between quite dissimilar commercial/industrial groups.

Looking through the lens of these findings at the social processes they reflect gives us an image of both evolution and turbulence. Evolution in labour markets is visible in the transfer from traditional materials-producing sectors to the growing information and service-providing sectors, in the trend of migration from large to smaller organizations, and in the high confidence many managers have in the transferability of their skills when making radical job moves. Turbulence is evident in the extraordinary frequency of moves to newly created jobs, the widespread reporting of job change because of company reorganizations, and the unpredictability of both in-company and out-company moves. By examining how the incidence of change and the reasons given for it vary across the managerial population sample, we have tried to move towards a deeper understanding of the nature and causes of job change. The origins of mobility we have located in the person and in the environment. Managers' motivational orientations toward job change are a closely blended weave of dispositions that might conventionally, but erroneously, be presumed to be inconsistent: idealism and opportunism, planfulness and impulse, intrinsic and extrinsic values, reactive and proactive choice. Personality and circumstance determine the balance of these elements. Gender, age, status, degree of managerial specialism, and motivational orientation are all interdependent and influential. Size and sector of company strongly affect the incidence of dissatisfactions, availability of internal career paths, and organizational stability and security. The causal origins of managerial mobility are thus too varied and interdependent to permit any simple generalizations, but many trends are clearly visible. Notably, high rates of radical change are to be found amongst women, younger junior status managers, specialists, value-pulled and dissatisfaction-pushed managers, and people in smaller and private sector organizations.

Managers' experience of job change

In Chapter 1 we raised the question of what managers feel when experiencing job change, and whether they find it onerous, dissatisfying, exciting or rewarding. One might expect that reactions would be as varied as the causes of change, but this is not the case. The experience is almost universally positive. Some anxieties precede job change, but these are not generally sufficient to justify mobility being characterized as a highly stressful life event. Stress is widely reported in the period immediately following job change but it is an experience so intertwined with highly positive reactions and satisfactions as to cast doubt upon the applicability of the stress concept, with all its connotations of impairment, to this kind of experience at the level of managerial employees (Fletcher *et al.*, 1979; Duckworth, 1985). We find stress being embraced as a welcome and indispensable part of the rewarding challenge of new job demands. One major reason for this is that most moves are upward in status – the most psychologically valued type of change, but even lateral moves are rated as overwhelmingly positive experiences. One type of job move, however, does stand out as a significant exception to this positive pattern: downward status moves. Though these moves are relatively scarce, the results imply that they are potentially injurious to managers' mental health. It is disturbing, if not surprising, to note that they are events which become increasingly common with age.

The positive experience of job change derives largely from the enlarged discretion, influence and challenge that new roles afford, but surrounding this psychologically all-important kernel of experience there is often to be found a layer of irritating, dissatisfying and sometimes even disturbing circumstances. These centre on a variety of factors. It is notable how unprepared managers are for the inefficiencies and insufficiencies of organizational systems, such as the quality of decision-making, training, communications and the like. That these should be found to be deficient is hardly surprising to anyone who has had experience of more than one organization, but that managers should expect to find things otherwise in their new settings suggests that many perennially entertain optimistic dreams of greener grass on the other side of the hill; dreams that no doubt help to sustain them through the risks and uncertainties of change. This point is especially noteworthy when one considers that these disappointments are being reported by many managers who are changing jobs *within* the same company. If such contextual factors are predictable sources of negative evaluation, it is less predictable and more worrying that so many managers should be equally negative about the social dimensions of their new settings: the boss and colleagues they must work alongside. They are particularly inclined to express negative judgements of senior management. As we shall see below, this often reflects the more general deficiencies that managers perceive in the organizational system, and which they are likely to lay at the door of top management.

The meanings of job change

The meanings of job change are highly personal. We would need to take an individualized biographical perspective to fully appreciate how they fit into the lives and careers of managers. It would also be desirable to monitor developments over an extended period of time to see what elements of change are sustained and which turn out to have been transient. This approach is closed to us here, but would be a worthwhile endeavour for future research. Here we have been able to take a broad view of general trends in the outcomes of job change and shed some light on individual differences. Of necessity we have been able to say more about short-term than long-term consequences, not just because our longitudinal method only encompasses a period of little over one year, but also because of the rapid rate of change experienced by many managers. For when some people are changing jobs every couple of years the long-term consequences of a single move would be difficult to discern by *any* methodology. Our results, however, do offer some scope for speculation about both short and long-run effects.

We have argued that job mobility can be a force for both stability and change: stability within the person in the continuous expression over time of elements of identity, and stability within the organization through the maintenance of established cultural custom and practice; change within the person through the transmutation or extension of personal qualities and dispositions, and change within the organization through the new adaptive behaviours that can reform roles and relationships. All these outcomes have been evident in our research. Let us look first at the personal sphere, and then at the organizational.

We have found unequivocal evidence that job mobility does change managers as people. Their needs, values and self-images develop, seemingly often pulled along in the wake of the expanded demands of their new roles, or in the case of an unhappy minority, depressed by diminutions of status and fulfilment. These have been interpreted as constituting, respectively, cycles of success (Hall, 1976), and for downward status movers, cycles of failure, in which job change is the mediating link. Our direct measures of these shifts show them to be small but significant over the limited time period we could measure them, though retrospective assessments of the impact of job change do tell us that managers recognize

211

job change to be an important cause of altered identity. Yet overall our findings argue for a cautious interpretation of personal change. The fundamental structure of personality is mostly unchanged and what we see are variations on the themes of individually anchored identity. In the midst of change managers find more security in their inner worlds than in the unpredictable externals of their environments. However, one of the most important and intriguing causal/mediating influences on stability and change we have found to be status. The indications are very strong that radical upward spiralling mobility is a primary route to the top, and that it is through the medium of altered status that much personal change is wrought.

Paradoxically, the propensity to innovate is one of the constants of managerial life, a product of the enduring characteristics of managers and their organizations. We see the roots of innovation in managers' powerful needs for challenge and success, and in the fluidity of the situational demands of the environments into which they move. These then are the constants that produce change, for it is apparent that when managers move into new roles many immediately enact behaviours which alter the configuration of tasks, procedures and relationships. But we must take care not to overestimate the magnitude or impact of innovation. The 'dynamic conservatism' of organizations is well known and understood (Vickers, 1965; Argyris and Schon, 1978; Brunsson, 1985), and one may expect most role innovations to be absorbed into the existing order without so much as a ripple to disturb the fundamentals of organizational design, goals and operations. There are many buffers against change in organizations, not least the adjustments a boss will make to accommodate the unaccustomed elements in the style of a new subordinate, circumscribing the scope of innovation, absorbing its impact and diffusing its power. However, if even only a small percentage of innovative acts have wider consequences for the functioning of enterprises then it would seem justifiable to say that job mobility, via role innovation, can be a revolutionary force within organizations.

The organizational context: the management of transition

If job change has the power to effect changes in identity as well as in organizational performance then how the transition process is managed has a vital bearing on the well-being and effectiveness of organizations. It would appear that few organizations recognize this. Human resource management seems to end at the point where it could most profitably begin, i.e. when the human resource has been secured. The new manager is a capital asset yet to be converted into a functional resource. This does not mean a lot of hand-holding and cosseting of newcomers is needed; quite the opposite, for most job-changing managers thrive on freedom and expanded horizons. But a good deal of attentiveness to the process of adjustment is required, to ensure that newcomers have access to the people and relationships they need to help them embed and amplify their personal effectiveness. It is important to receive reliable and informative feedback on what one is doing, so that one can acquire a sense of being empowered to act on one's environment in ways which will help to make it the kind of world one wants to work in.

So what happens in reality? Managers move into jobs whose intrinsic characteristics they value highly, but which are surrounded by relationships of doubtful conviviality and structures of manifest inefficiency. Resources and aids to learning and adaptation are negligible or valueless. Feedback from superiors on performance is largely absent. Future opportunities are as much at the mercy of uncontrollable exterior forces and biases as at the person's command through work behaviours. So how do managers respond to such circumstances? First, they immediately draw upon informal agencies rather than formal systems for insights into their new environments. Second, they cling to the known and familiar parameters of immediate work experience rather than approved organizational agents to appraise their performance. And third, they let their careers develop by following paths of least resistance or by unpredictable lurches into fresh opportunities rather than by planning and targeting job moves.

These effects are the product of four types of imbalance in organizational career development systems. One or more of the following seem to apply in most organizations. Career development is *neglected, restricted, mechanistic,* or *political*. Each of these is worth brief comment, for each holds distinctive dangers, as well as some potential advantages.

Without doubt the first of these, *neglect*, is the most general malady, where career development is largely left to the winds of chance and change. This may confer some advantages from a general 'ecological' perspective insofar as a natural selection operates amongst companies so that those that 'do it right' naturally reap the benefits of others' mistakes and neglect. But this optimistic view also requires the unfounded assumption of freedom of movement between organizations of differing types. The second malady, *restricted* career development, means that managers often are locked into organizations, or sub-systems of organizations, debarred from making the lateral or vertical moves that they would desire. The unintended advantage of restricted in-company movement from the individual's point of view, as we have seen, is that it acts as a stimulant to potentially advantageous out-company moves which otherwise might not have been contemplated. *Mechanistic* career development, where movement is determined by such criteria as length of service, age or qualifications, is the least common of the four maladies, but predictably an especially common feature of large bureaucratic organizations. The only advantage to mechanistic career development would seem to be that equality, if not equity, operates as a guard against uncontrolled power plays, though the evidence of organizational research suggests that bureaucracies are seldom immune from such politics (Crozer, 1964; Brown, 1978; Brunsson, 1985). And indeed the fourth and final feature is *political* career development, denoting the exercise of personal influence and favour in career systems. We have avoided calling this a malady, since political process is a necessary feature of all organizations (Pfeffer, 1981). At its best it is the 'mutual adjustment' on the basis of interpersonal knowledge and trust that can bind together organizational dynamics to good effect. But at its worst, it is the corrosive malady of unmoderated exercise of all the black arts of politics: nepotism, bribery, subterfuge, superficiality, concealed self-interest and gamesmanship.

Since this was not a study of organizations, but a study of managers, we cannot undertake a review of company practice in these areas, but through our sample we do receive some clear reflected images of organizational career development. From these, we see that there seem to be greater problems in almost all areas for medium-sized than for other organizations; neglect and restriction appear especially enervating maladies, leading managers to seek personal growth elsewhere.

We are not the first writers to point out that unthinking, unsystematic, and unplanned career development policies and practices have far-reaching and deleterious effects on organizational integration and development (Kaye, 1982; London and Stumpf, 1982); yet the management of job change remains one of the major unexploited areas of human resource development. The wider consequences for the effectiveness of the business and industrial community are worth pondering. If, as seems to be the case, failures in this domain are a cause of turnover amongst middle to senior ranking managers – i.e. it is often the best who are the first to leave the worst companies – and the direction of their migration is mainly toward smaller enterprises where they can find fulfilment more readily, then we arrive at an interesting population ecology model of organizational labour markets.

Large companies retain much managerial talent by locking them in with the golden handcuffs of job security, guaranteed benefits, incremental advancement and apparently diverse paths of opportunity, even though the opportunities for advancement to the highest levels may often be illusory for in-spirallers. Middle-size companies offer bright openings for hopeful managers but are unable to retain them after costly investments of time, training and experience to job mastery, because they fail to offer them real career development opportunities. Small companies provide fertile if

214

unstable ground for ambitious and self-directed managers, who either continue to migrate between small enterprises or move back into larger enterprises at higher levels than if they had experienced continuous careers within them. One could infer from this that managers' inter-organizational mobility achieves informally what formal career development systems fail to do. The 'stock' of managerial excellence is generally enhanced by this natural ecology of mobility, and the dynamism of organizations is maintained.

There is some truth in this analysis but we should not forget the costs. These accrue in three areas: (1) large companies which retain their managers but instead of capitalizing upon their talents inherit their growing disillusionment and underachievement; (2) companies of all sizes, but especially those in the middle-range, which attract and develop high quality managers but fail to retain them; they depart to discharge their cargo of knowledge and skills in some other port; a cost that is especially high for those companies who fail to recruit managerial talent into the organization at higher levels; (3) companies of all sizes which, because of their continual high rates of managerial turnover, are repeatedly paying for the cost of relatively unproductive time whilst new managers adjust to the demands of their jobs.

Women in management

Our further comment on women in management need only be brief since we have devoted a separate chapter to this issue. Much of our attention has focussed on the distinctiveness of their career paths, their situational constraints, and their motives. These findings add up to the conclusion that there is a profound sub-cultural difference in the organizational worlds of men and women managers. Superficially these are the same worlds – the same type of organizations and statuses – but the underlying differences in their experience and orientation seem crucial. The over-arching reason is that they are a small minority in management, and this has several important causes, corollaries and effects. Men's career paths have well charted traditions in management. Women come from different educational and biographical starting points, and consequently have to break in where others of their sex have not trodden before. Even if they face no overt discrimination at this point of entry it operates covertly in the sense that they are entering institutions whose terms of admission and criteria for acceptability have been set by the existing largely male population. Does this matter? It would not if one could assume that men and women do not differ in their interests, values and skills. We cannot make this assumption, and our findings have revealed some important differences in these areas.

Contrary to popular stereotypes, women seem to have in greater abundance than men many of the intrinsically oriented and achievement-directed values and motives that are conventionally identified with success. These we have speculated are attributable to the unequal obstacles that lie in the paths of men and women. In short, these drives form the basis for the self-selction and 'survival' of women into management. They need grit and determination to overcome the gender-selective barriers of cultural assumptions, the persistently unbalanced domestic division of labour, and the stifling inertia of organizational tradition. These same qualities are needed not just to break in but to survive, for women more often than not find themselves in male dominated work settings, though within these many are placed in ominously gender-segregated roles and supervisory responsibilities.

Upward status movement to upper-middle levels is available and achieved by women but the uppermost pediments of power are still male preserves, and this 'equality up to a point' is reinforced by women's lesser access to generalist roles, i.e. because the career ceiling of specialism is lower than for generalism. Women are highly conscious of prejudice and gender discrimination in their organizations' career development and decision-making practices, yet still they retain a higher degree of career satisfaction and optimism than their male counterparts. Is this delusory? No, it would seem to be justified by five trends we have observed in women's career development: (1) their continuing accession to formerly male roles; (2) their more spontaneous and 'existentialist' value-driven career orientations; (3) their greater willingness to undertake radical career moves; (4) their growing representation in the new organizations of post-industrial development; and (5) their retention of high levels of upward and radical career moves much later into their careers than men.

We have summarized these important differences in the career paths and patterns of men and women as suggesting that men represent the past and women the future of organizational society. The pattern of early mobility before settling down to a final resting place, much more a male than a female model, is more suited to a passing era when the loyalty of middle-aged managers could be taken for granted, and when organizations, their markets and wider environments evolved at a moderate pace in predictable ways. Such conditions no longer persist generally. To the extent that these conditions are diminishing then women represent the future face of management. Loyalty is increasingly a transacted commodity – to be given by managers to organizations only so long as their individual higher order needs are met and opportunity structures remain true to their promise.

216

Rapid change in the ecology of organizations means that today's managers need to have a broad view of these structures; they must anticipate future paths that extend beyond the boundaries of a role title, a single organization, or even a particular type of organization. The difficulties and dangers that women have to contend with to enter and survive in management have the effect of socializing them to fit this brave and uncertain new world of organizational life better than those men who expect the future to be like the familiar past, the past from which they and their senior male brethren derived their current norms and expectations.

At this point we shall put the managerial perspective to one side, though much more could be said about management in transition. It is time to consider the nature of transitions themselves from a more theoretical and experiential viewpoint. This will help us to understand better the management *of* transitions, by company agents, colleagues, and by the managers themselves as the centre of the change event.

Transitions and the study of organizational behaviour

Does this research bring us closer toward a theory of transitions capable of unifying insights from diverse other sources? We presented the model of the Transition Cycle (see Figures 1.1 and 5.1) as a descriptive and analytical device for this purpose, and argued that three assumptions are required to sustain this model: recursion, interdependence and discontinuity. Let us evaluate whether our findings justify these three assumptions.

Recursion, the idea that cycles are repeated events and that each cycle has a bearing upon the experience of the next, has been strongly in evidence in this study. Not only do managers experience multiple transitions in their career histories, but there are wide individual differences in the types of transition that they face. These can be linked to organizational characteristics and biographical factors. For reasons of circumstance, motivation, and demographically determined opportunity structure, some people are more prone to certain types of cycle than others. We can speculate that because of this people are socialized to develop differing expectations and varying willingness to undertake certain types of transition. Each cycle is thus a preparation for future change. Yet there would seem to be little justification for adopting a stochastic model which would predict chains of particular types of cycles, for we have seen that for some people sequences of active mobility reach a plateau of immobility earlier than others, and that some conventional incremental sequences of moves are unexpectedly disrupted by the need for radical change. We have identified many of the factors that generate these patterns, but our approach has been insufficiently idiographic to untangle all the skeins that weave the thread of individual career paths.

There would seem to be considerable scope for future case-based research to undertake this task, taking the Transition Cycle as a building block for analysing the shape of individual careers. This would help to shed further light on how the experience of particular sequences of cycles predispose people towards particular kinds of future experience of stability and change.

Interdependence *within* cycles has also figured in our analysis, i.e. how experience at one stage of the Transition Cycle affects experience at subsequent stages. The relationships are highly complex and again are mediated by individual and circumstantial differences. For example, anxiety before a change predisposes people toward personal change as a subsequent adjustment strategy, but both prior anxiety and subsequent adjustment are also linked with more enduring individual differences. Interdependence has also been evident in the association of high degrees of surprise at the encounter stage with subsequent role dissatisfaction and personal change rather than role innovation. There also seems to be a patterned interdependence of experiences around the Transition Cycle for particular types of job change; moves to newly created jobs and downward status moves represent examples of opposite extremes in this patterning. The unpredictability and high novelty of newly created jobs reinforces innovative adaptations and high satisfaction with outcomes, while enforced downward status moves produce both short and longer-term decrements in well-being: immediate dissatisfactions which convert into impaired psychological adjustment. But here too our understanding would be enhanced by more individualized research which articulated these linkages in greater detail.

Discontinuity, the assumption that different processes and experiences hold sway at each stage of the cycle, is also visible in our findings, so let us briefly summarize the predominant themes and events we have highlighted at each stage.

Commencing with preparation we can see that this is a misnomer if it means transitions consist of well-considered and planned events. Managers are ill-prepared for job changes insofar as they are manifestly often incapable of foreseeing them. Rationalistic theoretical models of choice and decision-making, such as expectancy-valence theory, would seem to have limited applicability under these circumstances. Yet neither would we want to advocate, as an alternative, a structuralist theory which says that the process is governed by exterior forces and opportunity structures. Our findings show that managers are low in their readiness for change, but this does not necessarily mean they are victims of circumstance rather than proactive agents. Between the theoretical extremes of planful choice and structural determinism lies the zone of bounded discretion and self-directed

218

opportunism. Effectiveness in this broad middle zone rests upon the resilience and resourcefulness of individuals, and we have seen that even through the most radical and unexpected of transitions managers retain high confidence in the transferability of their skills. When particular demands are highly novel and it is apparent that many new skills must be acquired, effective performance will be built upon the bedrock of much more general and enduring competencies, such as social and intellectual skills. These owe their existence to prior personal development and the continuity and growth that can be forged from familiar elements in past experiences. So we can infer that the apparently disparate raw materials of past experience of different types of Transition Cycle accumulate to give people a valuable platform of anticipatory socialization for departures into unexpected future change. The integrity of the personal system is the crucible for combining experience and for generating adjustment and competence.

Yet when we look at the encounter stage it seems that more particular and immediate experiences of change are not greeted with the familiarity they would seem to deserve. People are continually surprised and dismayed by their new environments. Their ability to find rewarding experience in the raw material of their new roles seems to be the saving grace of encounter, and derives from the generalized sense of competence we have been describing which buoys many people through the experience of change. Perhaps this is also partly responsible for the unjustified optimism they appear to have that their new organizations will be more efficient and their new co-workers more convivial than they actually find them; faith in oneself erroneously generalizes to faith in one's environment. It seems more justifiable to characterize this as disillusionment rather than stress. The first three months of settling in are described as stressful but a stress that is indissoluble from the most valued components of work experience. Stress = challenge in encounter, and therefore stress-coping = job performance. The low regard new role incumbents have for the organizational resources that are made available to them during this period no doubt has the effect of throwing them on their own resources and inducing them to resort to informal agents for sense-making in their new environments (Louis *et al.*, 1983). We shall be considering a little later what effects this may have upon the stabilization phase of the cycle.

The intervening adjustment phase we have characterized as the evolution of fit or misfit between person and role through the complementary but independent processes of personal change and role innovation. Their independence is more a theoretical than an empirical reality, for of the four modes of adjustment described in the theory of work role transitions (Nicholson, 1984) 'exploration' is more common than any other mode, i.e. simultaneous and correlated personal change and role innovation. People who are likely to adjust through role innovation are also likely to experience personal change, but as we have discussed earlier, the rhythms of these processes differ. Innovation is an immediate response to new demands, whereas personal change seems to have a longer time frame for development. In several respects these modes of adjustment are contingent upon individual characteristics and the form and circumstances of the transition, as predicted by the theory of transitions. For example, moving into roles of high discretion predisposes people toward role innovation as an adjustment strategy, and moving into roles of high novelty is associated with personal change. There is also some indirect support for the prediction that individuals with high desires for feedback will be more likely than others to experience personal change. As might be expected from this analysis, transitions of different types have differing outcomes. Radical job moves are accommodated by innovation, and bring consequent satisfaction. Jobs with enhanced growth potential heighten people's needs for growth.

There is also an intriguing suggestion that different aspects of identity are transmuted by forms of job change. Status changes, because they embody altered patterns of social relations, lead to perceived changes in the personality one displays to the world. Employer moves because they provide fresh social contexts in which no prior expectations of one's personality are held by others, require no comparable adjustment, but they do present the mover with a new normative environment of values and practices, hence we see people reporting changes in attitudes. It is also of interest to note that 'attitude' here seems to mean something more fundamental than the psychologist's general usage of the term, and personality something rather more mutable than conventional theoretical wisdom, for from people's reports the latter seem to be slightly *more* subject to change than the former. Our findings are indicative rather than conclusive in these areas. Further research is needed to verify these trends and identify the social and role processes that mediate the different types of personal change that accompany job mobility in its various forms. The role of mentors, role models, the demography and dynamics of the receiving work group, and organizational socialization practices are all potentially important mediating factors, but which have been analysed more theoretically in the literature than they have been systematically observed.

Finally, let us consider what the results allow us to say about the last two stages of the Transition Cycle: stabilization–preparation. First, some comment may be made about the general qualities of managerial work that have emerged here. The view we get is overwhelmingly favourable, in terms of the psychological and material benefits of managers' roles, and these benefits increase steadily in magnitude the higher one climbs the ladder of success. Top managers undoubtedly have the best jobs, on almost all dimensions. But there are more disturbing notes to this. In particular the organizational and management systems surrounding these highly satisfying roles are often deficient, especially in the quality of feedback and recognition that is given to people. Appraisal, evaluation and guidance are generally neglected, as we have described above, and this seems likely to be one reason for managers' disenchantment with their top management. We have also seen that managers' self-images, overwhelmingly positive when they describe themselves 'in general', shift in an ominously negative direction when they evaluate their 'selves at work'. The picture we receive is one of rather more guarded and mistrustful faces turned towards the world of work than is their natural outlook. It is not unreasonable to link this with the environmental shortcomings we have found in human resource systems, and the perceived deficiencies in the social sphere reported in the encounter stage. Heightened mistrust is an adaptive response to non-benign and unsupportive environments. We can see the reciprocal of this in how managers appraise their own stabilized performance, which seems to exhibit a much more caring involvement with functional and operational systems than with interpersonal concerns, and in particular, than with their subordinates. In short they themselves seem to be perpetuating the deficiencies in their organizations as 'humane' systems.

Yet, surprisingly perhaps, managers retain a high degree of commitment to their organizations. However, this should be regarded as 'provisional' commitment, for it seems that managers are vulnerable to sudden and unexpected disturbances, opportunities, and changes that lead them to quit. In short the 'loyalty' component of commitment is best regarded as a favourable mind-set rather than a reliable predictor of future behaviour. Another way of looking at stabilized relations between managers and their roles is through the notion of culture, for organizations differ considerably in the types of people they attract and retain, the kinds of responsibilities they give to managers, and the goals, resources and supports that make up the topography of their internal landscapes. The general image of hard-driving operationally-oriented rather than people-oriented cultures is generally confirmed by our analysis, though these emphases differ in important and subtle ways across organizations of different types. Large bureaucratic organizations in the public sector, and middle sized organizations of all types seem to create the least favourable environmental conditions. Life looks better in some of the newer growing areas of managerial employment.

To return to our starting point of attempting to evaluate the distinctiveness of processes at the four stages of the Transition Cycle, it cannot be said that we have fully addressed the issue. It remains an open question whether certain motivational, cognitive, or social theories are capable of illuminating equally what happens at all of the stages. It is probably also true to say that ours is not a full-blown stage theory in the sense that it depicts sharp and irreversible discontinuities between stages, or that each stage is inevitably experienced by all transitioners. In many areas these experiences shade into one another – for example encounters and adjustments may be multiple and concatenated – and we would expect there to be wide individual differences in the shape and content of Transition Cycles (see Nicholson, 1987a, for a review of these possibilities). However, it does seem that there are very many distinctive issues pertaining to the various temporal periods of the Transition Cycle for theory and research and it would seem advisable for future investigations to specify their field of vision accordingly. To make sense of an individual's experience of transition, a first step is to identify the person's temporal location in the change process and then to see what influences impinge in the present before tracing back to causal antecedents and forward to possible consequences. The notion of the Transition Cycle may prove to be a conceptual aid in such causal mapping.

Implications for theory and practice

Lifespan development

Work role transitions, in the language of lifespan development, are non-normative life events (Datan and Ginsburg, 1975). This means that for the most part they are neither clearly age-graded nor history-graded, i.e. with the possible exception of work entry and retirement they do not follow any evident culturally determined timetable for their onset. As we have seen they are continual, frequent, and often unpredicted happenings. We commented in Chapter 1 that the literature on lifespan development has generally had surprisingly little to say about job change, concentrating rather on major events outside the work sphere. The present research strongly argues for this deficiency to be remedied, for job changes clearly have great potential import for the development of identity. We have seen this in two ways. First, we have witnessed apparent alterations in people's work values, experiences, and psychological orientations with age and status. Second, we have seen how these differences may be due to the power of particular types of move to engender small but significant and cumulative shifts in these same qualities.

The more specific issue of how identity changes as a result of experiencing job mobility has been addressed in a number of ways. We have found support for those who argue for the general structural invariance of personality, as well as for the more phenomenological view that self-concepts are labile in response to environmental change. These two positions are not incompatible. In particular, we – like previous researchers – would wish to emphasize that people's needs for growth are responsive to expanded roles (Kohn and Schooler, 1983). This has an important corollary, for if needs for growth lead people to seek out further environmental change, by either innovation or selection (e.g. turnover in this sense is a form of selection), then we can see how any single job change can set in motion developmental sequences of change and growth. We have also noted the converse: how immobility or downward status moves can diminish psychological capabilities and shrink the horizons of perceived opportunity.

The writings of lifespan development which concern themselves with adults rather than children have much more to say about theory than practice, though it could be said that counselling psychology is the counterpart in practice to what is theory in the field of adult development. For counsellors, psychotherapists and other professionals helping people to make sense of and exert control over their lives, our research would recommend that the biographical analysis and self-exploration they undertake should accord a central role to reviewing discontinuities in work experience. The evolving course of people's relationship to work roles is an integral and central dimension of identity processes, and job changes are adjustment tasks of major life importance (Firth, 1985). Reviewing clients' past responses to work role changes might prove an effective means of extracting themes and variations in psychological states and coping strategies.

Careers

Many of these comments could be applied equally to the literature on careers for it is a field that has an overlapping domain of interest with lifespan development. Careers theorists are also concerned with life-long thematic patterns and the causes of change. It is even more surprising therefore, how little attention has been paid in writings on careers to individuals' experience of transitions, even though there is a great deal of theorizing about choice and selection processes as a product of person-environment fit/misfit (Brown and Brooks, 1984). Our research has some critical import for the study of careers. First, we can see that the conventional norms of occupational career development do not readily fit the experience of many managers, and that it is necessary to chart people's experience of multiple radical job changes to explain how the career that started at alpha later arrived at omega. Second, the unpredictability of many important changes makes rationalistic accounts of the choice process look implausible. Careers theory and research need to get closer to the

223

phenomenology of job change to do justice to the interaction of individuality, opportunity and external influence in career 'decision-making' at many more points of the journey between labour market entry and exit. To do this, merely mapping and matching individual and occupational characteristics is not enough – as a strategy for theory building its potential is extremely limited. Third, the ubiquitous phenomenon of the newly created job offers a particular challenge to careers theory. It encourages us to think about the process by which occupational roles evolve or are radically transformed over time, and to see role innovation as a constant force in the field of occupational and personal development. It also urges a greater theoretical and practical rapprochement between the study of careers and organizational processes, as we can now briefly consider.

We have argued that newly created jobs are the extreme manifestation of reciprocal change processes between individuals and organizations, whilst at the same time the ebb and flow of turbulence is buffered by stabilizing structures in both identity and institutions. Careers theorists seem to have put almost all their emphasis on the former, the individual, at the expense of the latter, the organization. Our results strongly recommend a more interactionist perspective for the study of career patterns and motives. It matters greatly whether mobility is in- or out-company, lateral or vertical, in terms of its causes and consequences, and for both the short- and the long-run of career development. It is entirely appropriate that psychologists in the careers field should devote their attention primarily to motivation and decision-making but this will always be unsatisfactorily abstract unless it is grounded in the context of what we know about organizations. The balance between initiation and response in career motives is inseparable from the balance of pressures and opportunities in organizations. This argument applies as much to stability as it does to change. For example we have seen that the relationship between career satisfaction and immobility is dynamic. For people who expect and desire change, failure to move jobs produces decrements in adjustment, which may in turn affect attitudes to future mobility. In passing, one may note that failure to experience an expected change could also be considered to be a transition. At the same time we have seen that career 'plateauing' may or may not be associated with career frustration (Veiga, 1981). Whether it is depends on where you are and how you got there. However, our results do support the increasing emphasis in the careers literature on self-esteem and self-efficacy. We would advocate that this be accompanied by closer attention to the complement of these concepts in organizations, i.e. the presence or absence of discretion, feedback and social support.

The implications of our findings for career practitioners – people who are charged with the responsibility of aiding the career decision-making process

224

– are twofold. First, the general insights we have sought to offer into the career motives, organizational influences, and career patterns of managers, can help to replace conventional but inaccurate paradigms of managerial careers with a new realism. This means helping managers to come to terms with the kinds of uncertainty and variety that typify life within and between organizations. Second, the conceptual framework of the Transition Cycle supplies an agenda for reviewing the immediate position of the client in vocational guidance or careers counselling; i.e. it is a method for analysing past patterns of experience and targeting the future.

Industrial/Organizational Psychology

This large and diverse field incorporates many of the concerns we have highlighted in this book, but the predominant tradition has been to approach them rather differently than we have here. We observed earlier that I/O Psychology has generally seemed more comfortable assuming stabilized rather than changing relations between people at work, and more prone to ahistorical than historical treatments, looking for law-like relationships between abstracted dimensions and factors. There are signs of movement in many areas of the field away from this paradigm, as scholars show increasing interest in change processes in people and organizations. However, we would hope the present study could contribute to knowledge in a number of familiar and well-researched areas by suggesting the possible value of applying a transitions perspective. Occupational stress is one such area, which we have seen has a quite different character in the period leading up to change than in the period following. Our results also support those who have suggested that the concept may have been overapplied in the field of management. When stress is so sought after and integral to the most valued aspects of occupational roles, then perhaps we need a different language from that of stress-coping to describe how people appraise and operate on themselves and their environments. Job design is another well-researched area with which we have been concerned. I/O Psychology has tended to be more absorbed with jobs at the lower more routinized end of the spectrum than with managerial work, though we would expect that many of the conclusions we have come to about adapting to novelty and discretion are widely generalizable. Indeed, the empirical literature on job redesign does appear to generally complement what we have found (Wall and Martin, 1986). However our work suggests there is room for some synthesis between job design theory and another major sub-field of I/O Psychology, leadership, for it does seem that, especially for managerial work, supervisory relations play an important part in the 'social construction' of role requirements. Innovation is a related factor of great moment here, but a

225

topic that has suffered serious neglect in the I/O Psychology literature (West *et al.*, 1986).

Recruitment, selection, placement, performance appraisal and kindred human resource management systems have enjoyed a long history of high quality research, though often more concerned with the technology of assessment than with more general theoretical aspects of person-organization linkages (Mowday *et al.*, 1982). The view we have taken of these is that these personnel measurement and control methods need to be seen within the context of changing relationships between people and organizations. This connects with the fast growing literature on organizational socialization (Feldman, 1976; Frese, 1982; Jones, 1986). Socialization has always been a quintessentially social psychological concept, though there seems to have been an implicit division of labour between the social science disciplines, with psychology restricting its interests to child socialization and sociology to adult socialization. Because of this the study of organizational socialization has been flourishing in the interdisciplinary environment of the business schools rather than in academic departments of applied psychology, which perhaps accounts for its neglect in relation to the traditional concerns of I/O Psychology. We would like to imagine that the present research could help to stimulate conceptual interchange between the study of human resource management systems and socialization processes. To assess the efficacy of these systems it is essential to know how they are complemented, undermined or overridden by the informal processes of adjustment. This means that the psychological demand characteristics of roles, the demography of work groups, the presence of agents and informants, and the expectations and needs of the person at each stage of the Transition Cycle, are all critical variables in predicting the outputs of systems designed to assess, review and control performance.

This is by no means an exhaustive review of the areas of I/O Psychology to which this research could be related. Indeed we would go so far as to say that a transitions perspective could be usefully applied to any part of the discipline that is concerned with individuals' responses to organizational environments. Job satisfaction, goal-setting, rewards and punishments, absence and accidents, adjustment to technological change and many other topics might be complemented by awareness of people's location on cycles of change and their adjustment processes.

The study of organizations and management

The individual manager's experience of change has been our main concern in this book, but we have repeatedly drawn attention to how this must be interpreted in relation to organizational contexts. It is an unfortunate but understandable fact that students of organizational behaviour tend to gravitate to one of two camps: those for whom organizational structure and process are relegated to the status of background variables, and those for whom individual differences are a source of unwanted and unexplained variance in the interpretation of more macroscopic forces and movements. Our methodology has placed us closer to the former psychological orientation rather than to the latter sociological position, but our research does identify areas in which a transitions perspective might offer scope for a much needed harmonizing of these two approaches.

The concept of organizational culture, although currently in danger of becoming fashionable to the point of disrepute, does offer a way forward. Culture is a necessarily fuzzy concept, denoting the shared values, meanings, assumptions and customary forms of conduct in a collective, but its value lies in its capacity to provide an important link between structure and process, and between individual and institutional forces. Role transitions are a primary means by which organizational systems renew, maintain and transform themselves. Movement into, through and out of the system is one of the most common and important sources of organizational learning (Hedburg, 1981; Sathe, 1985), for it facilitates the transmission of knowledge and skills, the incorporation and shedding of ideas and behaviours, and the redistribution of power and uncertainty. Role succession is the means by which the organization, as a socializing system, consolidates and extends its influence and thereby reproduces its culture. Thus we find most research on management succession has tended to evaluate the effects of job change on organizational performance (Allen and Panian, 1982), but from the research we have reported in this book we would argue that an alternative view needs to be balanced with perspectives that emphasize the hegemonic potency of organizations. Individuals are not just receptive media for the imprint of socializing forces but also are agents for change in their own rights, for, as we have seen, role innovation is a ubiquitous and potentially revolutionary force in organizations. Another way of putting this is that role change heightens, temporarily at least, uncertainty within the organizational system. So the net effects of job mobility will depend upon a number of the factors we have been looking at: (1) the rate of job change; (2) the form it takes; (3) the presence or absence of effective socializing structures and agents; (4) the motives and skills of the people changing jobs; and (5) the degree of latitude or control the individual can claim in the new role. The totality of these forces could be termed the 'mobility culture' of the organization and its configuration determines how job change reinforces or transmutes the organizational system. In short, organizational cultures contain the origins of their own future states.

Let us consider how this occurs. First, the *rate of job change* is directly controlled by the promotion and training practices of organizations, and by the level at which the organization is confronted with the need to replace personnel who leave the system. Second, the *form of change* has similar determinants, but additionally depends upon recruitment policies and practices, e.g. whether criteria for entry admit novices or experienced practitioners; and the existence of structural barriers/opportunities for movement, e.g. how readily individuals can transfer across functional or hierarchical internal boundaries. Third, the effects of *socializing structures and agents* depend on several factors: personnel induction-transfer programmes, socio-technical design, and organizational demography. These determine how much individuals are the targets of directive communication, how much they depend upon others for guidance on role performance, and how exposed they are to influential sub-cultural norms. Fourth, *the characteristics of the individuals changing roles* might appear to be the least organizationally dependent element in the mobility culture, but of course this transacts with the other elements we have been considering. In particular one can see that the motives and interests that accompany and sometimes steer people through in-company job changes, have already been shaped to some degree, by their prior exposure to their present organizational cultures. And for those entering the organization from outside one can see how recruitment processes exhibit a variety of conscious and unconscious biases favouring or discouraging the selection of people with self-concepts that are consonant with the organization's self-image. Fifth, a transactional perspective also needs to be adopted to understand the balance of *latitude and constraint in the new roles* people occupy, especially in managerial positions where role requirements are not entirely predetermined, but are the product of a 'negotiated order' (Strauss, 1978) which emerges out of interactions with superiors, colleagues and subordinates. But it would be a mistake to overextend this argument, for clearly organizations differ widely in how discretion is internally distributed (Jaques, 1976). In some, high decision latitude is a property, a reward almost, for achievement through the hierarchy, i.e. in such organizations high decisional scope is typically only a feature of the topmost jobs. In other types of organization 'mutual adjustment' is a much more customary mode of decision-making and performance at all levels of the system. These inter-organizational differences are the product of both structural aspects of design (Mintzberg, 1979) and cultural properties (Schein, 1985).

Kanter's (1984) contrast between 'segmentalist' and 'integrative' organizational cultures is a notable recent attempt to analyse how structural and cultural factors interdependently determine organizational performance, and she has emphasized how what we have termed the 'mobility culture' is a critical mediating link between these factors. Our research shares with Kanter's the implication that organizations need to be more aware of the content of their mobility cultures, and of their unintended and unplanned consequences. This is not to assert the unduly sanguine view that organizations can control and shape their structures and cultures at will. It is apparent from our research that the kinds of environments organizations inhabit, their past histories of growth, and the constraints imposed by ownership and size, all can exert an influence over the mobility culture which it would be difficult if not impossible to subvert or change. However, it seems likely that this question is not one that is usually even considered within organizations. People do not know what kinds of change are taking place within their own environments, still less what elements of the mobility culture might be susceptible to some form of control.

One main practical implication of the theory and research in this book is that organizations can readily undertake this task. The Transition Cycle may have some potential utility as a mapping tool, helping to point the way for the diagnosis of mobility cultures, and the formulation of action that will enhance individual and organizational effectiveness. Aggregating the rates and types of movement within and between sub-units would provide a more detailed and informative kind of accounting of human resource utilization than the simple statistics of recruitment and turnover which are customarily gathered. This would help to diagnose areas of undesirably high stability and instability, points where organizational learning or training investment are not being optimized, and blockages in the flow of expertise between and across levels of the total system. Using the model of the Transition Cycle more individualistically to investigate the qualities of people's experience in preparing for, encountering, adjusting to and achieving stabilized performance in new work roles, would also help to reveal the inner workings of the organizational culture and how it is being resourced by formal management systems and informal practices. This would help to expose discrepancies between the needs of valued personnel and the capacities of roles, supports, information systems and the immediate micro-culture to fulfil them. Such diagnostic application of a transitions perspective is likely to be especially valuable where a high premium is placed on team-building or sub-unit excellence, as has been recognized in recent studies of the effectiveness of Research and Development groups (Gerpott *et al.*, 1985).

Conclusion

It has become customary to the point of cliché for academics to conclude their papers and monographs with evidently self-serving recommendations for further research in their specialist areas. Unfortunately we can find no reason to break with this practice here, for we see the study of transitions as in its infancy, but with enormous potential for connecting theory with practice and for cutting across disciplinary boundaries in social science. Large scale investigations like ours are important in the early stages of development of a research area, by helping to establish descriptive and analytical frameworks, but smaller scale and more detailed studies are needed to specify particular processes, test and refine hypotheses, and to further develop concepts and theories. Many of the relationships we have observed directly or inferred here need to be cross-validated in other settings, i.e. within different cultures and with different occupational groups, and so help to establish the boundaries of generalizability from the present research.

It is important also to note that the study of transitions can benefit from a diverse range of approaches. Our work has targeted a large sample of managers through longitudinal survey methodology. It would also be profitable for future studies to take organizations as the units of analysis to investigate empirically the characteristics of mobility cultures and their effects. There is also a need for qualitative methods and biographical case studies of the lives and transitions of individuals and organizations, to enrich our understanding of how change processes are connected over time. Last, but not least, intervention and action research methods have considerable potential in the transitions field. One could say these are already plentiful under other guises, in fields such as vocational guidance and organization development, but the processes of adaptation to change receive patchy, unsystematic, and non-comparable treatment in these areas and would be helped, we would argue, by a clearer conception of the nature of the transition process.

There is no reason to expect work role transitions to become less frequent or important in the future; quite the contrary. In the late 1980s we stand amid a quickening flow of social, organizational, and informational change that affects almost every area of our lives. New technology promises to continue to revolutionize at an accelerating pace the way we work and live. Major economic, political and ecological changes are prophesied on a global scale, and there is much talk of how our survival will depend upon our ability to adapt and innovate. The study of transitions is a necessary response to this realization.

Appendix

One-way ANOVAs and LSDs (Scheffé tests*) on 5 samples

Samples: 1 = Women BIM Members   4 = Men BIM Members
            2 = Women BIM Fellows   5 = Men BIM Fellows
            3 = Women, Other

*Significant ($p < 0.05$) inter-group differences

Variable	F Ratio	Male vs female						Within female			Within male
		1/4	1/5	2/4	2/5	3/4	3/5	1/2	1/3	2/3	4/5
Biographical											
Age	114.68***	<	<	ns	ns	<	<	<	ns	<	<
Family	202.04***	<	<	<	<	<	<	<	ns	ns	<
Education	11.84***	>	>	ns	ns	ns	ns	ns	>	ns	ns
Professional qualifications	8.67***	ns	ns	ns	ns	>	>	ns	ns	ns	ns
Occupational											
Status	39.21***	ns	<	>	ns	<	<	<	<	>	<
Company size	1.58 ns	ns	ns	ns	ns	ns	ns	ns	ns	ns	ns
Role type (general)	53.68***	<	<	ns	<	<	<	ns	>	>	<

One-way ANOVAs and LSDs (Scheffé tests) on 5 samples

Samples: 1 = Women BIM Members   4 = Men BIM Members
          2 = Women BIM Fellows   5 = Men BIM Fellows
          3 = Women, Other

| | | *Significant (0.05) inter-group differences | | | | | | | | |
| | | Male vs female | | | | | | Within female | | |
Variable	*F* Ratio	1/4	1/5	2/4	2/5	3/4	3/5	1/2	1/3	2/3
Sex segregation										
Boss (female)	20.89***	>	>	ns	ns	>	>	ns	ns	<
Colleague help (")	16.58***	>	>	ns	ns	>	>	ns	<	ns
Previous job holder (")	14.72***	ns	>	ns	ns	>	>	ns	<	ns
Number of male colleagues	11.34***	<	<	ns	ns	<	<	ns	ns	ns
Number of female colleagues	2.20 ns	ns	ns	ns	ns	ns	ns	ns	ns	ns
Number of male subordinates	17.16***	<	<	ns	ns	<	<	ns	ns	ns
Number of female subordinates	6.54***	>	ns	>	>	ns	ns	<	ns	>
Number of male same job title	4.13**	ns	ns	ns	ns	ns	<	ns	ns	ns
Number of female same job title	18.29***	>	>	ns	ns	>	>	ns	<	<
Career history										
Number of employers	4.18**	ns	ns	>	ns	ns	>	ns	ns	ns
Employer changes	4.01**	ns	ns	ns	ns	ns	ns	ns	ns	ns
Up status changes	13.76***	ns	<	ns	ns	<	<	ns	>	>
Function changes	0.20 ns	ns	ns	ns	ns	ns	ns	ns	ns	ns
In-spiralling	9.97***	<	<	ns	ns	<	<	ns	ns	ns
Out-spiralling	6.08***	>	ns	>	>	ns	ns	ns	ns	ns

e-way ANOVAs and LSDs (Scheffé tests) on 5 samples

mples: 1 = Women BIM Members   4 = Men BIM Members
        2 = Women BIM Fellows   5 = Men BIM Fellows
        3 = Women, Other

*Significant (0.05) inter-group differences

		Male vs female						Within female			Within male
riable	*F* Ratio	1/4	1/5	2/4	2/5	3/4	3/5	1/2	1/3	2/3	4/5
ture expected											
change											
ties in post	5.82***	ns	>	ns	ns	ns	>	ns	ns	ns	>
nction	9.91***	ns	>	ns	ns	ns	>	ns	<	ns	>
omotion	9.49***	ns	>	ns	ns	ns	>	ns	ns	ns	>
ployer	6.03***	ns	>	ns	ns	ns	>	ns	ns	ns	>
loss	2.53*	ns	ns	ns	ns	ns	ns	ns	ns	ns	ns
st job change											
or anxiety	29.10***	>	>	ns	ns	>	>	ns	ns	ns	>
velty	4.29**	ns	>	ns	ns	ns	ns	ns	ns	ns	ns
scretion	2.16 ns	ns	ns	ns	ns	ns	ns	ns	ns	ns	ns
tisfaction	10.17***	<	<	ns	ns	<	<	ns	ns	ns	ns
rsonal change	3.14*	ns	ns	ns	ns	ns	ns	ns	ns	ns	ns
characteristics											
owth											
portunities	6.19***	ns	ns	>	>	ns	ns	<	ns	>	<
edictability	3.77**	ns	ns	>	ns	ns	ns	ns	ns	ns	<
wards	6.22***	ns	<	ns	ns	ns	ns	ns	ns	ns	<
ngenial people	1.26 ns	ns	ns	ns	ns	ns	ns	ns	ns	ns	ns
n-work fit	4.38**	ns	ns	ns	ns	>	>	ns	ns	ns	ns
cation	6.22***	ns	<	ns	ns	ns	<	ns	ns	ns	<

One-way ANOVAs and LSDs (Scheffé tests) on 5 samples

Samples: 1 = Women BIM Members   4 = Men BIM Members
          2 = Women BIM Fellows   5 = Men BIM Fellows
          3 = Women, Other

		*Significant (0.05) inter-group differences								
		Male vs female						Within female		
Variable	F Ratio	1/4	1/5	2/4	2/5	3/4	3/5	1/2	1/3	2/3
Work preferences										
Growth and development	15.02***	>	>	>	>	ns	>	ns	>	>
Predictability	3.23*	ns	ns	ns	ns	ns	ns	ns	ns	ns
Rewards	12.76***	<	<	<	<	ns	ns	ns	ns	ns
People	13.85***	ns	ns	ns	ns	>	>	ns	>	ns
Non-work fit	12.85***	>	ns	ns	ns	>	>	ns	ns	ns
Location	4.06**	>	ns	ns	ns	>	ns	ns	ns	ns
Self concept										
Adjustment	3.41**	ns	ns	ns	ns	ns	<	ns	ns	ns
" (at work)	5.02***	ns	ns	ns	ns	ns	<	ns	ns	ns
Dominance	5.34***	ns	ns	ns	ns	ns	<	ns	>	ns
" (at work)	4.73***	ns	ns	ns	ns	ns	<	ns	>	ns
Intellectual	12.09***	>	ns	ns	ns	>	>	ns	ns	ns
" (at work)	9.16***	>	ns	ns	ns	ns	>	ns	ns	ns
Trusting	2.31 ns	ns	ns	ns	ns	ns	ns	ns	ns	ns
" (at work)	3.95**	ns	>	ns	ns	ns	ns	ns	ns	ns
Sociable	11.48***	>	>	ns	ns	>	>	ns	ns	ns
" (at work)	2.69*	ns	ns	ns	ns	ns	ns	ns	ns	ns
Keep feelings to self	15.98***	<	<	ns	ns	<	<	ns	ns	ns
" (at work)	2.84*	<	ns	ns	ns	ns	ns	ns	ns	ns
Creative	2.22 ns	ns	ns	ns	ns	ns	ns	ns	ns	ns
" (at work)	2.34 ns	ns	ns	ns	ns	ns	ns	ns	ns	ns
Life uncertainty	0.13 ns	ns	ns	ns	ns	ns	ns	ns	ns	ns
" (at work)	1.29 ns	ns	ns	ns	ns	ns	ns	ns	ns	ns
Career development perceptions										
Performance	3.59**	ns	<	ns	ns	ns	ns	ns	ns	ns
Politics	1.91 ns	ns	ns	ns	ns	ns	ns	ns	ns	ns
Luck	2.08 ns	ns	ns	ns	ns	ns	ns	ns	ns	ns
Corporate planning	2.95*	ns	ns	ns	ns	ns	>	ns	ns	ns
Prejudice	30.65***	>	>	ns	ns	>	>	ns	ns	ns
Total significant differences (out of 65)		24	29	9	7	23	36	5	12	9

Notes

1 Men and women in transition

1 A more elaborated account of these interdependencies and how they relate to the notion of the Transition Cycle is provided in a forthcoming publication by one of the present writers (Nicholson, 1987 a, in press).
2 Advocates of Japanese management models, even in modified form (Ouchi, 1981) are swimming against this tide. The cradle to the grave paternalism of the Japanese corporation has always been antithetical to our cultural norms and seems decreasingly viable as a model of careers in turbulent and mobile Western societies.
3 Of course, an alternative is to 'change worlds' by moving to a different one, quitting one setting for another – the 'Exit' option in Hirschman's (1970) analysis of the turnover process (see also Watson and Garbin, 1981).
4 Similar models of phasic adaptation to work are to be found in Feldman (1976), Van Maanen (1976) and Katz (1980). This formulation differs from its predecessors in a number of respects, especially in the three assumptions we have set out, which embody a contingent treatment of the content of experience and behaviour at different stages. See also note 1 above.
5 This model has proved popular in other areas, notably reactions to unemployment. There are several problems with these extrapolations, not least the empirical basis for the original model and the validity of its assumptions, and its generalizability to other contexts and behaviours (cf. Hartley and Fryer, 1983).
6 The reader is referred to two series of volumes published by Academic Press: *Life Span Developmental Psychology* and *Life Span Development and Behavior*. These are regularly published collections of high level essays exploring specialized areas of theory and research into adulthood.
7 A limitation of these studies is that they record changes in job and personal characteristics over time but without any record of actual job changes between points of measurement. The processes of selection vs. socialization therefore have to be inferred from statistical analysis rather than from recorded behaviours.
8 By one reckoning the literature is very large, but diverse and diffuse (cf. Allen and Van de Vliert, 1984). Within this breadth very few writers pay close atten-

tion to *work* role transitions, though the topic is attracting increasing interest.

9 Our primary interest was in the outcomes of transitions and we targeted managers as a population on the assumption that their job changes would be more varied in form and outcome than other groups', such as industrial workers. A managerial sample was thus preferred partly because it offers opportunities for theory testing and development.

10 Names and addresses taken by random quota from alphabetically ordered lists of Members and Fellows.

11 This figure actually underestimates the numbers of women in BIM. Membership lists were incomplete at the time of the survey. In 1986 there were an estimated 1,699 women in a total membership of 66,228.

12 Dr Beverly Alban-Metcalfe of the Nuffield Centre for Health Services Studies, University of Leeds was responsible for this uniquely valuable extension of the original sample. See Alban-Metcalfe (1984 and 1985) for further discussion of issues in the career development of women managers.

13 The attained response rates for the mailed BIM samples were as follows:
    Members: male 34%; female 45%;
    Fellows: male 41%; female 49%.
These are underestimates of actual response rate, since an unknown number of questionnaires will have failed to reach sample members whose addresses on the BIM mailing list were incorrect or out of date. The geographical distribution of the BIM sample was as follows:

South East England	31%
Greater London	16%
North West England	9%
West Midlands	8%
South West England	8%
Scotland	6%
East Midlands	5%
Yorkshire and Humberside	6%
Northern England	4%
East Anglia	3%
Wales	3%
Northern Ireland	1%
Overseas	1%

See Alban-Metcalfe and Nicholson (1984) for details of occupational and other characteristics.

14 The CDS-II sample was derived from the CDS-I respondents who volunteered their names and addresses in response to a request at the end of the survey for people to participate in a follow-up survey; 1,700 (76%) did volunteer, and the response rate for the CDS-II was therefore 65% of this follow-up sample. Given the high mobility rate of the sample there is reason to assume that this underestimates the real response rate, since an unknown number of questionnaires

will have failed to reach people who had moved on. There are indications this could have been a sizeable number; for example it can be inferred from the fact that far fewer of the CDS-II than the CDS-I respondents' last job change was an employer move, 37% vs. 52%. There are no personal or job factors in the data that might account for this difference, so the simplest explanation is that many of our non-responding volunteers for the CDS-II had moved on, address unknown, diminishing the remaining proportion of employer changers whom we were able to reach.

15 See Alban-Metcalfe (1984) for further details of free comment data.

2 A managerial profile

1 The interquartile range for men was 39–54 years and for women, 32–47 years.
2 A detailed breakdown of these and other categories is to be found in Alban-Metcalfe and Nicholson (1984). See also summaries in Chapters 3 and 9.
3 We assessed our measures of status in various ways, experimenting with various computed indices to take account of size and length of organizational hierarchy (by combining levels 'up' and 'down'). These indices were compared with a more context free measure of status from the CDS-II, a single item asking people: 'If 20 represents the very highest rung in a ladder of success in your occupation or profession and 1 represents the very lowest level, what number would you say represents your current level?' Analysis revealed that our simple measures of levels 'up' was the best single measure, with the effects of organization size controlled statistically through multiple regression or analysis of covariance methods, rather than through any of several composite computed indexes we experimented with.
4 The time between the surveys varied since returns from Time 1 were spread over a two month period, and returns from Time 2 were similarly distributed.
5 This inventory was compiled by modifying some widely used life events scales reported in the literature. See, for example, Holmes and Rahe (1967).
6 Given the multiplicity of measures used in this study it is not possible to reproduce them all here, but the reader is invited to write to the authors for any further details that may be required beyond those that are supplied in text, tables and notes. This work preference scale was adapted from Bailyn (1980) who in turn had adapted her scale from Rosenberg(1957). The present scale consists of 17 Likert-type scales on a 5-point 'very important' to 'of no importance' response format.
7 Principally by factor analysis and scaling methods. These were conducted on sub-sets of the sample, and cross-validated on independent sub-sets.
8 Cronbach's alpha at Time 1 = 0.62, and at Time 2 = 0.69.
9 Cronbach's alpha at Time 1 = 0.65, and at Time 2 = 0.67.
10 Cronbach's alpha at Time 1 = 0.58, and at Time 2 = 0.57.
11 Likert-type response 5-point scales from 'very good' to 'very poor'.
12 Discrepancies were measured by collapsing the 'very important/important' and 'of little importance/of no importance' categories on the work preference scales

and the 'very good/good' and 'very poor/poor' categories on the work characteristics scales (giving values of 1 to 3 on both) and then subtracting work
characteristic ratings from work preference ratings. A figure of 0 indicated a
good fit, 1 a fair fit and 2 a poor fit.

13 Results not shown here; the sample exhibited high overall mean scores on the
Cook and Wall (1980) commitment scale, and Lodahl and Kejner's (1965)
work involvement scale.

14 Using a semantic differential format: bipolar four point response scale of the
form 'tense (very, quite) – relaxed (very, quite)', with a fifth 'not sure'
category.

15 T-test differences significant at the < 0.05 level, two-tailed test.

16 The scale of adjustment is derived from the following items: relaxed vs tense;
happy vs sad; fulfilled vs frustrated; confident vs unsure; optimistic vs pessimistic;
and contented with myself vs discontented with myself. Cronbach's alpha at
Time 1 = 0.72; Time 2 = 0.71. On this scale the difference between 'in general'
and 'at work' scores was highly significant ($p < 0.001$).

17 These groupings are based on category systems used in the literature (e.g.
Super, 1981; Lawrence, 1984) and on our desire for roughly equal groupings for
analytical purposes.

18 Multiple analyses of variance were used, using organization size as a covariate
(see note 3).

19 Scaled from self-perception items timid vs forceful; confident vs unsure;
ambitious vs unambitious; controlling vs casual: Cronbach's alpha at Time 1 =
0.60 and at Time 2 = 0.64.

20 Work characteristic items were scaled identically to work preference items (see
notes 8–10 above) with Cronbach alpha coefficients as follows:

	Time 1	Time 2
Growth	0.78	0.76
Predictability	0.69	0.69
Rewards	0.59	0.64

21 The time span of our longitudinal data is not sufficient to test this hypothesis
adequately, though some confirmatory indications are in evidence (see Chapter
6). Other studies over a longer time period (Kohn and Schooler, 1983;
Mortimer and Lorence, 1979; Brousseau, 1983) support this interpretation.

22 One of the items from a series of questions in the CDS-II designed to generate a
new measure of Snyder's (1974) concept of 'self-monitoring'. Since these items
failed to scale adequately no other results from this scale are presented in
this book.

23 See note 13.

24 See note 14.

25 One of the main scales derived from the work preference items, see page 29 and
note 8.

26 The analysis of variance results were as follows:
mean scores on need for rewards by dual career and sex:

	Single	Married, spouse not in full-time employment	Married, spouse full-time employed
Males	10.20 ($N =$ 20)	10.10 ($N =$ 440)	9.76 ($N =$ 151)
Females	9.53 ($N =$ 137)	8.57 ($N =$ 23)	9.42 ($N =$ 209)
Main effects	Dual career – $F =$	0.580, n.s.	
	Sex – $F =$	7.743, $p < 0.005$	
Interaction	Dual x Sex – $F =$	2.178, n.s.	

3 All change: mobility patterns in management

1 Cross cultural comparison and generalization is always fraught with dangers though there are many reasons for accepting that the British and American business worlds exhibit some common trends in management mobility, not least because of their considerable economic interdependence. They also share many of the same structural features characteristic of Western capitalism. The evidence of data on social and occupational trends on both sides of the Atlantic generally supports the idea that we experience common long-term trends in social and commercial development, though often with a time-lag in its occurrence in America and Britain. However the two cultures do differ in two respects which have an important bearing upon mobility. The first is size. The much larger geographical size of America means that intra-company transfers can involve major geographical relocation in a way that is much more rare in Britain. The concern in the US literature with in-company transfers reflects this fact (cf. Pinder and Das, 1979). The second difference is that in Britain there is a proportionately larger public sector. It might be surmised that intra-organizational mobility will be greater in public than private enterprises, generally confirmed by the data we present later in this chapter.

2 There is no standard practice in recording intra-organizational job changing, and indeed, it is easy to see why most organizations might not see the need to keep records of transfers in a form suitable for researchers. Employer change however can be simply and reliably recorded as 'wastage' or 'turnover', and bears an important and unambiguous relationship to other management systems, such as payroll and recruitment. The enormous preponderance of turnover over transfer studies in the literature reflects this differential accessibility of reliable mobility data to researchers. In passing one may also note that this reflects the regrettable tendency for organizational researchers to allow the amount of effort it requires to collect data to exert undue influence on their choice of dependent variables.

3 By a method developed by S. Rosenbaum of the Royal Statistical Society,

widely used in consumer and market research, which compares percentages taking account of their absolute magnitude and sample size.

4 Independent corroboration of this figure is to be found in a much less systematic but equally large scale readership survey carried out shortly before our surveys, by a British national newspaper with a largely middle-class and professional readership (Gordon and Wilson, 1982).

5 In the CDS-II, 12–15 months after the CDS-I, the sample was asked to report similarly on up to three job changes they might have experienced between the two surveys. Most of the analyses in this chapter are based upon the CDS-I career history data, though in almost every case findings have been cross-validated and corroborated on the smaller CDS-II data set.

6 This last statistic revealed a discrepancy between CDS-I and CDS-II findings: a lower proportion of job changes (37%) were employer changes in the CDS-II; see note 15 Chapter 1 for an explanation of this.

7 See note 2 above.

8 Measures were as follows:

Novelty:

'How different are the requirements of your present job from the one you held previously? i.e. before your last 'job change' (see definition as per p. 48).' Three items: (a) the tasks involved, (b) the skills required for the job, (c) the methods used to do the job; 4-point response scale: 'almost identical', 'only minor differences', 'major differences', 'almost completely different'. Cronbach's alpha at T1 = 0.82; at T2 an additional item was added, 'the interactions with others required for the job'; Cronbach's alpha for this 4-item was 0.78.

Learning:

Single item measure: 'how much did the job require you to develop major new skills?'; with a 4-point response scale: 'a great deal', 'quite a lot', 'not much', 'not at all'.

Transfer:

Single item measure: 'how much opportunity was there to use skills acquired in earlier job/training?'; 4-point response scale as for 'Learning' above.

9 Spearman's rho applied to these rankings revealed no significant correlation between them. However, intercorrelating the raw scores on these three measures across the total sample produced the following pattern:

	Learning	Transfer	
Novelty	+0.32***	−0.15***	(Pearson product moment correlations, 2-tailed test,
Learning	/	0.03 n.s.	*** = $p < 0.001$)

This shows that high novelty does involve high learning and low transfer, but that learning and transfer are independent of one another. Note that this result differs from the rank order correlation because the product moment relations are mediated by job change dimensions (see 10 below).

10 The results of 3-way analyses of variance with the self-concept scales adjustment and dominance and the single item 'confidence' held constant produced the following pattern:

	Novelty	Learning	Transfer
Main effects:			
Employer change	***	n.s.	**
Function change	***	***	
Status change (up)	***	***	***
Interactions:			
Employer × function	n.s.	*	n.s.
Employer × status	*	n.s.	n.s.
Status × function	n.s.	n.s.	n.s.
3-way interaction	n.s.	n.s.	*
Covariates:			
Adjustment	n.s.	**	***
Dominance	*	*	n.s.
Confidence	n.s.	n.s.	*
$N = 2,260$			

11 See note 10 above.

12 Hall also proposed (1971) that the experience of success and failure, along with other prolonged exposure to particular occupational conditions, forms and transmutes aspects of identity.

13 In the CDS-I respondents were offered a choice of 14 occupational areas plus an 'other' open category which yielded a further 15 job areas: 29 in all. See Alban-Metcalfe and Nicholson (1984) for details of these and Table 3.4 to see how the most populous job areas were categorized. Discriminant function analysis was used to verify the empirical viability of these eight categories and of the five Industry Group categories (see Table 3.5).

14 One can reason that the more tightly defined the group (and thus the larger the number of separate categories) the 'easier' it is to record moves between groups.

15 The total gains and losses aggregated across areas do not balance overall because we have excluded moves in and out of a few sparsely represented industry types which do not fit into the classification system. This also explains the reduced N in this table.

16 These tables (and similar ones in this and subsequent chapters) present in summary form the results of multiple analysis of covariance tests. First, tests were conducted within generic groups of independent variables (biographical,

occupational, industrial) against the dependent variables, and then analyses were repeated across those independent variables which emerged as most significant from each of these generic groups. Age was used as a covariate in all analyses. Tables only show those variables which emerged as reliable predictors (i.e. on both types of test: within and across generic groups). Interaction effects are shown by entries in tables combining two variables, e.g. 'younger males and females' in Table 3.6.

17 Family situation was coded: single with no children, married without children, married or single with children.

18 This dip is inexplicable from other data sources, but may not be a stable finding, since there were relatively few women in these older age categories.

19 See West *et al.* (1985), for a detailed discussion of this phenomenon, its outcomes and implications. See also Chapter 6.

20 Analyses of covariance yielded the following:

Employer change:
Main effects: Education ($p < 0.01$), Sex ($p < 0.001$), Family situation (n.s.)
Interactions: Sex $\times$ Family situation ($p < 0.01$)
Covariate: Age (n.s.)
For function change there were no significant main effects or interactions, and for speed of movement, no main effects but a significant three-way interaction ($p < 0.05$).

21 In analysis of covariance, there were main effects for sex ($p < 0.001$) and dual career ($p < 0.05$), but no significant interactions and no significant age covariance.

22 See note 20 above.

23 Table 2.2 shows the eight categories of organization size used in the CDS-I and CDS-II. Analysis of change was conducted by taking those managers who changed employers between Time 1 and Time 2 and for whom we had a record of company size at both times, and then cross-tabulating these two sets of company size data.

24 The confounding of status with size makes it particularly important to separate them analytically. These significant results are strongly confirmed for both status and size, each independently of the other.

25 Multiple analyses of covariance produced these findings, by comparing each of these move types with all other move types.

26 These analyses have been reported by Cawsey *et al.* (1985), showing (a) a significant negative correlation between upward status moves and employer moves, (b) positive correlations between both of these variables and actual status, with the correlation between employer moves and status the larger of the two.

27 These results come from multiple regression analysis in which the following variables were regressed on status: company size, age, sex, number of upward status moves (out of last five moves), number of employer changes (out of five), and all the work preference and self-concept scales. All the demographic and mobility variables, and Adjustment and need for growth entered the stepwise

regression with significant Beta weights. Other self-descriptive scales failed to enter the equation. $R = 0.628$, $df = 7,2131$.

28 No difference in status for employer changers vs other job movers between the CDS-I and CDS-II in discriminant function analysis.

29 See note 27 above.

30 Analysis of covariance comparing upward status movers with other movers yielded significant F ratios for directional change scores on these two scales, with Time 1 scores on these scales entered as covariates to avoid the well-known statistical artifacts in change score data of ceiling and floor effects, and regression to the mean (see Johns, 1981).

31 T-tests comparing Time 1 to Time 2 upward status movers with other movers on their scores on all self-description scales at Time 1. None of these was significant.

32 Analyses as in note 31 and 32 above, using employer change vs. other job change as the criterion. All t-tests were non-significant with one exception: employees with high need for rewards were more likely than others to change employers (i.e. a positive finding on path F in Table 3.11).

4 The causes of mobility

1 These labels were omitted from the questionnaire scale so as not to 'lead' respondents, and items were randomly ordered to avoid response set.

2 The overall pattern is of generally low intercorrelations, indicating that many independent dimensions are represented by these items. Factor analysis confirms this by failing to indicate that reliable scales could be constructed from these items. The intercorrelations of the principal items were as follows:

	A1	B5	C8	
B5	0.18***			
C8	−0.18***	−0.42***		
D11	0.11***	−0.03	0.03	*** $p < 0.001$

3 The question form and response distribution were as follows: 'Now please think about your career to date. Overall how satisfied are you with your progress to date?'

Very satisfied	21.9%
Satisfied	36.7%
Somewhat satisfied	24.9%
Neither satisfied nor dissatisfied	5.0%
Somewhat dissatisfied	7.9%
Dissatisfied	2.1%
Very dissatisfied	1.4%

$(N = 1,072)$

4 Veiga (1981) has drawn a similar distinction between two kinds of plateaued managers whom he terms 'deadwoods' and 'solids'. These he found could be empirically distinguished on a number of variables, such as career impatience, exposure and visibility (deadwoods lower than solids on all of these) but did not

differ in their satisfaction. However he found both plateaued groups were more dissatisfied than an upward mobile comparison group.

5 Table 4.2 shows only significant zero-order correlations ($p < 0.05$, two-tailed tests). Canonical correlation analysis between the work history and career types measures were performed, confirming that there are distinctive patterns underlying these associations.

6 This inference is made from a non-significant zero-order correlation between employer changing and career satisfaction ($r = -0.037$) and a positive significant ($p < 0.001$) positive correlation between upward status change and career satisfaction ($r = +0.156$).

7 See note 16, Chapter 3.

8 See Table 9.1 for empirical confirmation of the linkage between generalism and status achievement. We can infer from this that many high status managers who now describe themselves as generalists started their careers as specialists, and helped to bring about their conversion to generalism and status attainment by radical job changing.

9 Pilot interviews for this part of the CDS-I were conducted by Dr Beverly Alban-Metcalfe with a sample of working managers attending MBA and other management courses.

10 Analysis of these data revealed that people's reasons for their last job move were representative of their reasons for job moves in general (i.e. the previous four moves): the percentage distributions of reasons were almost identical for all previous job changes. Accordingly, in the text we shall only report the results for managers' last job change. Table 4.4 also combines the most 'important' and 'secondary' reasons, since these did not differ from one another in their distribution.

11 This oversight was unfortunate, and perhaps illustrates the dangers of over-reliance on pilot interviews when, for one reason or another, they may have hidden sources of bias. In this case one can surmise that the pilot sample came from exceptionally stable organizational environments. However, we can also take comfort from the fact that apart from this omission and a couple of extreme minority responses ('retirement', 'start own business', 'illness' and 'no choice', all given by less than 3% of the sample) our precoded list fitted extremely closely with reasons elicited by the free-response format of the CDS-II, thus allowing the same coding categories to be used.

12 Although the coding system was corroborated, the rank order of reasons comes out rather differently in the CDS-II to the CDS-I. This is due to the different method of questioning used to elicit reasons. Without the prompting stimulus of a list of reasons, the free response method has the advantage of allowing the most psychologically salient reasons to rise to the surface more clearly, but the disadvantage of not prompting people to think about non-salient or socially undesirable reasons.

13 For more detailed statistical analysis of these data and discussion of their implications for cognitive theory the reader is referred to Nicholson, West and Cawsey (1985).

244

14 See Roberts (1975) and Speakman (1980) for expositions of the structuralist perspective on careers.

15 The questioning format for expectations in the CDS-I and recent job changes in the CDS-II does not allow the two categories of functional change and redundancy to be reliably compared over time. For this analysis it is essential to compare like with like, and only on these three measures could exactly comparable indices be constructed.

16 See note 13. The contingency tables from which these results are derived can be converted into the equivalent of correlation coefficients (phi coefficient). These coefficients are between 0.2 and 0.3; highly significant on a sample this size but predicting only a fraction of the variance in actual job change.

17 Hall (1976) is one writer on the subject who has recognized this by adopting a similarly broad and non-assumptive definition of career.

5 Experiencing the Transition Cycle

1 Several theoretical strands in social psychology converge on this insight which has long been a tenet of symbolic interactionist theory, as represented by such writers as Mead, Cooley, Becker and Strauss (see Meltzer *et al.*, 1975, for a review of this tradition). It is also a theme in the modern social ethnography, of writers like Garfinkel, Goffman and Harré, and also in social identity theory where psychologists have been challenging traditional trait views of personality (Tajfel, 1978; Turner and Giles, 1981).

2 We found this often to be the case in our studies of graduate entry and adjustment to life in a large UK oil company (Nicholson and Arnold, 1985; Nicholson, 1987b).

3 Since all are at different stages of the Transition Cycle, and, as we have seen, people are not very good at predicting the onset of the next cycle, the only way to gather comparable data from all respondents is by asking them to think back to their last job change.

4 Based upon analysis of covariance, controlling for the effects of status and function changes.

5 These category labels were omitted on the original survey form and the item order randomized to avoid response set. The item content was empirically derived from an intensive study of the adjustment experiences of graduates entering industry, see note 2 above.

6 From content analysis of free response data.

7 For example, by coding surprise 1 and 0 and aggregating across the range this percentage represents the proportion with scores of more than 0.

8 See Arnold (1985) for parallel and corroborative data on graduates' surprises in their jobs.

9 Correlation between total surprise score and satisfaction with work life in the past year = −0.21.

10 These form a highly consistent scaled measure of satisfaction. Cronbach's alpha = .846 The three negative items shown in Table 5.4 fail to scale as a single

measure or with any of the satisfaction items though they do intercorrelate fairly highly; see note 13 below.

11 Correlations amongst these were as follows:

	Satisfaction	Stress	Difficulties: family	Difficulties: social
Stress	0.44 ***	—		
Difficulties: family	0.49 ***	0.45 ***	—	
Difficulties: social	0.39 ***	0.42 ***	0.75 ***	—

$N = 2,267$; *** $p < 0.001$

12 MANACOVA yields highly significant main effects on all three of these items for employer change and status change, but not function change, and with no significant interaction effects. Age, sex, and status were held constant as covariates. Age and sex are significantly predictive of stress (low age and female), and age and status of the two 'difficulty' measures (low age and high status). The unexpected finding that these adjustment difficulties are lower among those changing employers than for those transferring jobs within organizations, indicates that these difficulties are not problems of life-space adjustment generally, but reflect how immediately intrusive are new *work* demands for the managers, i.e. one can imagine these demands to take the form of extra work load, longer working hours, more business-related social events and the like, rather than problems of relocation, childcare, schooling, new circles of friends etc.

13 These outcomes are conceived as (a) dimensional, and (b) orthogonal. Cutting each dimension at its notional midpoint produces this two-by-two typology.

14 Van Maanen and Schein's (1979) notion of 'custodial' responses to socialization has similar meaning.

15 Pun intended. To determine changes in one's environment often takes 'determination' of character. Need for control could be said to subsume this psychological 'determination'.

16 This is less tautological than it might appear, for the two are conceptually and empirically independent. Discretion is usually determined by external agencies, such as superiors and socio-technical systems, while innovation is a chosen behavioural strategy of the role incumbent. However, the relationship does become tautological when these agencies *require* innovation in role performance, as Brett (1984) has suggested may be the case in some jobs.

17 Analogous dimensions are widely recognized in personality theory (cf. Schutz, 1967; Witkin, 1978; Costa and McCrae, 1980).

18 Induction-socialization practices were not measurable in this study, but the reader is referred to Van Maanen and Schein (1979) and Nicholson (1984) for

19 Cronbach's alpha = 0.82 (CDS-I) and 0.84 (CDS-II).

20 These findings are derived from multiple regression analyses which identify independent predictors of the dependent variable: role innovation. Further details of these analyses can be found in West (1987).

21 The five dimensions are: 'Acting independently of my boss; Setting my own work targets/objectives; Choosing the methods for achieving objectives/targets; Choosing the order in which different parts of the job are done; Choosing whom I deal with in order to carry out my work duties.' Cronbach's alpha for this measure at Time 1 was 0.92 and 0.93 at Time 2.

22 This represents a correlation of 0.20 (Time 1 data).

23 Again this was measured retrospectively on a scale with high internal reliability (see Chapter 6 note 9 for discussion of this variable).

24 See note 20 above.

25 By repeating the analyses described in note 20 above, using reports of innovation at Time 2, and predictor variables from *both* Time 1 and Time 2 – again see West (1987) for fuller details.

26 Regression analysis using change in innovation scores from Time 1 to Time 2 as the dependent variable, and changes in work characteristics, work preferences and self-concept scores (Time 1 to Time 2), including Time 1 scores on these variables as independent variables, thus controlling for the effects of regression to the mean. See West (1987).

27 Based on discriminant function analysis (see West, 1987).

28 See West, Farr and King (1986) for discussion of the differences between creativity and innovation, and how these relate to the characteristics, processes and products of innovation.

6 Outcomes of job change

1 This is one of the oldest lines of development in psychology's history as a biological science, encompassing both the psychoanalytic and the anthropometric traditions. Although there has been much public and at times acrimonious debate between these two schools, they have in common a structuralist conception of human personality development. The latter group, as represented in the work of Cattell (1950) and his successors, continues to be highly influential in industrial psychology.

2 This approach owes its greatest debt to the interactionist conceptions of Kurt Lewin (1935) and Gordon Allport (1937). More recent writings draw upon phenomenological theories in sociology and psychology which promote ethnogenic and 'aleatoric' views of psychic organization and functioning (Gergen, 1980).

3 All scales were factor analysed and tests for internal reliability conducted at both Time 1 and Time 2. The factor structure of all our main scales was almost identical at both times. There were other measures that failed to scale consistently, but this was due to their general psychometric inconsistency rather than their

structural instability, and these scales have been omitted from this book.

4 We compared intercorrelation matrices for all self-description scales at Time 1 and Time 2 for those respondents for whom we had complete records at both times ($N = 1,020$) and tested for significant differences between matched pairs of correlations from the two data sets. None of these 10 pairs of correlations differed significantly at the 0.05 level, on a 2-tailed test. One did on a 1-tailed test: the correlation between need for growth and need for predictability fell from 0.45 to 0.38 ($t = 1.910$). This minor reduction in a strongly positive association cannot be taken as evidence of structural instability. Therefore our results concur with the conclusion of Mortimer *et al.* (1982), who found structural stability by using confirmatory factor analysis techniques.

5 These correlations were as follows: adjustment 0.66; dominance 0.65; need for growth 0.55; need for predictability 0.46; need for rewards 0.59, i.e. less than half the variance in people's Time 2 scores is predictable from their Time 1 scores. The lowish correlation for need for predictability shows this to be the most prone to change over time.

6 It is also possible to test for 'absolute change', which is level change ignoring the direction of movement. This is actually another way of looking at normative change, and indeed testing for absolute level change produces highly significant results on all scales: t values between 29.69 and 36.01 for the five main scales, and only slightly less high values for individual items. Clearly there is a good deal of personal change going on, but much of it cancels itself out when one measures directional level change. However, when we come to try to see how life events and job change predict both types, directional level and absolute change, there is little to choose between them in the number of significant predictive relationships. In other words, much of the absolute change is either error or the product of multiple influences beyond the scope of this study, and what absolute change is predictable from life events and job changes tends to be systematically in one direction or another according to the nature of the intervening event.

7 Tested by stepwise regression with job change entered as the first predictor at step 1 so that only events associated with personal change independent of job mobility are revealed. Time 1 scores were also entered at the first step (i.e. to predict Time 2 scores) to ensure that directional level changes are not artifacts of initial scores (Johns, 1981).

8 Here we deviate from Mortimer *et al.* (1982) analytical model for measuring change. Their fourth method is 'ipsative change' – alterations in individuals' rank ordering of scores on items or scales over time, e.g. whether a person who is higher on dominance than adjustment at Time 1 retains this precedence at Time 2. This is assessed by Spearman's rho, and Mortimer *et al.* found high ipsative stability to be the norm. We have obtained similar results for one year change data from another (unpublished) study, but have not repeated this test here. Neither Mortimer *et al.* nor, to our knowledge, any other studies in the organizational literature make use of self-assessed change as a criterion. It is unfortunate that we only measured this in the CDS-I, denying us the oppor-

tunity to see how it relates to change as measured by the other methods we have used.

9 These were developed in our investigation of graduate entry and adjustment to work in an oil company (see Chapter 5, note 2), where we found results on similar scales concurrently validated by content analysed interview responses on personal change from the same subjects at the same time.

10 See note 9.

11 This does not hold for measures of absolute change; see note 6 above.

12 i.e. there is more variance to be explained than there is for level change; also larger effects are to be expected because the item wording asks people to assess change attributable to work adjustment.

13 Analysis of covariance main effects are shown in this table, with other move types held constant as covariates.

14 Employer change was most strongly associated with our record of geographical relocation between Time 1 and Time 2.

15 These scales were identified by regression analysis, so by implication the omitted scales failed to predict change (i.e. need for predictability, adjustment, dominance etc.).

16 Discriminant function analysis with stepwise entry of independent predictors. Table 6.5 shows only those items and scales entering the equation with significant values.

17 Table 6.7 summarizes the results of analysis of covariance performed on change scores, controlling for status and organizational size.

18 As per note 17, with other dimensions of job change (status and function) held constant as covariates.

19 As per note 18, but here the dependent variables are Time 2 scores with Time 1 scores controlled as covariates, i.e. change scores which avoid artifactual statistical effects due to original Time 1 scores.

20 Analysis as per Table 6.8 (see note 18), with additional controls for age (through covariance).

21 Of the 30 downward status moves in the second survey, 12 reported a period of unemployment. T-tests between the two groups of those who did and did not experience a period of unemployment revealed no significant differences on any scales or items. Given the small sample size it remained a possibility that unemployment might still be having an effect so a further comparison was made between all those job movers who experienced a period of unemployment in the time between the two surveys and those who did not ($Ns = 50$ and 353 respectively). T-tests showed that those who experienced some unemployment scored significantly lower than others in their Time 1 ratings of their jobs. They showed a significantly greater increase on these measures over the time between the two surveys than the job movers who did not experience unemployment, suggesting that they found more satisfaction in their new jobs. This confirms that the group differences we have found are not attributable to unemployment experience.

22 These measured outcomes were usually less than one year later, for many of the

job changes we recorded between the CDS-I and II had occurred only shortly before Time 2. This implies that we have been able to pick up people's immediate evaluations of jobs, but probably for many the time was insufficient for us to discern the personal change that these moves may engender.

7 The cutting edge of change – the case of newly created jobs

1 Published reports elsewhere describe some of the findings in this chapter. West *et al.* (1987) relate these to the theory of work role transitions (Nicholson, 1984); and West and Nicholson (1986) consider their managerial implications.
2 Data from 171 people providing information about origins of their newly created jobs were transcribed onto index cards, which were subject to *ex post facto* classification. This was conducted repeatedly with inter-rater checks to arrive at an economical, reliable and comprehensible classification system. This was not a difficult outcome to achieve, since the origins of newly created jobs are highly distinctive (though not mutually exclusive – 13 of the 171 cases fell into more than one category).
3 In some ways this sub-category may be the hardest to detect. It is likely that many people who did not indicate they were in newly created jobs might have done so had they been prompted to consider this dimension to organizational process. Following this reasoning it would seem likely that a good many of the 42 uncodable cases of newly created jobs are of this type, those cases where people gave no information that would permit classification.
4 These were treated separately because they differ radically from other newly created jobs in several ways; most importantly in operating outside the organizational and institutional framework of paid employment.
5 Using t-tests (2-tailed) to assess differences between those moving to newly created jobs and other job movers; in both cases t-values were significant at the < 0.001 level. Similar comparisons were made for industry group and job area using chi-square analysis. There were differences across industry groups ($p < 0.05$) but not across job areas.
6 Comparisons using t-tests (2-tailed) on individual scales were significant at $p < 0.001$ level.
7 Sex differences between groups were confirmed by chi-square analysis ($p < 0.001$); other biographical differences were confirmed using t-tests.
8 To investigate differences in perceived job characteristics, individual characteristics, and job change outcomes between those moving into newly created jobs and those moving into existing jobs in both CDS-I and CDS-II, variables on which there was a significant group difference on t-tests were entered into stepwise discriminant function analyses. Those variables which still significantly discriminated between groups are reported here.
9 See note 8 above.
10 See note 8 above.

11 Based on analyses of covariance of change scores controlling for status, organization size, and CDS-I scores on the same variables.
12 Analyses similar to those described in note 8 above produced the findings shown in Table 7.3.
13 By paired t-tests (2-tailed) on identical scales in the CDS-I and CDS-II.
14 Determined by t-tests (2-tailed); $p < 0.05$.

8 Organizational career development – the management experience

1 See Chapter 2 and Alban-Metcalfe and Nicholson (1984).
2 3-point scale collapsed to two for ease of presentation.
3 As in previous tables with this format, results are derived from multiple analyses of covariance (see note 16, Chapter 3). Age and status are used as covariates in all analyses, because of their pervasive influence on these dependent variables, and independent variables have been grouped as follows for separate analyses: age and sex, type and status, sector and size, sex and job area, sex and industry group.
4 Only measured in the CDS-II, see note 13 Chapter 2.
5 See Chapter 3 and Chapter 4, where it appeared that managers are especially likely to quit medium size companies because they fail to offer fulfilling roles and development opportunities.
6 Analyses per note 3 above.
7 It is important to note that these repeated size effects are independent of managerial status.
8 Two categories of this 4-point response scale are collapsed in this table.
9 The analyses of sex differences in self-descriptions, described in Chapter 2 (p. 41) would seem to indicate that women are generally more motivated to see interpersonal supports than men.
10 4-point scales collapsed to two in Table 8.8, and 3-point scales reduced to two in Table 8.9 by omitting the middle response category 'somewhat useful' (whose percentages can be calculated by subtracting the two shown from 100).
11 MANACOVA's controlling for status show managers who change employer in particular draw informal sources for learning about procedures and methods upon more than do other movers. T-testing in- versus out-spirallers shows that out-spirallers make more use of colleagues than in-spirallers for standards of performance and methods/procedures information, but not for attitudes etc.
12 As per note 3 above.
13 The same kind of analysis as shown in Table 8.10 was repeated on the CDS-II scales which relate to these processes (i.e. the measures which are shown in Table 8.9).
14 One may tentatively speculate that this betokens differences in organizational culture at different stages of the enterprise's life cycle (Kimberly and Miles, 1980; Schein, 1985). It is perhaps characteristic of new industries and younger managers to be fast moving, and task oriented in a culture of self-reliance. This

is perhaps stretching these data a little far, though it is consistent with some of our later findings on industry differences in organizational culture (see Table 8.15).

15 5-point response scale collapsed to two in this table, with the scale midpoint, 'moderate', omitted. Percentages for this response category = 100 minus the sum of the two percentages shown.

16 See note 3 above.

17 This measurement of culture does not attempt to capture the deeper shared assumptions that Schein (1985) considers to be the basic content of culture. This would not be amenable to the 'surface' methods of questionnaire response. Our more modest aim here was to get managers to describe the predominant operating 'style' of their organizations, based upon the premise (observable in item content) that this is often a function of organization-environment linkages and dependencies (Pfeffer and Salancik, 1978).

18 As note 15 above, but the omitted scale mid-point is 'not sure'. It can be seen that no more than 13% gave this response to any one item. This indicates that managers seemed to have little difficulty in describing their organizations in these terms.

19 See note 3 above.

20 This was by far and away the most strongly linked factor. Independently of size, and holding age and status constant as covariates, every one of these items yielded significant F-ratios for industry group, and most of them highly significant (four with $p < 0.001$, three with $p < 0.001$, and one at $p < 0.05$). This is not due to high collinearity amongst items, as can be seen by the different pattern of results for items, and the fact that for no other independent variables were there such strongly and consistently significant results. We did examine item covariance on this measure by means of factor analysis. This confirms that there is little overlap between these items; their average intercorrelation is 0.08; the highest between any two items was 0.51, but most were between 0.1 and 0.3. Thus it is not surprising that factor analysis and scaling failed to produce well defined scales, though there is some clustering of the 'competitive' types and the 'solid' type items. This failure to scale is entirely satisfactory, since the items were designed to measure conceptually independent aspects of organizational functioning.

21 In this characterization of group differences there are some striking similarities with Miles and Snow's (1978) typology of organizations' strategic cultures.

22 The results for 'sector' and 'size' are completely independent, through the statistical controls applied by analysis of variance, i.e. these are both main effects, with no significant interaction term.

23 We did not separate size from industry group in analyses, since this would render the latter meaningless as a variable, on the reasoning that some industry groups are consistently larger than others and therefore size is, in a sense, intrinsic to their character. However, because of the importance and controversial nature of some of these findings additional analyses controlling for size were conducted, verifying that the findings for government were not just a reflection of size.

9 Women in management

1 See note 12, Chapter 1. The authors would also like to thank Dr Beverly Alban-Metcalfe for her helpful comments on this chapter.

2 Tested by two analyses of covariance, with number of children as the dependent variable, and age and status as covariates. Sex is a highly significant main effect in both analyses.

3 Poole *et al.*'s (1981) study of British management actually found fewer managers came from working class backgrounds than in previous management surveys, but it is nonetheless to be expected that these origins will still be more common amongst male than female managers. Unfortunately we have no way of testing this proposition. However, Poole *et al.* do confirm that technical rather than collegiate educational paths predominate amongst their male sample, i.e. they are very different from our female sample here.

4 T-tests on status for these two comparisons (for Members and Fellows separately) confirm there is no significant difference between the sexes' status, either overall or within size categories.

5 The content of these categories is described in Chapter 3.

6 Each cell represents a significant t-test result for male–female differences, analyses conducted separately within the seven job areas shown. The job area 'line management' was excluded because there were too few women (15) for meaningful analysis.

7 This line of argument would follow from Deci's (1975) theory that extrinsic rewards and motives mitigate the motivational force of intrinsic rewards.

8 A series of analyses of variance were conducted to evaluate family situation and dual career as alternative causes of age and sex effects. Some marginally significant results did emerge from this, but none sufficient to account for the much larger and independent age and sex effects we have reported in this and previous chapters.

9 We interviewed a senior representative of the BIM to discover if there were any apparent differences in the motives for joining the BIM of males and females. It was reported to us that none were apparent though BIM membership is probably at higher levels generally in the core business and industrial sectors where women have not been numerous.

Bibliography

Ainsworth, M.D., Salter and Bell, S.M. (1974). Mother–infant interaction and the development of competence. In K. Connolly and J. Bruner (Eds.), *The Growth of Competence*. New York: Academic Press.

Alban-Metcalfe, B.M. (1984). Current career concerns of female and male managers and professionals: an analysis of free-response comments to a national survey. *Equal Opportunities International, 3*, 11–18.

(1985). The effects of socialization on women's management careers: a review. *Management Bibliographies and Reviews, 3*.

Alban-Metcalfe, B.M. and Nicholson, N. (1984). *The Career Development of British Managers*. London: British Institute of Management.

Allen, M.P., Panian, S.K. and Lotz, R.E. (1979). Managerial succession and organizational performance: a recalcitrant problem revisited. *Administrative Science Quarterly, 24*, 167–80.

Allen, M.P. and Panian, S.K. (1982). Power, performance, and succession in the large corporation. *Administrative Science Quarterly, 27*, 538–47.

Allen, V.L. and Van de Vliert, E. (1984). *Role Transitions: Explorations and Explanations*. London: Plenum.

Allport, G.W. (1937). *Personality*. New York: Holt, Rinehart and Winston.

Argyris, C. and Schon, D.A. (1974). *Theory in Practice: Increasing Professional Effectiveness*. San Francisco, CA: Jossey-Bass.

(1978). *Organizational Learning: An Action-Learning Perspective*. Reading, MA: Addison-Wesley.

Arnold, J.A. (1985). Tales of the unexpected: surprises experienced by graduates in the early months of employment. *British Journal of Guidance and Counselling, 13*, 308–19.

(1986). Getting started: how graduates adjust to employment. *Personal Review, 15*, 16–20.

Ashridge Study (1981). Women in management – actual and potential. *Industrial Relations Review and Report, 239*, 9–10.

Bailyn, L. (1980). *Living with Technology: Issues at Mid-Career*. Cambridge, MA: MIT Press.

Baltes, P.B., Reese, H.W. and Lipsitt, L.P. (1980). Lifespan developmental psychology. *Annual Review of Psychology, 31*, 65–110.

Bamber, G. (1986). *Militant Managers?* Aldershot, Hants: Gower.

Barron, R.D. and Norris, G.M. (1976). Sexual divisions and the dual labour

254

market. In D. L. Barker and S. Allen (Eds.), *Dependence and Exploitation in Work and Marriage*. London: Longman.

Beechey, V. (1986). Women's employment in contemporary Britain. In V. Beechey and E. W. Hitelegg (Eds.), *Women in Britain Today*. Milton Keynes: Open University Press.

Birch, S. and McMillan, B. (1971). *Managers on the Move*. London: British Institute of Management.

Blanchard, K. and Johnson, S. (1982). *The One Minute Manager*. New York: Morrow.

Blau, B. F. (1984). *Sex Segregation in the Workplace: Trends, Explanations, Remedies*. Washington, DC: National Academy Press.

Brayfield, A. H. and Crockett, W. H. (1955). Employee attitudes and employee performance. *Psychological Bulletin, 52*, 396–424.

Brett, J. M. (1980). The effect of job transfer on employees and their families. In C. L. Cooper and R. Payne (Eds.), *Current Concerns in Occupational Stress*. London: Wiley.

  (1984). Job transitions and personal role development. In K. Rowland and J. Ferris (Eds.), *Research in Personnel and Human Resource Management*, Volume 2. Greenwich, CT: JAI Press.

Brett, J. M. and Werbel, J. D. (1978). *The Effect of Job Transfers on Employees and their Families*. Technical Report to the Employee Relocation Council, Washington, DC.

Britain 1986: An Official Handbook. London: HMSO.

Brousseau, K. R. (1983). Toward a dynamic model of job-person relationships: findings, research questions, and implications for work system design. *Academy of Management Review, 8*, 33–45.

Brown, D. and Brooks, L. (Eds.) (1984). *Career Choice and Development*. San Francisco: Jossey-Bass.

Brown, R. (1986). *Social Psychology: The Second Edition*. London: Collier Macmillan.

Brown, R. H. (1978). Bureaucracy as praxis: toward a political phenomenology of organizations. *Administrative Science Quarterly, 23*, 365–82.

Brown, W. and Sisson, K. (1983). Industrial relations in the next decade. *Industrial Relations Journal, 14*, 9–22.

Brunsson, N. (1985). *The Irrational Organization*. Chichester: Wiley.

Buchanan, B. (1974). Building organizational commitment: the socialization of managers in work organizations. *Administrative Science Quarterly, 19*, 533–46.

Campion, M. A. and Mitchell, M. M. (1986). Management turnover: experiential differences between former and current managers. *Personnel Psychology, 39*, 57–69.

Cattell, R. B. (1950). *Personality*. New York: McGraw Hill.

Cawsey, T. F., Nicholson, N. and Alban-Metcalfe, B. M. (1985). Who's on the fast track? The relationship between career mobility, individual and task characteristics. Proceedings of the Academy of Management, 45th Annual Meeting, San Diego.

Clarke, D. G. (1966). *The Industrial Manager, His Background and Career Pattern*. London: Business Publications.

Bibliography

Clements, R.V. (1958). *Managers: A Study of their Careers in Industry*. London: George Allen and Unwin.

Clutterbuck, D. (1985). *Everyone Needs a Mentor*. London: IPM.

Colantuono, S.L. (1982). *Build Your Career*. Amherst, MA: Human Resources Development Press.

Cook, J.D. and Wall, T.D. (1980). New work attitude measures of trust, organizational commitment and personal need fulfilment. *Journal of Occupational Psychology, 53*, 39–52.

Cook, J.D., Hepworth, S.J., Wall, T.D. and Warr, P.B. (1981). *The Experience of Work: A Compendium and Review of 249 Measures and Their Use*. London: Academic Press.

Cooper, C.L. and Marshall, J. (1978). *Understanding Executive Stress*. London: Macmillan.

Costa, P.T. and McCrae, R.R. (1980). Still stable after all these years: personality as a key to some issues in adulthood and old age. In P.B. Baltes and O.G. Brim (Eds.), *Life-Span Development and Behavior*, Volume 3. New York: Academic Press.

Crozier, M. (1964). *The Bureaucratic Phenomenon*. Chicago: University of Chicago Press.

Cullen, J.B. (1983). An occupational taxonomy by professional characteristics: implications for research. *Journal of Vocational Behaviour, 22*, 256–67.

Datan, N. and Ginsburg, L.H. (Eds.) (1975). *Life-Span Psychology: Normative Life Crises*. New York: Academic Press.

Davidson, M.J. (1985). *Reach for the Top – A Women's Guide to Success in Business and Management*. London: Piatkus.

Davidson, M.J. and Cooper, C.L. (1983). *Stress and the Woman Manager*. London: Martin Robertson.

Dawis, R.V. and Lofquist, L.H. (1984). *A Psychological Theory of Work Adjustment*. Minneapolis: University of Minnesota Press.

Deci, E.D. (1975). *Intrinsic Motivation*. New York: Plenum.

Drucker, P. (1955). *The Practice of Management*. London: Heinemann.
(1973). *Management*. London: Heinemann.
(1985). *Innovation and Entrepreneurship*. London: Heinemann.

Dubin, R., Hedley, R.A. and Taveggia, C. (1976). Attachment to work. In R. Dubin (Ed.), *Handbook of Work, Organization and Society*. Chicago: Rand McNally.

Duckworth, D.H. (1985). Is the 'organizational stress' construct a red herring? A reply to Glowinkowski and Cooper. *Bulletin of the British Psychological Society, 38*, 401–5.

Dunnette, M.D. (1973). *Work and Non-Work in the Year 2001*. Monterey, CA: Brooks-Cole.

Dyer, L.D. (1973). Implications of job displacement at mid-career. *Industrial Gerontology, 17*, 38–46.

Eichdorn, D.H., Clausen, J.A., Haan, N., Honzig, M.P. and Mussen, P.H. (Eds.) (1981). *Present and Past in Middle Life*. London: Academic Press.

Erikson, E.H. (1950). *Childhood and Society*. New York: Norton.

Esland, G. and Salaman, G. (Eds.) (1980). *The Politics of Work and Occupations*.

256

Milton Keynes: Open University Press.

Evans, P. and Bartolomé, F. (1980). *Must Success Cost So Much?* London: Grant McIntyre.

Feldman, D.C. (1976). A contingency theory of socialization. *Administrative Science Quarterly, 21*, 433–52.

Feldman, D.C. and Brett, J.M. (1983). Coping with new jobs: a comparative study of new hires and job changers. *Academy of Management Journal, 26*, 258–72.

Fineman, S. (1983). *White Collar Unemployment: Impact and Stress.* Chichester: Wiley.

Firth, J. (1985). Personal meanings of occupational stress: cases from the clinic. *Journal of Occupational Psychology, 58*, 139–48.

Fletcher, C. and Williams, R. (1985). *Performance Appraisal and Career Development.* London: Hutchinson.

Fletcher, B., Gowler, D. and Payne, R.L. (1979). Exploding the myth of executive stress. *Personnel Management, 11*, 30–4.

Fothergill, S. and Vincent, J. (1985). *The State of the Nation.* London: Pan Books.

French, J.R.P., Caplan, R.D. and Van Harrison, R. (1982). *The Mechanisms of Job Stress and Strain.* Chichester: Wiley.

Frese, M. (1982). Occupational socialization and psychological development: an underemphasized research perspective in industrial psychology. *Journal of Occupational Psychology, 55*, 209–24.

(1984). Transitions in jobs, occupational socialization and strain. In V.L. Allen and E. Van de Vliert (Eds.), *Role Transitions: Explorations and Explanations.* London: Plenum.

Fromm, E. (1942). *Fear of Freedom.* London: Routledge and Kegan Paul.

Frost, P.J., Moore, L.F., Louis, M.R., Lundberg, C.C. and Martin, J. (1985). *Organizational Culture.* Beverly Hills, CA: Sage.

Fryer, D.M. and Payne, R.L. (1984). Pro-active behaviour in unemployment: findings and implications. *Leisure Studies, 3*, 273–395.

Fulk, J. and Cummings, T.G. (1984). Refocusing leadership: a modest proposal. In J.C. Hunt, D.M. Hosking, C.A. Schriesheim and R. Stewart (Eds.), *International Managerial Behaviour: Leadership Perspectives.* Oxford: Pergamon.

Gergen, K.J. (1980). The emerging crisis in life-span developmental theory. In P.B. Baltes and O.G. Brim (Eds.), *Life-Span Development and Behavior*, Volume 3. New York: Academic Press.

Gerpott, T.J., Domsch, M. and Pearson, A.W. (1985). *R & D Professionals' View of Criteria for Intrafirm Job Mobility.* Institute for Personnel management, University of West German Armed Forces, Hamburg.

Glaser, B.G. and Strauss, A.L. (1971). *Status Passage.* Chicago: Aldine.

Gordon, J. and Wilson, P. (1982). What makes people change jobs? *Personnel Management, 14*, 22–5.

Grusky, O. (1963). Managerial succession and organizational effectiveness. *American Journal of Sociology, 69*, 21–31.

Guerrier, Y. and Philpot, N. (1978). *The British Manager: Careers and Mobility.* London: British Institute of Management.

Hakim, C. (1979). Occupational segregation: a comparative study of the degree and pattern of the differentiation between men and women's work in Britain, the United States and other countries. Research Paper No. 9, Department of Employment. London: HMSO.

Hall, D.T. (1971). A theoretical model of career subidentity development in organizational settings. *Organizational Behavior and Human Performance, 6*, 50–76.

(1976). *Careers in Organizations*. Pacific Palisades, CA: Goodyear.

Halsey, R.H. (1978). *Change in British Society*. Milton Keynes: Open University Press.

Handy, C. (1984). *The Future of Work*. Oxford: Blackwell.

Harré, R. and Secord, P.F. (1972). *The Explanation of Social Behaviour*. Oxford: Basic Blackwell.

Hartley, J. and Fryer, D. (1983). The psychology of unemployment: a critical appraisal. In G.M. Stephenson and J.H. Davis (Eds.), *Progress in Applied Psychology*, Volume 2. Chichester: Wiley.

Hedburg, B. (1981). How organizations learn and unlearn. In P.C. Nystrom and W.H. Starbuck (Eds.), *Handbook of Organizational Design*. London: Oxford University Press.

Herriot, P. (1984). *Down From the Ivory Tower: Graduates and Their Jobs*. Chichester: Wiley.

Herzberg, F. (1968). *Work and The Nature of Man*. London: Staples Press.

Hickman, C.R. and Silva, M.A. (1985). *Creating Excellence*. London: Unwin.

Hill, J.M. and Trist, E.L. (1955). Changes in accidents and other absences with length of service. *Human Relations, 8*, 121–52.

Hirschman, A.O. (1970). *Exit, Voice and Loyalty*. Cambridge, MA: Harvard University Press.

Holmes, T.H. and Rahe, R.H. (1967). The social readjustment scale. *Journal of Psychosomatic Research, 11*, 213–18.

Hoppock, R. (1935). *Job Satisfaction*. New York: Harper and Brothers.

Hopson, B. and Adams, J. (1976). Towards an understanding of transition: Defining some boundaries of transition dynamics. In J. Adams, J. Hayes and B. Hopson (Eds.), *Transition*. London: Martin Robertson.

Houser, J.D. (1938). *What People Want From Business*. New York: McGraw Hill.

Hunt, J.W. and Collins, R.R. (1983). *Managers in Mid-Career Crisis*. Sydney, Australia: Wellington Lane Press.

Institute of Manpower Studies (1986). *UK Occupation and Employment Trends to the 1990's*. Brighton: IMS.

Jaques, E. (1976). *A General Theory of Bureaucracy*. London: Heinemann.

Jennings, E.E. (1967). *The Mobile Manager: A Study of the New Generation of Top Executives*. New York: Appleton.

Johns, G. (1981). Difference score measures of organizational behavior variables: a critique. *Organizational Behavior and Human Performance, 27*, 443–63.

Jones, G.R. (1983). Psychological orientation and the process of organizational socialization: an interactionist perspective. *Academy of Management Journal, 8*, 464–74.

258

(1986). Socialization tactics, self-efficacy, and newcomers' adjustments to organizations. *Academy of Management Journal, 29*, 262–79.

Jurgensen, C.E. (1948). What job applicants look for in a company. *Personnel Psychology, 1*, 433–45.

Kanter, R.M. (1977). *Men and Women of the Corporation*. New York: Basic Books.

(1984). *The Change Masters*. London: Unwin.

Katz, R. (1978). Job longevity as a situational factor in job satisfaction. *Administrative Science Quarterly, 23*, 204–23.

(1980). Time and work: toward an integrative perspective. In B.M. Staw and L.L. Cummings (Eds.), *Research in Organizational Behavior*, Volume 2. Greenwich, CT: JAI Press.

Katz, D. and Kahn, R.L. (1980). *The Social Psychology of Organizations*, 2nd edition. Chichester: Wiley.

Kaufman, H.G. (1974). *Obsolescence and Professional Career Development*. New York: AMACOM.

(1982). *Professionals In Search of Work*. New York: Wiley.

Kaye, B.L. (1982). *Up Is Not the Only Way*. Englewood Cliffs, NY: Prentice Hall.

Keller, R.T. and Holland, W.E. (1981). Job change: a naturally occurring field experiment. *Human Relations, 34*, 1053–67.

Kemp N.J. and Cook, J.D. (1983). Job longevity and growth need strength as joint moderators of the task design-job satisfaction relationship. *Human Relations, 36*, 883–98.

Kilmann, R.H., Saxton, M.J. and Serpa, R. (Eds.) (1985). *Gaining Control of the Corporate Culture*. San Francisco: Jossey-Bass.

Kimberly, J.R. and Miles, R.H. (Eds.) (1980). *The Organizational Life-Cycle*. San Francisco: Jossey-Bass.

Kirjonen, J. and Hanninen, V. (1986). Getting a better job: antecedents and effects. *Human Relations, 39*, 503–16.

Kohn, M.L. and Schooler, C. (1983). *Work and Personality*. Norwood, NJ: Ablex.

Korman, A.K., Wittig-Berman, U. and Lang, D. (1981). Career success and personal failure: alienation in professionals and managers. *Academy of Management Journal, 24*, 342–60.

Langrish, S. (1981). Why don't women progress to management jobs? *The Business Graduate, 11*, 12–13.

Latack, C. (1984). Career transitions within organizations: an exploratory study of work, nonwork, and coping strategies. *Organizational Behavior and Human Performance, 34*, 296–332.

Lawrence, B.S. (1984). The implicit organizational timetable. *Journal of Occupational Behaviour, 5*, 23–35.

Legge, K. (1973). Obsolescence of people – in context. *Management Decision, 11*, 27–49.

Lemkau, J.P. (1983). Women in male-dominated professions: distinguishing personality and background characteristics. *Psychology of Women Quarterly, 8*, 144–65.

Bibliography

Lewin, K. (1935). *A Dynamic Theory of Personality*. New York: McGraw Hill.

Lewis, C. (1985). *Employee Selection*. London: Hutchinson.

Liebermann, S. (1956). The effects of changes in roles on the attitudes of role occupants. *Human Relations, 9*, 467–86.

Lockwood, B. and Knowles, W. (1984). Women at work in Great Britain. In M.J. Davidson and C.L. Cooper (Eds.), *Women at Work: An International Survey*. Chichester: Wiley.

Lodahl, T.M. and Kejner, M. (1965). The definition and measurement of job involvement. *Journal of Applied Psychology, 49*, 24–33.

London, M. and Stumpf, S.A. (1982). *Managing Careers*. Reading, MA: Addison-Wesley.

Louis, M.R. (1980). Surprise and sense-making: what newcomers experience in entering unfamiliar organizational settings. *Administrative Science Quarterly, 25*, 226–51.

Louis, M.R., Posner, B.Z. and Powell, G.N. (1983). The availability and helpfulness of socialization practices. *Personnel Psychology, 36*, 857–66.

Mangham, I. and Silver, M.S. (1986). *Management Training: Context and Practice*. London: ESRC.

March, J. and Simon, H. (1958). *Organizations*. New York: Wiley.

Marshall, J. (1984). *Women Managers: Travellers In A Male World*. Chichester: Wiley.

Marshall, J. and Cooper, C.L. (1976). The mobile manager and his wife. *Management Decision, 14*, 4–48.

Martin, J. and Roberts, C. (1984). *Women in Employment: A Lifetime Perspective*. London: HMSO.

Maslow, A.H. (1954). *Motivation and Personality*. New York: Harper and Row.

Melrose-Woodman, J. (1978). *Profile of the British Manager*. London: BIM.

Meltzer, B.N., Petras, J.W. and Reynolds, L.T. (1975). *Symbolic Interactionism: Genesis, Varieties and Criticism*. London: Routledge and Kegan Paul.

Merton, R.K. (1957). *Social Theory and Social Structure*. Glencoe: Free Press.

Miles, R.E. and Snow, C.C. (1978). *Organizational Strategy, Structure and Process*. New York: McGraw-Hill.

Mintzberg, H. (1973). *The Nature of Managerial Work*. New York: Harper and Row.

(1979). *The Structuring of Organizations*. Englewood Cliffs, NJ: Prentice-Hall.

Mischel, W. (1968). *Personality and Assessment*. New York: Wiley.

Mitchell, T.R. (1974). Expectancy models of job satisfaction, occupational preference and effort: a theoretical, methodological and empirical appraisal. *Psychological Bulletin, 81*, 1053–77.

Mobley, W.H., Griffith, R.W., Hand, N.H. and Meglino, B.M. (1979). Review and conceptual analysis of the employee turnover process. *Psychological Bulletin, 86*, 493–522.

Bibliography

Moore, W.E. (1969). Occupational socialization. In D.A. Goslin (Ed.), *Handbook of Socialization Theory and Research*. Chicago: Rand McNally.

Moreland, R.L. and Levine, J.M. (1983). Socialization in small groups: temporal changes in individual-group relations. *Advances in Experimental Social Psychology, 15*, 137–92.

Mortimer, J.T. and Lorence, J. (1979). Work experience and occupational value socialization: a longitudinal study. *American Journal of Sociology, 84*, 1361–85.

Mortimer, J.T. and Simmons, R.G. (1978). Adult socialization. *Annual Review of Sociology, 4*, 421–54.

Mortimer, J.T., Finch, M.D. and Kumka, D. (1982). Persistence and change in development: the multidimensional self-concept. In P.B. Baltes and O.G. Brim (Eds.), *Life-Span Development and Behavior*, Volume 4. New York: Academic Press.

Mowday, R.T., Porter, L.W. and Steers, R.M. (1982). *Employee-Organization Linkages*. London: Academic Press.

Newcomb, T.M. (1958). Attitude development as a function of reference groups: the Bennington study. In E.E. Maccoby, T.M. Newcomb and E.L. Hartley (Eds.), *Readings in Social Psychology*, 3rd edition. New York: Holt, Rinehart, and Winston.

Nicholson, N. (1984). A theory of work role transitions. *Administrative Science Quarterly, 29*, 172–91.

(1987a). The transition cycle: a conceptual framework for the analysis of change and human resources management. In J. Ferris and K.M. Rowland (Eds.), *Personnel and Human Resources Management*, Volume 5. Greenwich, Conn: JAI Press.

(1987b). Good and bad practice in graduate development. *Personnel Management*, February, 34–38.

Nicholson, N. and Arnold, J.M. (1985). *The Graduate Development Project*. Unpublished report, MRC/ESRC Social and Applied Psychology Unit, University of Sheffield.

Nicholson, N., Brown, C.A. and Chadwick-Jones, J.K. (1976). Absence from work and job satisfaction. *Journal of Applied Psychology, 61*, 728–37.

Nicholson, N., West, M.A. and Cawsey, T.F. (1985). Future uncertain: expected vs. attained job mobility among managers. *Journal of Occupational Psychology, 58*, 313–20.

O'Leary, V.E. (1974). Some attitudinal barriers to occupational aspirations in women. *Psychological Bulletin, 81*, 809–26.

Ouchi, W.G. (1982). *Theory Z*. New York: Avon.

Parker, S.R., Brown, R.K., Child, J. and Smith, M.A. (1981). *The Sociology of Industry*, 4th edition. London: George Allen and Unwin.

Payne, G. and Payne, J. (1983). Occupational and industrial transition in social mobility. *British Journal of Sociology, 34*, 72–92.

Pedler, M., Burgoyne, J. and Boydell, J. (1978). *A Manager's Guide to Self-Development*. New York: McGraw Hill.

Pfeffer, J. (1981). *Power in Organizations*. Marshfield, MA: Pitman.

Pfeffer, J. and Salancik, G.R. (1978). *The External Control of Organizations.* New York: Harper and Row.

Pinder, C.C. (1977). Multiple predictors of post-transfer satisfaction: the role of urban factors. *Personnel Psychology, 30*, 543–56.

(1981). Mobility and transfer. In H. Meltzer and W. Nord (Eds.), *Making Organizations Human and Productive.* New York: Wiley.

Pinder, C.C. and Das, H. (1978). Corporate transfer policy: comparative reaction of managers and their spouses. *Relations Industrielles, 33*, 654–65.

(1979). Hidden costs and benefits of employee transfers. *Human Resource Planning, 2*, 135–45.

Pinder, C.C. and Moore, L.F. (Eds.) (1980). *Middle Range Theory and the Study of Organizations.* London: Martinus Nijhoff.

Pinder, C.C. and Walter, G.A. (1984). Personnel transfers and employee development. In J. Ferris and K. Rowland (Eds.), *Research in Personnel and Human Resources Management*, Volume 2. Greenwich, Conn: JAI Press.

Poole, M., Mansfield, R., Blyton, P. (1981). *Managers In Focus.* Aldershot: Gower.

Porter, L.W. and Steers, R.M. (1973). Organizational, work, and personal factors in employee turnover and absenteeism. *Psychological Bulletin, 80*, 151–76.

Premack, S.L. and Wanous, J.P. (1985). A meta-analysis of realistic job preview experiments. *Journal of Applied Psychology, 70*, 706–19.

Rabinowitz, S. and Hall, D.T. (1977). Organizational research on job involvement. *Psychological Bulletin, 84*, 265–88.

Report on the Census of Production (1982). London: HMSO.

Richards, E.W. (1984). Undergraduate preparation and early career outcomes: a study of recent college graduates. *Journal of Vocational Behavior, 24*, 279–304.

Roberts, K. (1975). The developmental theory of occupational choice: a critique and an alternative. In G. Esland, G. Salaman and M. Speakman (Eds.), *People and Work.* Milton Keynes: Open University Press.

Rogers, C.R. (1961). *On Becoming a Person.* Boston: Houghton Mifflin.

Rosenberg, M. (1957). *Occupations and Values.* Glencoe, Ill: Free Press.

Sathe, V. (1985). How to decipher and change corporate culture. In R.H. Kilmann, M.J. Saxton and R. Serpa (Eds.), *Gaining Control of the Corporate Culture.* San Francisco: Jossey-Bass.

Schein, E.H. (1971a). The individual, the organization, and the career: a conceptual scheme. *Journal of Applied Behavioral Science, 7*, 401–26.

(1971b). Occupational socialization in the professions: the case of the role innovator. *Journal of Psychiatric Research, 8*, 521–30.

Schein, E.H. (1978). *Career Dynamics: Matching Individual and Organizational Needs.* Reading, MA: Addison-Wesley.

(1985). *Organizational Culture and Leadership.* San Francisco: Jossey-Bass.

Schneider, B. and Schmitt, N. (1986). *Staffing Organizations*, 2nd edition. London: Scott Foresman.

262

Bibliography

Schutz, W.D. (1967). *Firo-B*. Palo Alto, CA: Consulting Psychologists Press.

Sell, R.R. (1983). Transferred jobs: a neglected aspect of migration and occupational change. *Work and Occupations, 10*, 179–206.

Selyé, H. (1956). *The Stress of Life*. New York: McGraw-Hill.

Sheehy, G. (1976). *Passages*. New York: Dutton.

Snyder, M. (1974). Self-monitoring of expressive behaviors. *Journal of Personality and Social Psychology, 30*, 526–37.

Social Trends (1985). London: HMSO.

Speakman, M.A. (1980). Occupational choice and placement. In G. Esland and G. Salaman(Eds.), *The Politics of Work and Occupations*. Milton Keynes: Open University Press.

Stewart, R. (1967). *Managers and Their Jobs*. London: Macmillan.

(1982). *Choices for the Manager*. Englewood Cliffs, NJ: Prentice-Hall.

Strauss, A.L. (1959). *Mirrors and Masks: The Search for Identity*. Glencoe, Ill: Free Press.

(1978). *Negotiations*. San Francisco: Jossey-Bass.

Super, D.E. (1957). *The Psychology of Careers*. New York: Harper and Row.

(1981). Approaches to occupational choice and career development. In A.G. Watts, D.E. Super and J.M. Kidd (Eds.), *Career Development in Britain*. Cambridge: Hobsons Press.

Tajfel, H. (1978). *Differentiation between social groups: studies in the social psychology of intergroup relations*. London: Academic Press.

Tavris, C. and Offir, C. (1977). *The Longest War: Sex Differences in Perspective*. New York: Harcourt, Brace Jovanovich.

Toffler, A. (1970). *Future Shock*. London: Bodley Head.

Turner, J.C. and Giles, H. (1981). *Intergroup Behaviour*. Oxford: Blackwell.

USA Bureau of Labor Statistics (1980). Washington, DC.

Van Maanen, J. (1976). Breaking-in: Socialization to work. In R. Dubin (Ed.), *Handbook of Work, Organization, and Society*. Chicago: Rand McNally.

Van Maanen, J. and Schein, E.H. (1979). Toward a theory of organizational socialization. In B.M. Staw (Ed.), *Research in Organizational Behavior*. Greenwich, CT: JAI Press.

Veiga, J.F. (1981). Plateaued versus nonplateaued managers: career patterns, attitudes, and path potential. *Academy of Management Journal, 24*, 566–78.

(1983). Mobility influences during managerial career stages. *Academy of Management Journal, 26*, 64–85.

Vickers, G.C. (1965). *The Art of Judgement*. London: Chapman and Hall.

Vroom, V.H. (1964). *Work and Motivation*. New York: Wiley.

Wall, T.D. and Martin, R. (1987). Job and work design. In C.L. Cooper and I.T. Robertson (Eds.), *Industrial Review of Industrial and Organizational Psychology*. Chichester: Wiley.

Wanous, J.P. (1980). *Organizational Entry*. Reading, MA: Addison-Wesley.

Warr, P.B. (1987). *Work, Unemployment and Mental Health*. Oxford: Oxford University Press.

Bibliography

Watson, C.A. and Garbin, A.P. (1981). The job selection process: a conceptual rapprochement of labor turnover and occupational choice. *Human Relations, 34*, 1001–11.

Watts, A.G. (1981). Career patterns. In A.G. Watts, D.E. Super and J.M. Kidd (Eds.), *Career Development in Britain.* Cambridge: Hobsons Press.

Watts, A.G., Super, D.E. and Kidd, J.M. (Eds.) (1981). *Career Development in Britain.* Cambridge: Hobsons Press.

Weiss, H.W. (1978). Social learning of work values in organizations. *Journal of Applied Psychology, 63*, 711–18.

Werbel, J.D. (1983). Job change: a study of an acute job stressor. *Journal of Vocational Behavior, 23*, 242–50.

West, M.A. (1987). A measure of role innovation at work. *British Journal of Social Psychology, 26*, 83–85.

(1987). Role innovation in the world of work. *British Journal of Social Psychology, 26*, in press.

West, M.A. and Nicholson, N. (1986). Coping with the job that no-one did before. *Personnel Management*, July, 38–41.

West, M.A., Nicholson, N. and Rees, A. (1985). Downward mobility, unemployment and psychological adjustment among professionals. Memo No. 762, MRC/ESRC Social and Applied Psychology Unit, University of Sheffield.

(1987). Transitions into newly created jobs. *Journal of Occupational Psychology, 60*, 97–113.

West, M.A., Farr, J.L. and King, N. (1986). Innovation at work: definitional and theoretical issues. Paper presented at the American Psychological Association Annual Convention, Washington DC.

Witkin, H.A. (1978). *Cognitive Styles in Personal and Cultural Adaptation.* Worcester, MA: Clark University Press.

Wortman, P. (1982). Women in management. In H.J. Bernadin (Ed.), *Women in the Work Force.* New York: Praeger.

Yogev, S. and Brett, J. (1985). Patterns of work and family involvement among single- and dual-earner couples. *Journal of Applied Psychology, 70*, 754–68.

Ziller, R.C. (1976). A helical theory of personal change. In R. Harré (Ed.), *Personality.* Oxford: Blackwell.

Zurcher, L.A. (1977). *The Mutable Self.* Beverly Hills, CA: Sage.

Author Index

Author index

Subject Index

absorption 106–16
accounting 24
achievement 45, 66, 140
adaptation 2; individual 6; *see also* adjustment
adjustment 8–15, 112, 141, 158, 168; to change, 2, 52, 73, 93, 117, 140; modes of 7, proactive 6; processes 6; psychological 33–44, 45, 52, 53, 68, 99, 121–39, 151, 156, 202, n238; reactive 6; in the Transition Cycle 96–8, 105–14; to transition 1, 8, 118–39
administration 24, 53, 54, 67, 81, 164–84, 192, 198
adulthood 12
advancement 29, 30–1, 43, 122, 154, 174
advertising 23, 153, 161–84
age 22, 32–9, 45, 79, 130, 190; and career paths 79–83; and innovation 107; and job demands and performance 161–69; and mobility 57–60; and organizational culture 177–84; and perceived career influences 176–7; and self-concepts, 32–44; and sources of learning 170–5
anxiety 1, 98–100, 114–15, 128, 150, 202; about fit with family life 99–100; performance 96, 99; about relationships 98–9; transition 99–100, 127
armed forces 23
attitudes 2, 72, 113, 117, 126–9, 138; *see also* work attitudes
authority 104
autonomy 36; *see also* job discretion

banking 23
bereavement 7, 10
biographical characteristics 19, 22, 130, 201; associated with mobility 57–60; and sex 186–91
bosses 14, 126, 160, 170–84, 194–200
British Institute of Management 18, 46, 186–204, n236; Fellows of 18, 47, 186, 187; Members of 18, 47, 186, 187

career 2, 9, 17, 25–7, 37, 72–95, 96, 223–5; advisors 92, 224–5; choice 5, 72, 74, 79, 93; counselling 15, 92, 158, 224–5; cultures 16; development 19, 88, 92, 94, 95, 214, 224–5, model of 157–9, 181–4, organizational 157–84; development survey 18; dissatisfaction 79, 83; dual-career 23, 41, 60; entry 12; exit 12; exploration 58; fulfilment 65; frustration 65; goals 74, 84, 88, 126–9, 202; influences 151–6, 173–7, 203; literature 57, 223–5; managerial 5, 60, 69; mid-career 12, 78; mobility 58–60, 62–5, 139; as myth 88–93; paths 7, 12, 16, 41, 42, 64, 66, 72–83, 152, 157, 215; patterns 60, 69, 73, 201; plateau 74, n243; preferences 9; problems 74–83; in public sector 71; satisfactions 74, 78–83, 93, 151; success 39; types 72–83, 88, 93; upwardly mobile-career 64
CDS I 19, 22, 24, 28, 38, 40, 41, 49, 53, 54, 56, 58, 59, 60, 67, 83, 84, 85, 86, 89, 90, 91, 99, 100, 102, 110, 111, 122, 123, 126, 129–37, 141, 142, 144, 146, 147, 148, 149, 151, 153, 154, 155, 156, 159, 161, 165, 166, 167, 168, 169, 170, 172, 173, 175, 176, 187, 188, 189, 190, 191, 193, 194, 195, 196, 197, 198, 199, n235–53
CDS II 19, 26, 28, 37, 53, 54, 56, 74, 83, 85, 86, 89, 90, 91, 100, 101, 141, 142, 147, 148, 149, 151, 153, 156, 159, 160, 163, 164, 165, 168, 169, 171, 172, 175, 176, 178, 179, 180, 183, n235–53
challenge 28, 30–1, 40, 86, 87, 104, 122, 123, 129–37, 138, 142, 150, 154, 219
change 1; and the manager 2–7; *see also* job change

269

Subject index

sources of learning 170–5; private 23,
62–5, 67, 70, 148, 161–84; public 23,
62–5, 67, 70–1, 148, 161–84, 194
innovation 13, 16, 31, 127, 140, 142,
143, 149, 178, 179, 212, 220, 208–30,
n247; content 13; role 13, 106, 109–14,
117, 129, 130, 141, 150, 151
insurance 23
interdependence 8, 218
intra-organizational moves 15, 45, 99,
100, 103, n239; *see also* transfers and
job moves
inter-organizational moves 99, 100, 101,
103, 155

job, areas 54–5, 61–5, 67, 80–3, 161–84,
192–4, 198; change 2, 5, 6, 7, 16, 22,
27, 72, 73, 125–39, causes of 15, 83–8,
definition of 48, effects of, on personal
change 125–39, expectations of 55, 61,
66, 73, 88–93, meanings of 211–12,
outcomes of 15, 107, 117–39, involuntary 6, 7, 85, reasons for 48, 73, 83–8,
201, n244, stress of 99–100, types of
48–55, 73, 78–83, 109, 161–84;
changers 129–39, *see also* job mobility,
managerial job change, work role transitions; characteristics 1, 13, 20, 21,
32–44, 106–16, 149–56, 202; demands
13, 160, 161–9; design 45, 50, 72, 225;
discretion 70, 107–16, 129, 142, 149,
150, 151, 154, 155, 164; immobility
122–39; involvement 37–9; location 29,
30–1, 40, 42, 84, 121, 122, 129, 201;
longevity *see* job tenure; loss 7, 28, 154;
managerial 159–84, 208–30, qualities of
159–64, theory and practice 208–30;
mobility 2, 6, 18, 118, 122–39, and personal change 125–39; moves 12, downward status 16, 48–71, 85, 104–5, 118,
125–39, 218, employer 46, 48, 48–71,
78–83, 85, 86–95, 99, 104–5, 125–39,
201, 205, 209, function 48–71, 80–3,
86–95, 125–39, 144, 146, 209, inter-
organizational 61–2, 99–100, 101, 103,
125–39, 150–3, 209, *see also* job
moves, employer, intra-organizational
15, 45, 64, 99–100, 103, 125–39, 150–
3, 209, *see also* transfers, lateral 12, 13,
48–71, 125–39, newly created job 16,
110, 118, 140–56, 195, 209, 218,
n250–1, radical 50–2, 67–8, 99, 117,
125–39, 203, 209, 220, spiralling 49–
71, 78–83, 86–8, 201, 205, upward

status 12, 48–71, 104–5, 125–39, 144,
146, 201, *see also* job change; novelty
107–16, 128, 142, 147, 151, 152, 153,
n240; relocation 7, 10, 47, 106, 126;
satisfaction *see* satisfaction, job; security
29, 30–1, 40, 43, 140, 178; tenure 48,
129, 130, 149, 175–6; types 22, 23

leadership 14
leisure 3, 25–7
life, changes 5, 7; circumstances 22; cycle
13, 43; events 10, 12, 26–8, 83, 85,
118, 154, n237, associated with job
change types 86, associated with personal change 123–5; satisfactions 25–7
lifespan, development 2, 12, 118, 137,
222–3, n235

management 4, 14; consultants 18, 157;
development 43; education 24; line 53,
54, 55, 61, 67, 70, 81, 192; middle-
management 25; services 24, 54, 67, 70,
81, 164–84, 198; study of 226–9
managerial, job change 2, 6, 17, 20, 208–
30, experience of 210–1, extent of 208–
11; careers 5, 53, 157–84; status 192–3;
succession 45, 73, 228
managers, and change 2–7; general- 4, 24,
61–5, 67–8, 70, 79–83, 109, 161–84,
192–4; married- 26, 187–91; self-
concepts 31–4; senior-managers 2, 29,
30–1, 121, 122, 164; single-managers
25, 26, 41
manufacturing 3, 23, 153, 161–84
marital status, and mobility 57–60, 67–8,
187–91; and self-employment 152–6
marketing 24
market research 148, 153
marriage 7, 25, 26, 28, 187–91
material rewards at work 36–44, 121–39,
149–56; *see also* earnings, salary
media 4, 22, 55; *see also* communication
media
men 7, 12, 70, 185–204; biographical
characteristics of 22; functional types 24;
in management 39–44; and mobility 49–
71; self-concepts of 39–44; in transition 1;
work needs of 39–44
mental health 16, 28, 139
methodology 2
mid-career 12, 78
mining 23
mobility 6, 15, 16, 20; attained 88–95;
causes of 72–95; expected 88–95; pat-

271

Subject index

women (*cont.*)
  factors 191–4, status of 191–4, 204–7;
  and mobility 49–71; married 23, 187–
  204; role conflict of 187, 188; and
  segregation 194–204; self-concepts of
  39–44; single 42, 187–204; work needs
  of 39–4; *see also* gender
work, attitudes 36; characteristics 30–1,
  34–44, 121–39, n238; context 101–5;
entry 32, 96; and family life 42, 152–6;
life outside 26, 29, 40; motivation 21;
needs 35–44; and non-work roles 42;
performance 14; preferences 29–31,
121–39, 201, n237; role 9, transitions
8–15, 12, 96–116, 129–39, theory of
106–16, 117–18, 128, 138, *see also* job
change; transitions